UNDERSTANDING RELATIONSHIP PROCESSES

Series Editor
Steve Duck, *University of Iowa*

This series of books on the theme **Understanding Relationship Processes** provides a coherent and progressive review of current thinking in the field. Uniquely organized around the notion of relational competence, the six volumes constitute a contemporary, multidisciplinary handbook of relationship research for advanced students and professionals in psychology, sociology, communication, family studies, and education.

Volumes in the Series

1. INDIVIDUALS IN RELATIONSHIPS

2. LEARNING ABOUT RELATIONSHIPS

3. SOCIAL CONTEXT AND RELATIONSHIPS

4. TRANSACTIONAL DYNAMICS OF RELATIONSHIPS

5. DISRUPTED PROCESSES OF RELATIONSHIPS

6. CHALLENGING RELATIONSHIPS

LEARNING ABOUT RELATIONSHIPS

EDITED BY
STEVE DUCK

LEARNING ABOUT RELATIONSHIPS

UNDERSTANDING RELATIONSHIP PROCESSES SERIES
VOLUME 2

SAGE Publications
International Educational and Professional Publisher
Newbury Park London New Delhi

For information address:

SAGE Publications, Inc.
2455 Teller Road
Newbury Park, California 91320

SAGE Publications Ltd.
6 Bonhill Street
London EC2A 4PU
United Kingdom

SAGE Publications India Pvt. Ltd.
M-32 Market
Greater Kailash I
New Delhi 110 048 India

Printed in the United States of America

Library of Congress Cataloging-in-Publication Data

Main entry under title:

Learning about relationships / [edited by] Steve Duck.
    p. cm — (Understanding Relationship Processes Series: v. 2)
    Includes bibliographical references (p. 213-237) and indexes.
    ISBN 0-8039-5157-4 (cl.) — ISBN 0-8039-5158-2 (pb)
    1. Interpersonal relations. 2. Interpersonal relations in children. I. Duck, Steve. II. Series.
    HM132.L4   1993
    302—dc20   93-16834

93 94 95 96 10 9 8 7 6 5 4 3 2 1   MAY 1 7 1994

Sage Production Editor: Diane S. Foster

Contents

Series Preface

This short series **Understanding Relationship Processes** attends to recent calls for an attention to process in relationships. A close look at the nature of processes in relationships will reveal that, over and above the importance of change, temporality, and an orientation to the future, beneath most process thinking on relationships lies the implicit notion of competent use of knowledge across time. For example, this assumption is true of many elements of the work on relationships, such as the (competent) transition to marriage, (skilled) conflict management, (appropriate) self-disclosure in relationship development, and (orderly) organization or (satisfactory) maintenance of relationships diachronically. The assumption also is contained in discussion of intimacy assessment of couple creation (by which authors evaluate the degrees of intimacy or progress that are adequate, allowable, suitable, or competent) and is latent in discussion of relationship breakdown where discussions treat breakdown as failure or incompetence, contrasted with skill or competence.

Such competence is evident in, and constrained by, a variety of levels of influence on behavior. In focusing on some of these topics, this series moves conceptually outward; that is, the series begins with the contributions of individuals and their developmental experiences to relationships, and moves toward the social context and interpersonal interaction. Individuals bring into relationships their individual characteristics and factors that reflect their point in the life cycle and their developmental achievements. Individuals are influenced by the social setting (situational, cultural, linguistic, and societal) in which the relationship takes place; they are constrained and influenced by the structural, transactional, behavioral, and communicative contexts for their relationships; and they sometimes conduct the relationships in dysfunctional environments or disrupted emotional contexts. The series takes the contextual themes in sequence and deals with the latest research and thinking that address these topics.

Accordingly, each volume focuses on a particular context or arena for relationship activity. The first three volumes of the series deal respectively with the following topics:

Individuals in Relationships. Volume 1 deals particularly with the ways internal or intrapersonal context is provided by structures of the mind or of knowledge that are prerequisite for success in relationships; however, rather than focusing on such things as if they were the end of the story, the chapters place such knowledge styles and structures in context by referring frequently to behavioral effects of such structures.

Learning About Relationships. Volume 2 covers especially the skills and experiences in childhood that lay the groundwork for competence as a properly functioning relater in adult life; the volume emphasizes the wide range of social sources from which development of competence is derived and the richness of the social sources from which developing minds acquire their sense of relationship competence.

Social Contexts and Relationships. Volume 3 focuses especially on the social structural constraints within which relationships are located and the ways the two partners must negotiate and deal with the dialectical and interior pressures created by such contexts. Other volumes in the series deal with the dynamics of relational transactions, overlooked elements of relating, and challenging contexts for relating.

STEVE DUCK

Volume Preface

This is the second volume in a short, self-contained series whose goal is to explore the recent growth of theory and research into personal relationships. The first volume deals with the knowledge, knowledge structures, and prototypic cognition that an individual is presumed to have before a relationship with another person can be possible. This second volume deals with the sources for this knowledge and the influences on it as the individual grows up. The volume focuses on those strong exterior social sources, such as parents and peers, from which development of social knowledge is first derived and later practiced in developing relationships with others.

Whereas Volume 1 lays out individual processes but essentially takes them as a given for adults, Volume 2 explores their origins and their development in childhood. The volume deals with the ways experiences in the early part of life influence a person's approach to relationships. It thus focuses on the origins of attitudes to others and the shaping of beliefs or styles for use in relationships. Its emphasis is on "normal" processes and development rather than, say, on the inculcation or training of relational competence through intervention programs.

Although Volume 1 focuses mostly on the *minds* of individuals, Volume 2 begins to focus the series also on the development of competent *behavior,* as well as mental development. In the course of early development, the child learns not only *that* but *how,* and the development of knowledge about relationships also is buttressed in the normal course of daily life by the experience of conducting them, the experience of others as social beings, and some assessment of one's own worth and value to other people.

Rather than focus on cognitive development as the basis for the growth of relational capacities, about which much has already been written elsewhere, this book attends to the growing research on the contexts in which children have their relationships with others, such as their growing and changing experience of their own competency and abilities with peers and the influence of parents on their sense of self and self-worth as a social object for others.

The guiding themes for authors here were to consider those styles and experiences that have a lasting effect on the way a person conducts relationships. Such a task necessarily involved the authors placing their work in the context of the "big picture" of relationships, while also focusing primarily on the issues that arise in exploring the topic per se. Thus although each chapter reviews issues within the developmental literature, authors also were encouraged, where possible, to point out the implications for later life. While treating the development of children's social competence in its own right, therefore, the volume attempts to identify those processes in development that have lasting effects, as well as those that are "local" to childhood itself. The volume thus emphasizes the continuities of developmental experiences on the individual through life, as well as illuminates the processes at the particular point of life and particular circumstances that are the explicit focus of each chapter.

The opening chapter, by Judi Beinstein Miller, explores the ways early experiences of relationships with parents create expectations that assimilate later experience in interpersonal events and provide a basis for the person to form an impression of his or her worth to others. Using an object relations perspective, Miller describes both the development of expectations and their subsequent influences on relationship learning. The emphasis on continuity of experience is an important one, but as Miller concludes, there is much to be learned also about the discontinuities that shape the child's learning about relationships.

Pursuing the issues of continuity and discontinuity, Kim Bartholomew, in Chapter 2, deals specifically with attachment theory and its proposals about the development of attachment styles in infancy that may carry over to adult relationships. In a careful consideration of the relationship between early attachment patterns and patterns established in adult relationships, Bartholomew develops her schema for conceptualizing attachment styles and reviews evidence relative to it. Her conclusion is that the evidence does indicate that individuals' constructions of their childhood experiences play an important role in the structuring of their experiences of quality in adult relationships too.

Picking up somewhat on this theme, Martha Putallaz, Philip Costanzo, and Tovah Klein explore, in Chapter 3, the experiences of mothers in childhood and the ways these experiences, in turn, affect their rearing of their own children. In a sense this exciting work looks at the intergenerational transmission of attachment styles and shows that attachment style affects one's relationships with not only other adults but also with one's offspring and that it does so in a way that also affects *their* social development. Reviewing evidence from studies of child abuse, remembered peer relationships, and remembered parent-child relationships, Putallaz et al. systematically review a number of related areas in search of evidence of patterns. The discussion of these issues is quite captivating, and the authors present a number of interesting ideas for the development of this powerful work.

Taking this theme further, Rosemary Mills and Kenneth Rubin explore, in Chapter 4, the ideas that parents have about relationships as influences on the ways they deal with children. Noting the significance of the fact that children grow up in families that have their own ways of representing and thinking about relationships, Mills and Rubin develop an interesting case for the influence of parental beliefs on parenting technique and so add something to the analysis presented by the previous authors in terms of individual reactions to experience. The chapter shows clearly that a child's social competence with peers is a product of parental influences in a degree that merits serious attention.

Greg Pettit and Jacquelyn Mize continue this theme in some ways, in Chapter 5, by reviewing the work that looks at the way parents *directly* teach their children about relating. The focus here is on the style of the interactions between parents and children as much as it is on the content, and the argument is developed by reference to some intriguing work that disentangles the influence of style and substance in the equation. Pettit and Mize develop a model that will help us illuminate the mechanisms of transmission (from parents to children) of approaches to social relating.

In Chapter 6, Gary Ladd, Karen Le Sieur, and Susan Profilet also explore such mechanisms and offer a way of linking together the two presently separate research areas of family-child relations and child-peer relations. They give a careful and intriguing analysis of some family effects on peer relationships in terms of the parents' roles as influencers of the child's social experience. Distinguishing among parents as designers of the social environment, parents as mediators of play opportunities and relationships with specific peers, parents as supervisors of ongoing interactions with peers, and parents as consultants and advisors about relational matters, Ladd et al. develop a useful picture of the role of parents' influences on peer relationships. They end their chapter by pointing out some intriguing ways to develop this line of thinking as we develop ways to help children to better relationships.

In Chapter 7, Peter Smith, Louise Bowers, Valerie Binney, and Helen Cowie deal with the learning about relationships associated with the bullying and victimization that can occur in school playgrounds. For some 25% of the typical day, children at school are engaged in play or "time out" activities that permit much peer interaction. At these times, a certain amount of rough-and-tumble play is quite common. Bullying and victimization go further than this and demonstrate some of the real consequences of individual and family experiences that the rest of the book illustrates. By asking whether bullies lack social skills, whether

bullying may serve some adaptive purpose, and whether bullying is a status-seeking activity, Smith et al. investigate a number
of issues related to the questions of why some children become
victims and others become bullies. The authors present a review
of several areas of literature and also of some lines of work
showing that bullies and victims are clear subgroups with distinct identities and prior histories of attachment or relationship
learning in the family.

The volume as a whole presents a compelling catalogue of the
specific ways a child's social relational learning is shaped and
molded by developmental and family experiences that continue
right through childhood (and doubtless beyond). A major feature
of the chapters here is the development, in different lines of
work, of the comprehension of the tragedies and triumphs that
are foretold in childhood experiences.

As with the first volume in this series, the chapters in this
second volume not only demonstrate and review some important points about a specific aspect of relationships—in this case
the loci of the learning that takes place about relationships—but
also touch on the fact that none of this learning occurs in a life
devoid of context. The processes of learning about relationships
are processes in themselves, and yet they can be understood
fully only in the context of other matters such as knowledge of
individual cognitive structure and awareness of social structures
and contexts. These, too, influence the ways people address their
own experiences and make sense of them vis-à-vis other people's
experiences. Accordingly Volume 3 of the series adds to this
progression by dealing with social contexts for relationships.

STEVE DUCK

Learning From Early Relationship Experience

Judi Beinstein Miller

Behavior in relationships is influenced strongly by prior relationship experience, as is illustrated amply by research in this volume. Whether internalized generally as attachment security or specifically as lessons in sharing, consistencies in past experience can influence future interaction by providing frameworks for interpersonal understanding and guidelines for responding to partners. As shown in this chapter, early relationship experience can be particularly influential because of its potential to create expectations that assimilate later interpersonal events. Unless later events are very different from earlier ones, expectations created by the former are likely to persist, as appears to happen with friendship expectations of liked versus disliked children (Patterson, Kupersmidt, & Griesler, 1990) and with parenting expectations of toddlers whose attachments in infancy have been secure versus insecure (Main, Kaplan, & Cassidy, 1985). In this chapter I review evidence for the formative influence of early relationship experience. Using an object relations perspective, I describe the development

1

of relationship expectations and their influence on subsequent relationship learning. The first part develops a conceptual perspective for relationship learning that is based on object relations theories. The second part contains illustrations of specific relationship lessons from infancy, preschool, and grade school and factors that facilitate or hinder their internalization. The final part suggests implications of early relationship experience for subsequent relationship learning and calls attention to the importance of studying discontinuities, as well as continuities, in relationship experience.

As a prelude to describing relationship learning, it will be helpful to clarify what is meant here by the term *relationship* and what it means to learn about relationships. Because the term *relationship* is used conventionally to apply to people who influence each other's behavior, relationships themselves can be construed as constraints, or limitations that partners place on each other's behavior. Some constraints (e.g., for obedience) can be experienced as restrictive and negative, whereas other constraints (e.g., for self-disclosure) can be experienced as liberating and positive. Interpersonal constraints make mutual predictability and understanding possible because they limit behavior. Particularly in close relationships where interpersonal constraints are stable, partners know what to expect of each other and for that reason feel free to be themselves. Because relationships entail interpersonal constraint, they make a difference in the ways we think, feel, and act. Particular relationships make particular differences, due to the nature of their constraints. We expect different treatment from parents than peers, from mother than father, from Friend A than Friend B; and we expect to treat them differently as well. Even within the same relationship, we know that constraints change as we negotiate new understandings and joint endeavors. Long-term negotiations can transform our relationships markedly, as occurs during adolescence, when children and their parents redefine control over decisions in daily life. From an objective viewpoint also the constraints of relationships are apparent because it is common to infer the character of a relationship from partners' mutual influence—for example, the care evident in compromises, sacrifices, and gestures of loyalty. Knowledge about relationships, which creates expectations for behavior in relationships, therefore can be described as knowledge about these constraints and one's own experience and observations of relationships as major contributors to knowledge.

If it is assumed that relationships can be described as constraints, then learning about relationships is largely a matter of learning these constraints—for example, that enemies and friends will treat us differently and that we should treat them differently in return. Relationship learning occurs when prior expectations about relationships are adjusted to accommodate new relationship experience—for example, when an enemy treats us well and we question our previous understanding of his or her feelings toward us, or when a parent turns us into a confidante by sharing previously undisclosed details of his or her life. Learning about relationships implies a change in prior expectations due to some felt discontinuity in relationship experience. Discontinuities are experienced by partners in developing relationships as their interdependencies and expectations for mutual support grow. Discontinuities among relationships are experienced by children as they become aware of expectations for behavior in different types of relationships—for example, with teachers versus parents or siblings versus friends. More generally, relationship learning occurs whenever people (a) are exposed to novel relationship constraints and (b) recognize these as being different from prior relationship constraints. Factors that *increase* exposure and sensitivity enhance relationship learning by creating awareness of discontinuity. Factors that *decrease* exposure and sensitivity perpetuate a status quo by maintaining continuity in relationship expectations. Thus experiences of discontinuity result in new understandings and/or expectations, whereas experiences of continuity maintain prior understandings and expectations. Object relations theories are germane to relationship learning because they address factors that contribute to recognition of continuity and discontinuity in relationship experience.

An Object Relations Perspective
on Relationship Learning

Object relations theories are about internalized relationships
with people (objects) and their influence on external relationship behavior. Object relations theories are particularly concerned
with factors that shape internal representations of relationships
and maintain continuity in expectation. Childhood experiences
are regarded as especially important because these provide
relationship lessons early in life when there is little other contradictory experience. If lessons are particularly painful, they
are repressed and made unavailable for conscious inspection
even though they continue to influence behavior unconsciously.
It is the primacy and unconscious influence of early experience
that make it tenacious.

Object relations theories make use of several related constructs to express relationship knowledge, both conscious and
unconscious, including object relations schemata (by Raush,
Barry, Hertel, & Swain, 1974; or more simply, object relations, by
Chodorow, 1978), working models of relationships (by Bowlby,
1988), and mental representations of attachment (by Main et al.,
1985). Although these constructs derive primarily from psychoanalytic theory (see Westen, 1991, for a review of major clinical
contributions to object relations theories), they are compatible
with notions of schematic knowledge that are used by cognitive
psychologists for internal models of repeated experience with
similar events (Bretherton, 1985). One common characteristic
is that they refer to experienced-based expectations for interpersonal interaction and for intentions and feelings that accompany
interaction. Consequently they imply individual differences in
knowledge that is acquired for understanding and engaging in
interpersonal relationships. A second characteristic is that they
are structured and become increasingly complex as individuals
mature. Consequently they imply a general pattern in styles by
which relationship knowledge develops, regardless of individual
differences in expectations. A third characteristic is that they
are created in circumstances where constraints are strong and

easy to perceive. Among these circumstances is interpersonal conflict, where opposition between partners highlights difference in perspective and goal. These characteristics of relationship knowledge (that it is experienced-based, follows a general pattern of development, and is fostered by conflict) can be elaborated further to develop a framework for describing relationship learning.

1. Experienced-Based Expectations for Interaction

Bowlby (1988) proposed that early relationship experiences influence later experience by means of "working models." According to his theory of attachment, the infant builds an initial model of its attachment figure and self, based on treatment it receives from the attachment figure or caretaker. The model provides generalizations about the caretaker's past responses to the infant's needs for security, which create expectations for future responses by the caretaker when similar needs arise again. These expectations serve as guidelines for adapting to the caretaker because the infant learns to behave in anticipation of the caretaker's response—for example, by seeking proximity to the caretaker if it anticipates support and by distancing itself if it anticipates rejection. Expectations for support and rejection thereby are reinforced by the behavior of the infant. The behavior of the caretaker can, of course, change and lead to revision of the infant's expectations, which is indicated by the term *working model.* The behavior of other attachment figures in the infant's environment can provide alternative expectations for treatment as well. Nonetheless, tendencies for mothers to become major attachment figures and to maintain fairly stable attachment relations with children (Main et al., 1985) suggest that treatment from mothers can have a disproportionately large influence on the infant's later behavior.

Research by Ainsworth, Blehar, Waters, and Wall (1978) provides evidence for three models of infant attachment, each associated with a different pattern of parental treatment. *Secure attachment* occurs in children whose mothers are predictably responsive and helpful when frightening situations arise. *Anxious avoidant attachment* occurs in children whose mothers are predictably unresponsive and whose rebuffs promote avoidance of contact, even after separation. *Anxious resistant attachment* occurs in children with unpredictable mothers, who sometimes are responsive and sometimes are not, an inconsistency that creates anxiety in their children about being separated and exploring novel situations. According to Bowlby (1988), these patterns, once formed, tend to persist, become a property of the child, and direct its expectations of other relationships unless disconfirming or other novel experience results in revision of expectations.

Chodorow (1978), whose work was strongly influenced by Bowlby's (1969) early writing, provides an example of gender differences in early relationship experience and their influence by means of internal object relations on later relationship behavior. She depicts the origin of object relations in the first few months of life, when the infant, regardless of gender, comes to recognize its primary caretaker, usually the mother, as separate from itself and internalizes a relationship with her. At this point its object relations are defined by interaction with its mother and so are relatively simple. Within the next few years, males become aware of being sexual opposites of their mothers and therefore define themselves as more distinct and separate from her than females do. The males repress their attachment to her (in the context of resolving oedipal conflict) but are ready to find a substitute primary love object in adulthood. Females, in contrast, retain their mothers as primary love objects throughout childhood. This retention provides them with a greater sense of connectedness than males have but complicates their transition to heterosexual love. The transition to heterosexual love requires them to transfer their primary object choice to men, which they achieve partly by superimposing their relations with fathers over relations with mothers. According to Chodorow, because girls emerge from childhood with more complex object relations than boys do, their relational capacities (e.g., for empathy and perspective taking) are extended. A more complex internal world of object relations makes them more permeable externally and capable of learning about others.

Explanations for the influence of early relationship experience on later experience rely on the directive influence of relationship knowledge, such as internal object relations and working models. Knowledge from childhood, even among adults, is believed to affect attachment behavior—for example, in love relationships. Hazan and Shaver (1987) demonstrated small to moderate correlations between adult attachment styles in love relationships and memory for relationships with parents. They explained these correlations with reference to expectations of loved ones that were derived from early experience and that predisposed later behavior in consistent directions. Continuity in expectations by this explanation is maintained by recent relationships, as well as by memory for past relationships. Other explanations include behavior by the loved one as a reinforcing response to the individual's predisposed behavior. Bartholomew (1990; Chapter 2, this volume), for example, proposes that initial attachment behaviors are maintained due to the behavior they evoke from interaction partners. Affiliative behaviors evoke affiliativeness, and hostile behaviors result in distance. In these cases, tendencies for behavior to elicit confirmatory feedback increase the likelihood of people maintaining continuity in expectations.

Relationship knowledge influences later relationship experience also because it affects perceptions of social encounters. Particularly when intentions are ambiguous, they tend to be interpreted in accordance with previous experience. Aggressive children, for example, tend to attribute ambiguous provocations by a peer to the peer's hostility more often than do nonaggressive children (Dodge, 1986), and socially rejected children do worse at detecting group norms and behaving in group-oriented ways than do socially accepted ones (Putallaz & Heflin, 1986). Moreover, children's expectations and interpretations of play have been found to be more strongly correlated with each other than either has been with their actual play behavior (Cillessen & Ferguson, 1989). Prior experience of interpersonal constraint, which is stored in memory, is used to interpret current interaction.

Reminiscent of the relationship between interpretations and expectations is Kelly's personal construct theory (Kelly, 1970). One of Kelly's basic tenets is that interpretations of social behavior are constructed out of expectations; and research has demonstrated the manifestation of these interpretations in behavior. For example, Adams-Webber (1979) summarizes evidence that observers can identify accurately the personal constructs of interactors from samples of their social behavior and that predictions about a target person's behavior can be improved by having information about the target's personal constructs. Moreover, evidence for greater similarity in personal constructs of friends rather than neutral associates (Duck, 1973) suggests that mutual understanding and validation in friendship might reinforce relationship knowledge and contribute further to continuity in relationship experience.

2. General Patterns of Growth in Relationship Knowledge

Despite individual differences in relationship learning, there is a tendency for internal object relations to become increasingly complex as discontinuities in experiences are accommodated by previous expectations. The newborn may not distinguish itself from its environment, but by the end of its first year its attachment behaviors in anxiety-provoking situations are often different with mothers and fathers, even though concordance of behavior occurs as well (Fox, Kimmerly, & Schafer, 1991). Infants recognize differences in their relationships but have limited understanding of these constraints.

Growth of interpersonal understanding appears to proceed in developmental stages whereby increasingly complex perspectives of interpersonal relations are formed as simpler ones are adjusted to accommodate social experience. Selman (1980), for example, describes five developmental levels of interpersonal understanding. At Level 0 (ages 3 to 6) children's concepts of relations are relatively egocentric, and others' points of view are difficult for them to differentiate. At Level 1 (ages 5 to 9) they recognize differences in their own and others' points of view but are limited by expecting influence to be unilateral rather than reciprocal. By Level 2 (ages 7 to 12) children can put themselves in each other's shoes and know that their partner will do the same, but they have difficulty taking a third person's view of their relationship and recognizing it as a system of mutually shared experiences, which they do at Level 3 (ages 12 to adult). Finally at Level 4 they can abstract the mutual experiences of many relationships, communicate this knowledge objectively, accept changes in partners' perspectives, and recognize that people grow out of, as well as into, relationships. According to this developmental scheme, a 7-year-old whose behavior and beliefs reflect unilateral understanding (e.g., that a friend is someone who will participate in activities you enjoy and that conflict between friends is caused by one and felt by the other) would be considered as competent, but an adolescent with the same behavior and beliefs would not. By adolescence, behavior and beliefs should reflect reciprocal, as well as unilateral, understandings (e.g., that a friend is someone with whom there is intimacy and mutual sharing and that conflict in friendships is, in fact, between persons and not due solely to one or the other).

According to object relations theories, learning about interpersonal constraints and achieving new levels of interpersonal understanding are facilitated by having complex and permeable object relations because these aid accommodation of new experience. When object relations are insufficiently differentiated and flexible to accommodate a new experience, then the experience is assimilated to prior expectations without perception of its novelty. A child with enemies alone, for example, has less reason to find humor in being teased than a child with friends and enemies. More generally, the detection of nuances in interaction depends on prior experience with similar interaction events. Because socially well integrated children are more likely than less well integrated children to have exposure to variety in interaction, they are also more likely to develop complex object relations earlier than less well integrated children.

Evidence for a connection between levels of interpersonal understanding and interpersonal competence is provided by comparisons of interpersonal understanding among socially well integrated and less well integrated children. Children's levels of understanding, as revealed by their responses to hypothetical interpersonal dilemmas, correlate positively with their IQ and social acceptance, as well as with their age (Pellegrini, 1985). When interpersonal understanding is compared among disturbed and normal youths, disturbed youths are found to lag behind, although their sequence of progression through levels is the same (Gurucharri, Phelps, & Selman, 1984). Levels of understanding are associated additionally with knowledge of strategies for negotiating interpersonal conflict. These strategies, which range from impulsive behaviors such as hitting or grabbing to collaborative efforts such as third-person perspective taking and reflective dialogue, also are associated with social adjustment (Yeates, Schultz, & Selman, 1991). Development of interpersonal competence thus appears to be determined, at least in part, by ability to accommodate new relationship experience with increasingly mature interpersonal understandings.

Work by Raush and his colleagues (1974) suggests that growth in interpersonal understanding is a continuous process that affects interpersonal competence long after childhood. Following Piaget (1970), they argue that having flexible (permeable) and differentiated (complex) object relations schemata aids accommodation of interpersonal differences—in this case, between spouses—better than having undifferentiated and rigid ones. As an example they describe a husband who has had little interpersonal experience with women other than his mother prior to marriage. Because he has never heard his mother express wishes opposing his father, his concepts of women do not include direct confrontations. When his own wife states wishes in opposition to his own, he thinks this is not the way a wife behaves and wonders whether she loves him. Of course he needs to learn that all women are not like his mother, which would have been facilitated by experience with a larger variety of women. Opportunities to form subsets of expectations would make subsequent, additional distinctions easier to draw.

As indicated by these examples, factors that interfere with perception of constraint limit relationship learning. Anxiety is another such factor because it fosters rigid expectations, which are more difficult to adjust than are flexible ones. Bowlby (1988), for example, notes that anxious attachments can obstruct the updating of working models because such attachments encourage defensive exclusion of discrepant information. Raush and his colleagues (1974) note clinical evidence that severe anxiety or its threat inhibits recognition of new experience because anxiety-provoking events get assimilated to schemata associated with earlier anxieties. Interference with learning could be one reason for correlations between measures of social competence and anxiety. For example, children whose attachments in infancy have been anxious have less competent peer relations in preschool than do children whose attachments have been secure (Erickson, Sroufe, & Egeland, 1985; Sroufe, 1983). Adolescents and children whose scores are higher in use of aggressive conflict tactics manifest higher anxiety than do those whose scores are lower (Kashani, Deuser, & Reid, 1991). Anxiety could both hamper accurate social perception and stimulate dominant responses, which in the case of aggressive youngsters would be aggressive responses.

3. Acquisition of Relationship Knowledge in Interpersonal Conflict

The third characteristic of relationship knowledge is that it is acquired most readily where constraints are strong or for other reasons easy to perceive. *Interpersonal conflict,* in which there is opposition between partners and often interference with each other's goals, is among the most important of these circumstances. As indicated by Shantz (1987), the concept of *conflict* is central to most major theories of human development because conflict fosters change for better or worse. In interpersonal conflict, partners discover differences in their expectations, including differences in expectations they may have of each other. Because the process of working through conflict includes exchanges of reasons for opposition, conflict can clarify the nature of interpersonal constraints (e.g., why one wishes the other to act against his or her will), lead to new understanding, and foster mutually satisfying outcomes. In this way conflict provides opportunities for partners to adapt former interpersonal understandings and to negotiate changes in their relationship. Especially for young children, little conflicts such as disagreements would be major vehicles for learning about differences in perspective. Expression of disagreement (in addition to agreement) is also a way that children as young as 3-6 years find common ground and develop friendship (Gottman, 1983). Having disagreements, it should be noted, is not the same thing as getting into fights; the latter entails aggression, which does not always accompany the former. Getting into fights is a socially incompetent way of responding to opposition, as indicated by findings that angry, reactive aggression precedes rejection by peers (Dodge, Coie, Pettit, & Price, 1990). Children even as young as age 4 have less intense conflicts and better resolutions with friends than with neutral associates (Hartup, Laursen, Stewart, & Eastenson, 1988).

The idea here is that learning about relationships is a matter of acquiring new relationship expectations, which is retarded or accelerated by individual differences in exposure and sensitivity. This notion provides a framework for describing early relationship learning and its implications for later relationship experience. In the following section, I provide examples of relationship knowledge that is acquired in infancy, childhood, and adolescence, particularly in conflict, and suggest ways in which this knowledge makes subsequent relationship learning easier or more difficult, with the result of limiting or furthering continuity in experience.

Development of Relationship Expectations

Lessons From Infancy

To differentiate varieties of relationship constraint, infants first must experience themselves as separate from others. Chodorow

(1978) describes this as occurring in the first few months of life, when the child becomes aware of repeated departures by its mother. The experience of separateness occurs in the context of conflict because the infant's expectations for closeness get frustrated. Recognition of separateness increases the infant's felt dependency on its mother, attachment to her, and awareness of her separate interests and activities, which oppose its own. But in most instances it learns to wait for her because it anticipates receiving satisfaction. Thus the infant's initial differentiation of self and recognition of need for its mother occur because its expectations for love get frustrated. Its object relations change as it recognizes her separateness and separate interests, which recognition forms the foundation for taking the interests of others into account. The infant's relationship with its mother forms a prototype for experiencing other objects as separate, which is why the dependability of its mother in providing secure attachment affects its relationships with others.

Sometimes infants experience more devastating loss of attachment figures than simple short-term departures. In some cases their bonds are severed altogether by prolonged institutional care. Children who suffered these losses were of particular interest to Bowlby because clinical observations had linked maternal deprivation to unhealthy personality development (Bowlby, 1988). In other cases their bonds are disrupted for moderately long periods but later reestablished. Bowlby generalized the response of these children by a sequence of protest, despair, and detachment, which he likened to mourning in healthy adults. In still other cases, as those described by Ainsworth and her colleagues (1978), bonds are not severed, but secure attachment is frustrated daily by rejection, ineptness, or inconsistent behavior of the attachment figure. These children become anxiously attached and either insatiable or avoidant of contact, depending on the consistency of their treatment. In still other cases, security is threatened by stressful family circumstances, such as separation and divorce, which increase risk for social maladjustment (Patterson, Vaden, & Kupersmidt, 1991). In each case, conflict is the context in which expectations for lack of contact and comfort are formed.

By the end of the first year, attachment systems appear to be firmly established. Infants have formed expectations of treatment from attachment figures, which are reflected by their behavior in the Strange Situation (Ainsworth et al., 1978). The *Strange Situation* is a laboratory procedure for observing responses of infants to a toy and a stranger, following presence and absence of a parent. When the parent returns after a brief departure, most infants seek contact, but after being comforted resume their play and other exploration of the environment. Anxiously attached infants behave in predictably different ways. The *avoidant infant* directs its attention away from the parent. The *resistant infant* directs its attention constantly at the parent and away from other aspects of its environment. These patterns remain relatively stable, as indicated by 6-year-olds' reunion behavior with parents after a 1-hour separation (Main et al., 1985). Children rated as *securely attached* in infancy behave affectionately, confidently, and responsively toward the parents, whereas children rated as *insecurely attached* do not. Those who have been judged avoidant tend to ignore the parent; those who have been judged resistant try to control the parent. Although stability in children's responses has been attributed to their temperament rather than to treatment (Lamb & Nash, 1989; Rowe, 1989), changes in infants' emotionality have been shown to be contingent on changes in parents' stressful circumstances and communication (Belsky, Fish, & Isabella, 1991), a finding that suggests an important role of treatment regardless of temperament. By the end of the first year, then, children differentiate their caretakers from other people and have expectations for treatment that appear to influence their subsequent behavior.

Between 1 and 2 years of age, children begin to acquire knowledge about feelings, intentions, and social rules that are conveyed by family members' communication. During this time they become *responsive* to expressions of distress and anger, *anxious* in response to disapproval, and *concerned* about others' perspectives and standards (Zahn-Waxler & Radke-Yarrow, 1990).

Much of their learning occurs from observing or being involved in family conflict. Dunn and Munn (1985) cite examples from two observational studies of mother-sibling triads in which the second-born child was 14-24 months old. When these children were witnessing conflict between their mothers and older siblings, many would engage in supportive behaviors for one or the other. When engaged in sibling conflict themselves, they would draw attention to their sibling's transgressions, such as aggression and teasing. Their behavior indicated increasing awareness of constraint, which the authors attributed to mothers' justifications for prohibitions (e.g., "You shouldn't tease because teasing hurts feelings") as much as to punishment for transgression.

Between 1 and 2 years of age, children are learning also to adjust their responses to the behavior of different peers. When paired with two different partners over a series of play sessions, previously unacquainted toddlers develop patterns of interaction with one partner that differ significantly from patterns with the other (Ross & Lollis, 1989). When paired with same-age, younger, or older peers, they behave in predictably different ways as well, presumably to accommodate developmental differences in communication (Brownell, 1990). Younger toddlers paired with older toddlers are more interactive and positive than are younger toddlers in same-age dyads; and older toddlers paired with younger toddlers make greater efforts to engage their partners than do older toddlers in same-age dyads. By the time they enter preschool, children have acquired awareness of individual differences in behavior and basic, though minimal, skills for negotiating their differences.

Lessons in Preschool

Preschoolers go on to elaborate their relationship knowledge in peer groups as they learn to make friends, cooperate in joint activities, and resolve interpersonal conflicts. Those who acquire social acceptance in this context will learn, if they have not already learned, to perceive basic emotions such as happiness and sadness accurately (Denham, McKinley, Couchoud, & Holt, 1990), to treat peers positively rather than negatively (Ladd, Price, & Hart, 1988; Masters & Furman, 1981), and to test alternative problem-solving strategies in resolving interpersonal conflict (Rubin & Krasnor, 1986). Conflicts during this period will focus most often on control of objects, though interpersonal actions and facts also will become subjects of dispute (Shantz, 1987). Children will learn that simple insistence and disagreement are met by simple insistence and disagreement but that reasons for opposition are met by compromise and an end to conflict. In experiencing the consequences of their actions, these children will learn how to coordinate their goals for mutual satisfaction. Factors that influence their learning will contribute consequently to their social acceptance.

The relationship knowledge that preschoolers bring from home is among the more important factors affecting their subsequent learning. Two kinds of knowledge will influence their learning readiness: generalizations from their attachments and specific lessons in interpersonal relations.

A central proposition from object relations theories is that generalizations formed from past relationship experience provide expectations for future interaction. According to attachment theory, children with secure attachments should enter preschool with greater interest in the new social environment and greater confidence in exploring it than should children with insecure attachments. Their dependably good treatment from caretakers, unlike that of insecurely attached children, would have predisposed them to behave positively and assertively and to expect similar behavior from others. With fewer anxieties about interpersonal relations than insecurely attached children, they would be more predisposed to learn about others by listening to what they say and watching what they do. Securely attached children, therefore, would be expected to display greater social competence in preschool than their insecurely attached counterparts, an expectation supported by longitudinal studies of attachment. Sroufe (1983), for example, used observations and teacher ratings to compare the social behavior of preschoolers whose attachment status had been determined in infancy. Among other findings, securely attached children were rated higher in expression of positive feelings, empathy, and social competence and lower in expression of negative feelings and aggression than were insecurely attached children. They also were described as having more friends than insecurely attached children and behaving more compliantly. Similar results have been obtained in other studies. For example, Booth, Rose-Krasnor, and Rubin (1991) ascertained the attachment status of 20-month-old middle and lower class children and then analyzed their play behavior with a previously unknown, securely attached peer when they were 4 years old. Children with insecure status expressed more negative feelings and tended to behave more aggressively than did children with secure status. Cohn and her colleagues (Cohn, Patterson, & Christopoulos, 1991) point out, however, that most longitudinal evidence comes from only two major research programs and so should be regarded tentatively.

Children also learn specific lessons from observing or listening to family members, including how to communicate their feelings and wishes, how to gain group acceptance, and how to resolve disputes. In some cases these lessons are learned incidentally by observing models provided by parents. As an example, Denham, Renwick, and Holt (1991) coded task interaction of mothers and preschoolers and then correlated the behavior with teacher ratings of the children's social behavior. They found that mothers who expressed positive feelings, allowed autonomy within limits, and provided clear and confident instructions tended to have children whose social behavior was positive and assertive as well. As another example, Pettit, Dodge, and Brown (1988) compared the social competence and status of preschoolers according to their social problem-solving abilities and their mothers' endorsements of aggression in problem solving. The results suggested that maternal aggressiveness interferes with children's social competence because it limits the children's repertoire of solutions to social problems. In a similar study, Pettit, Harrist, Bates, and Dodge (1991) collected teachers' ratings of social behavior for kindergartners whose interaction with family had been observed during the previous summer. The researchers found positive correlations between teachers' ratings of the children's aggressiveness and earlier observations of coercion and interference in family interaction.

Parents also provide lessons purposively, as when they give instructions for getting along with others. Russell and Finnie (1990) found that mothers of liked children suggested group-oriented strategies for gaining entry to groups of unknown children more often than did mothers of rejected or neglected children. Dunn, Brown, and Beardsall (1991) coded references to feelings in conversations between 3-year-olds and their families and 3 years later tested the children's affective perspective-taking ability. They found that conversations about causes and consequences of feelings were particularly likely to occur during conflicts and that children with greater exposure to talk about feelings at age 3 could recognize emotion better at age 6 than could youngsters with less exposure. Although direct and incidental lessons such as these differ from attachment experiences, they also can facilitate children's social acceptance by providing guidelines for social understanding and interaction.

In grade school, youngsters continue to build their relationship knowledge on foundations of family and early peer experience. Their object relations will be more complex than before preschool because expectations of peers and teachers will be added to those for family members, which themselves will have been updated. Children now have reason to differentiate vertical relationships with adults from horizontal relationships with peers (Hartup, 1989). Relationships with adults have provided, and continue to provide, protection, security, and basic social know-how (e.g., not to hurt others' feelings), whereas relationships with peers facilitate elaboration of social skills (e.g., for cooperation and competition). By the end of preschool, children also have begun to make distinctions among their peer relationships because their experience with friends and nonfriends has been different. As indicated earlier, friends will have shared more agreements and disagreements, less intense conflicts, and better conflict resolutions than nonfriends will have shared (Gottman, 1983; Hartup et al., 1988).

By the end of preschool, expectations of relationships will be more consistent for some children than for others. Securely attached children will have made friends fairly easily in preschool, whereas insecurely attached children will have had difficulty adjusting socially. Research by Erickson et al. (1985) suggests that children categorized as anxious/avoidant in infancy have particular difficulty in preschool regulating their feelings and behavior. Their behavior is hostile and impulsive, and they give up easily. Children categorized as anxious/resistant in infancy have particular difficulty with self-confidence and distractions. They behave passively and do not pay attention easily to classroom activities. Correlations between attachment to parents and acceptance by peers are not perfect, however. Not all children experience consistency in attachments to mothers and fathers (Main & Weston, 1981), and not all experience consistency in relationships with parents and peers (Erickson et al., 1985). Prosocial behavior generally earns children social acceptance from peers, and antisocial behavior earns them rejection (Ladd et al., 1988), which can alter their expectations of relationships. Nonetheless, because children's expectations influence their interpretations of each other's behavior (Cillessen & Ferguson, 1989), confirmation of expectations is a more likely outcome than disconfirmation. Most children, therefore, will begin grade school with generally good or bad expectations of others, although some will begin with a more complex set of expectations.

Lessons in Grade School

From kindergarten to eighth grade perspective-taking and problem-solving skills mature steadily and interpersonal intimacy, loyalty, and mutuality become increasingly important. According to Selman's (1980) developmental scheme, it is during this time that children learn to be self-reflective and put themselves in each other's shoes. In other words, they can evaluate themselves from the perspective of others and discover how to create a good impression. Conflicts over control of objects decrease markedly, and conflicts over interpersonal control increase (Shantz, 1987). They learn that impression making and interpersonal influence, like rules of games, are negotiated and, through their friendships, acquire information and practice to negotiate competently (Fine, 1981). A major developmental achievement is behavioral flexibility, which requires sensitivity to feedback and a growing repertoire of problem-solving and negotiation strategies.

Sensitivity to feedback depends on accurate perception of others' feelings and motives, and accurate perception develops with age and social integration. Rothenberg (1970), for example, asked third and fifth graders to listen to tapes of conversations between adults and to identify the feelings and motives. She also collected ratings by teachers and peers of the children's interpersonal adjustment. Fifth graders proved to be more socially sensitive than third graders, and children with higher interpersonal adjustment ratings proved to be more socially sensitive than those whose ratings were lower. Rothenberg attributed these correlations to a probable two-way influence between interpersonal adjustment and social sensitivity. Interpersonal adjustment both facilitates and is facilitated by social sensitivity.

Problem-solving skills also have been demonstrated to be a function of age and social integration. Asarnow and Callan (1985) asked fourth- and sixth-grade boys whose peer ratings were extremely positive or negative to generate and evaluate solutions for problems that youngsters have in getting along. Boys with positive status generated more strategies altogether than did boys with negative status and more often mentioned assertive strategies and strategies that entailed consequential thinking (e.g., If I hit him, I'll get in trouble). Younger boys and boys with negative status generated more aggressive solutions than did older boys and boys with positive status. Boys with negative status also rated aggressive responses more positively and positive responses more negatively than did boys with positive status, a finding that may reflect differences in their social sensitivities.

Pellegrini (1985) examined the contributions of both interpersonal understanding and problem-solving skills to positive peer reputations among fourth to seventh graders and found that these skills made only moderately independent contributions. Each added an increment to positive peer reputation, but understanding and problem-solving skills were themselves intercorrelated. These results are consistent with the idea that interpersonal understanding provides a foundation for interpersonal problem solving but will not result in competence by itself. A similar conclusion can be derived from research by Yeates et al. (1991), who interviewed elementary school and junior high school students about interpersonal problems that children often face in school. They asked students to define each problem, generate a strategy for solving it, predict the strategy's effect, generate obstacles to the strategy's effectiveness, and devise a criterion for the strategy's effectiveness. Each answer was scored according to the developmental level of interpersonal understanding it represented, and scores were averaged to form an estimate of interpersonal negotiation strategies development. Estimates were higher for older than younger students and correlated positively with teachers' ratings of actual interpersonal problem-solving behavior and social adjustment. The latter scores, in turn, correlated positively with peer status.

Results from studies of problem solving suggest that children become increasingly aware of nuances in interpersonal constraint as they get older and learn, particularly in conflict, how to negotiate constraint effectively. Because opportunities for learning are afforded by peer interaction, better integrated children will have more opportunities to develop sensitivity and to experiment with strategies than will less well integrated children. Children whose anxieties have interfered with relationship learning may now be at a double disadvantage because they will have limited opportunities to learn and practice the very behavior that furthers social competence. These children, particularly those who are aggressive, will continue to have difficulty managing common social problems, such as peer provocation and group entry, due to their ineptness at processing social cues and avoiding conflict escalation (Dodge, Pettit, McClaskey, & Brown,

1986; Putallaz & Heflin, 1986). Their social ineptness and unacceptability are likely to be mutually reinforcing, as indicated by stability in patterns of social behavior and status, at least from second to fifth grade (Hymel, Rubin, Rowden, & LeMare, 1990). Lessons from earlier peer relationships have limited their subsequent learning.

Relationships with parents continue to have an influence on peer relationships. Parental supportiveness and warmth are associated with peer acceptance, and aversive parental discipline with peer rejection. Putallaz (1987) demonstrated the former association in a study of first graders and mothers at play. Mothers who were positive, agreeable, and open about their opinions and feelings (with other mothers, as well as their children) had children who behaved similarly and were accorded high social status. Patterson et al. (1990) found that self-perceptions of competence, companionship, and support from parents correlated positively with peer ratings among third and fourth graders, although rejected aggressive children tended to overestimate their competence. East (1991) provided evidence for a similar relationship among sixth graders, whose high peer ratings in sensitivity and sociableness were associated with high levels of parental support. In contrast, Dishion (1990) reported low sociometric ratings for boys who experienced aversive parental discipline. Low peer ratings were an apparent consequence of antisocial behavior, which was encouraged by parental example. Hart, Ladd, and Burleson (1990) obtained consistent results from correlations between first and fourth graders' expectations of conflict resolution strategies, sociometric status, and mothers' discipline styles. Children who expected to get their way using unfriendly assertive strategies and who were not well liked tended to have mothers who endorsed power assertive discipline styles. Aversive control by parents can provide a model for children to get their way and control their environment. More generally, Patterson and his colleagues (1989) argue that delinquency and related problems in adolescence develop from coercive parental behavior in childhood. Children whose parents are coercive learn to control family members through coercive behavior and later employ similar behavior with peers. Their aggressiveness earns them social rejection, which stimulates their joining deviant peer groups where their antisocial behavior is reinforced. Not all antisocial children become delinquents in adolescence, but those who do are likely to have long histories of peer rejection, according to Patterson and his colleagues.

Children learn other lessons about relationships during their grade school years besides negotiating conflict. Intimacy becomes increasingly important in friendship up until adolescence (Berndt, 1986; Jones & Dembo, 1989), when it is correlated with interpersonal competence (Buhrmester, 1990). Learning to establish and maintain intimate relationships through self-disclosure, loyalty, and mutual responsiveness, therefore, might help compensate for earlier difficulties with interpersonal conflict.

During their grade school years, children learn about relationships from other sources besides family and peers. The media are particularly important sources of incidental learning about social roles (e.g., in occupations) and intimacy behaviors (e.g., between romantic partners). Firsthand experience with family and peers, however, provides the most enduring lessons because it reinforces expectations on a daily basis. By assimilation of many such experiences and accommodation of still others, adolescents acquire working models of relationships that they carry into adulthood. These models will continue to provide interpretive frameworks and guidelines for relationship behavior.

Cumulative Lessons
of Relationship Experience

A growing body of research links relationship experience in adulthood with early relationship experience. Kobak and Sceery (1988) found that affect regulation and interpersonal relations of college students, as described by peers, could be predicted by their memories of parental relations. Those with memories of secure attachments were considered to be the most positive and resilient, those classified as dismissing of attachment the most hostile, and those classified as preoccupied with attachment the most anxious. Hazan and Shaver (1987) found that romantic love, conceptualized as attachment styles, had consistent associations with memories of parents. Adults with secure love styles remembered their parents in more positive terms than did adults with avoidant or anxious styles. McCrae and Costa (1988) found small but significant correlations between adults' personality scores and their memories of parents. Those who remembered their parents as loving and attentive scored lower in neuroticism and higher in extraversion, conscientiousness, and openness to experience than did adults whose memories of parents were less positive. Putallaz, Costanzo, and Smith (1991) found that mothers' parenting intentions and behaviors could be predicted from their memories of early peer relations. Mothers with memories of social anxiety were particularly concerned about their children avoiding the negative things that they had experienced and, along with mothers whose memories were positive, scored higher in nurturance than did mothers with memories of social rejection. Although results such as these can be explained as reconstructions to fit current experience, longitudinal evidence confirms a connection between parental care in childhood and social adjustment in adulthood. Parental warmth and affection at age 5 have been associated with friendship and stable marriage in adulthood (Franz, McClelland, & Weinberger, 1991). Within the same sample, paternal involvement in child care and maternal tolerance of dependence and inhibition of aggression have been associated with empathic concern in adulthood (Koestner, Franz, & Weinberger, 1990). These results exclude influences from infancy, which are the focus of attachment theory but are nonetheless consistent with object relations predictions of continuity.

Memories of peer relations are associated also with behavior in adulthood, as illustrated in my own research. In a series of three studies, I compared young adults' endorsements of conflict responses according to their memories of peer relations in grade school, junior high, and high school (Miller, 1989). I had expected memories of social acceptance to encourage self-confidence and assertiveness in conflict, and memories of social rejection to encourage self-consciousness and conflict avoidance, for example, through acquiescence. I had not expected the influence of their memories to be strong because other factors affect behavior as well, including recent experience that updates working models, but I did expect the influence of peer memories to be systematic.

In an initial study, 40 undergraduates who had been classified as assertive or acquiescent were interviewed about their peer relations while growing up. They were questioned about their popularity in grade school, junior high, and high school and about experiences of being teased, feeling left out, and having friendships discontinued. On the basis of this information, they were divided into two groups—those who indicated having little social acceptance and those who indicated having at least some. Acquiescent students tended to fall into the former group, whereas assertive students tended to fall into the latter.

In the second two studies, Likert scales were used to quantify memories of peer relations, including memories of popularity, prestige, and friendship quality. In these studies four types of responses were written for each of 10 hypothetical conflicts with friends, and undergraduates were asked to rate the likelihood of using each one. In this way it was possible to estimate their expectations of using aggressive, assertive, tactful, and acquiescent responses to conflict. Results from these studies confirmed and extended those from the first. The better the students' memories of popularity, prestige, and friendship quality, the more likely they were to endorse assertive responses of every type and the less likely they were to endorse acquiescent ones. Because students from the third study had additionally responded to Fenigstein, Scheier, and Buss' (1975) Self-Consciousness Scale, it was possible also to ascertain the relationship between their memories and conflict responses on the one hand

and levels of private self-consciousness, public self-consciousness, and social anxiety on the other. The poorer the students' memories of peer relations, the higher their self-consciousness scores. Public self-consciousness, in particular, was associated with poorer memories, higher ratings of acquiescent conflict responses, and lower ratings of assertive and aggressive ones. Thus the lessons they had learned from earlier relationship experience appeared to influence their self-consciousness, which also affected their conflict responses. These were correlational results, however, and could have been interpreted in other ways. As demonstrated by connections between social competence and acceptance in childhood, young adults' memories of poor peer relations could be due to poor social skills that persist until adulthood. Their memories also could be a consequence of reinterpreting the past to be consistent with current relationship experience. Because working models integrate current with past experience, inconsistencies might be handled by aligning the past with the present.

Equally possible is that sociability has a strong heritable component (Lamb & Nash, 1989; Rowe, 1989) and that connections between parental treatment and later relationship behavior reflect common genetic influences. According to this line of reasoning, individuals are born with predispositions to be outgoing and cooperative that are channeled by subsequent experience. Cooperative children, who are easy to raise and comfort, will elicit more positive responses from peers than uncooperative, anxious, and inconsolable ones. Continuity in experience is afforded by the individual's constant stimulus value across a variety of social circumstances.

Developmental evidence has not ruled out these alternative explanations, and each may explain part of the continuity in relationship experience. Equally important, however, are discontinuities in experience, which suggest a role for factors beyond genetic ones. Belsky, Fish, and Isabella's (1991) evidence for parental circumstances that predate changes in infant emotionality provides one example. Infants whose positive affect increased and negative affect decreased from 3 to 9 months of age had parents who were psychologically healthy, who had good marriages, and whose interaction with the infant was harmonious. Those who scored high in positive affect and low in negative affect at 9 months, regardless of earlier ratings, were classified most often as securely attached, whereas those who scored high in negative affect and low in positive affect were classified most often as insecurely attached. Similarly discontinuity between attachment in infancy and competence in preschool has been associated with parental behavior (Erickson et al., 1985). Mothers of children with secure attachments in infancy but behavior problems in school were observed to be somewhat ineffective in helping their children solve problems and cope with frustration. Mothers of children with insecure attachments in infancy but without problems in school were observed to encourage exploration, to act warmly and supportively, to supply appropriate play materials, and to structure play tasks carefully. Thus it appears as though new relationship lessons can be learned under appropriate circumstances, in which cases earlier expectations are changed to accommodate new experience.

By adulthood, working models of relationships, styles of learning, and modes of relating will have been updated many times to accommodate diverse lessons from interaction with different people in different contexts. For some, such as currently secure adults with memories of insecure attachments in childhood, models will have been fundamentally rethought (Main et al., 1985). Complex and sometimes internally contradictory, the working models of most will continue to be updated as new relationships are formed and older relationships change. Although some relations (e.g., painful and other conflictual relations) will be defensively hidden from conscious awareness, these will continue to influence current behavior according to object relations theories (Westen, 1991). Consequently people will not always have access to prior experience, and this lack can create complications for self-understanding and subsequent

learning. In contrast, complexity and flexibility of object relations can facilitate relationship learning—for example, recognition of changes in partners' expectations or realization of growing
out of relationships.

Relationship learning, then, can be depicted as an ongoing,
progressive accommodation of prior knowledge about constraint in
relationships. Learning depends on exposure to novel constraints
and capacity to recognize these as different from prior constraints, which is why social integration and complex object
relations can facilitate learning, whereas social isolation and
anxiety can inhibit it. When relationship experience is assimilated to prior knowledge, novel constraints are not recognized
as different and behavior does not change accordingly. Assimilation processes, therefore, can prevent or prolong acquisition of
social skills, which retards social success. Some children take
longer than others to discover the effectiveness of group-
oriented strategies, and this delay may limit their success in
gaining entry to new groups. Some children take longer than
others to realize that opposition requires explanation, which
may limit their success in achieving compromise. Some take
longer than others to recognize that physical aggression does
not earn friends, and this delay may limit their peer status.
Factors such as social isolation and anxiety, which encourage
assimilation rather than accommodation processes, therefore
afford continuity in experience.

Continuity in experience, which is a manifestation of assimilation processes, has received particular research attention because of interest in the long-term impact of early relationship
experience. Developmental evidence for continuity in social
experience is strongest for childhood, especially for aggressive-
rejected children, but is beginning to accumulate for adulthood
as well. Research results do not imply invariance in social out-
look and behavior throughout life, but rather that outlooks and
behavior change gradually due to the force of prior expectations. According to object relations theories, prior expectations
can be difficult to alter due to their history of reinforcement,

internal organization, and potential association with anxiety. Continuity, rather than discontinuity, in experience is to be expected because assimilation is a simpler, less threatening process than accommodation of novelty. Accommodation of experience, however, makes acquisition of skills and understandings possible, and we are only beginning to demonstrate some of the factors that facilitate or inhibit accommodation processes. As evidence for continuities in relationship experience accumulates, it may be productive to investigate discontinuities. By studying experiences of discontinuity, we may be able to identify circumstances that facilitate relationship learning and thereby social adjustment.

From Childhood to Adult Relationships: Attachment Theory and Research

Kim Bartholomew

Attachment theory, as developed by Bowlby (1973, 1980, 1982), Ainsworth (Ainsworth et al., 1978), and others, is a way of conceptualizing "the propensity of human beings to make strong affectional bonds to particular others" (Bowlby, 1977, p. 201). The theory leads to two bold hypotheses: (a) Attachment behavior characterizes human beings throughout life and (b) patterns established in childhood parent-child relationships tend to structure the quality of later adult-adult relationships. Attachment theory therefore offers a promising theoretical framework for understanding why some people have difficulties in forming and maintaining satisfying bonds in their adult relationships and why some people even seem to avoid this presumably "natural" inclination.

AUTHOR'S NOTE: I wish to thank Fraser Archibald, Steve Duck, Antonia Henderson, and Elaine Scharfe for their helpful comments on earlier versions of this chapter.

Bowlby asserts that "attachment behavior is held to character-ize human beings from the cradle to the grave" (1977, p. 203). Attachment processes have been investigated extensively in parent-child relationships, but until recently, relatively little attention has been paid to the role of attachment processes in adult relationships. Following up on the seminal work of Hazan and Shaver (1987), however, a growing body of research has applied an attachment perspective to the study of adult personal relationships. Although doubtless many aspects of adult relation-ships are independent of attachment processes, attachment the-ory provides a new perspective on a number of important dimensions of relationship functioning—including conflict res-olution, provision of support, and breakups. Moreover, the qual-itatively different patterns of attachment identified in childhood may be parallel to patterns that characterize adults.

Attachment theory may provide a useful framework for under-standing adult relationships independent of any claims of conti-nuity between childhood and adult relationship patterns. But the more exciting (and controversial) implication of the theory is that relationship patterns established in the family of origin tend to be carried forward into adult personal relationships. More specifically, Bowlby hypothesized that the quality of child-hood relationships with caregivers results in internal represen-tations of attachment relations that become integrated into the personality structure and thereby provide the prototype for later social relations. Consistent with this hypothesis, the quality of early parent-child relationships has been found to be predictive of a range of psychosocial outcomes in later childhood (Bretherton, 1985), and recent research is providing growing evidence for the intergenerational transmission of specific attachment patterns, presumably as mediated by parenting practices (e.g., Fonagy, Steele, & Steele, 1991; Ward & Carlson, 1991). There is as yet no direct evidence of continuity from parent-child to adult-adult relation-ships, and it will be some time before such evidence is available. However, extrapolating from the childhood attachment litera-ture, it is possible to predict developmental pathways that may lead to specific patterns of problems in adult personal relation-ships. The theory can also guide explorations of the mechanisms that underlie continuity in relationship patterns and the potential avenues through which these patterns can be changed.

In this chapter I briefly review the basic principles of attachment theory and summarize relevant findings from the childhood attachment literature. I then selectively review work applying an attachment perspective to adult relationships, with particular attention to work of mine that integrates previous research in parent-child and adult attachment. Specific mechanisms that may mediate the relationship between early attachment patterns and patterns established in adult relationships are then explored. Finally I discuss some caveats of present work in adult attachment and suggest some directions for future work in the area.

Overview of Attachment Theory and Research

Attachment theory was developed originally by Bowlby to explain the emotional distress caused by unwilling separation and loss from particular others (Bowlby, 1973, 1980, 1982). Bowlby proposed that an attachment system has evolved to maintain proximity between infants and their caregivers under conditions of threat. The attachment system is organized homeostatically: It is especially prone to activation when the infant is afraid, hurt, ill, or tired, and, under such conditions, the infant will emit attachment behaviors such as crying and clinging to establish contact with the attachment figure. More recent formulations also view the attachment system as functioning continuously to provide a so-called *secure base* from which young children can engage in exploration of the environment. From the perspective of the individual, the goal of the attachment system is the regulation of a sense of *felt security* (Sroufe & Waters, 1977). The attachment system thus is proposed to have "its own internal motivation distinct from feeding and sex, and of no less importance for survival" (Bowlby, 1988, p. 27).

The quality of early attachment relationships is seen as rooted largely in the history of interactions between infants and their primary caretakers (or attachment figures). Especially crucial is the degree to which infants learn that they can rely on their attachment figures as sources of security and support. From a laboratory procedure designed to observe the behavior of infants toward their caretakers under conditions of increasing stress (the Strange Situation), Ainsworth and her colleagues have identified three distinct patterns of infant attachment: secure, ambivalent, and avoidant (Ainsworth et al., 1978). *Secure* infants appear to perceive their caretakers as reliable sources of protection and security. These infants actively seek contact with their caretakers when distressed and are readily soothed and reassured by that contact. Secure infants also tend to explore the environment confidently under nonthreatening conditions. In contrast, infants showing an *anxious-resistant* or *ambivalent* attachment pattern show ambivalent behavior toward the caretaker when distressed. These infants intersperse contact seeking with angry resistant behavior and are not easily comforted. Finally infants showing *avoidant* patterns of attachment actively avoid contact with the caretaker when distressed. Thus neither ambivalent nor avoidant infants appear to successfully use their caretakers to gain security when distressed. In addition, both groups of insecure infants show deficits in using their attachment figures as a secure base for exploration.

The dimension of caretaking behavior that seems to be related most strongly to infant attachment patterns is *sensitivity to the infant's signals* (Ainsworth, 1982; Ainsworth et al., 1978). Ainsworth found that (a) mothers of securely attached infants tended to be consistently responsive to their infants' signals, (b) mothers of infants classified as ambivalent tended to be inconsistent and inept in dealing with their infants, and (c) mothers of avoidant infants tended to be relatively cold and rejecting toward their infants. Consistent with these findings, Egeland and Farber (1984) demonstrated relationships between attachment classifications at 12 months and mothers' sensitivity in feeding situations when their infants were 3 and 6 months (see also Grossmann, Grossmann, Spangler, Suess, & Unzner, 1985).

In the early years, continuity in the quality of attachment appears to be mediated largely by continuity in caregivers' treatment of children. But over time, children are hypothesized to internalize their experiences with caretakers such that early attachment relations come to form a template for later relationships outside the family. Bowlby argues that children construct "working models" or internal representations of themselves and others, and he describes the basic process through which such internal representations come to be formed:

> Confidence that an attachment figure is, apart from being accessible, likely to be responsive can be seen to turn on at least two variables: (a) whether or not the attachment figure is judged to be the sort of person who in general responds to calls for support and protection; (b) whether or not the self is judged to be the sort of person towards whom anyone, and the attachment figure in particular, is likely to respond in a helpful way. . . . Once adopted, moreover, and woven into the fabric of the working models, [the model of the attachment figure and the self] are apt henceforward never to be seriously questioned. (Bowlby, 1973, p. 204)

These working models are dynamic cognitive structures that guide expectations about relationships and interpretations of experiences in relationships. They are expected to operate largely automatically and outside of conscious awareness. On the assumption that the need to maintain stability and coherence of one's internal models of reality is a basic human motive (cf. Epstein, 1987), people are hypothesized to process social information and to act so as to obtain feedback that confirms their internal models of themselves and others (see Caspi & Elder, 1988; Swann, 1983, 1987). Although representational models formed during childhood and adolescence tend to be self-perpetuating over time, they also are expected to be open to revision based on new experiences that contradict established models. For instance, heightened frequency of life stresses among low-income families has been associated with infants shifting from secure to insecure attachments within a 6-month period (Vaughn, Egeland, Sroufe, & Waters, 1979).

Individual differences in infant attachment suggest that, by 12 months of age, infants have formed expectations of their attachment figures. However, the low concordance found between infant attachment patterns with each parent (e.g., Main & Weston, 1981) suggests that these early models tend to be relationship specific. More recent work has begun to directly address general working models of attachment in young children (Main et al., 1985). For instance, Cassidy (1988) confirmed that 6-year-old children classified as securely attached showed positive conceptions of themselves (see also Easterbrooks, Davidson, & Chazan, 1991). In contrast, those classified as avoidant tended to insist on unrealistic levels of personal perfection in interviews (although this finding was not replicated on standard self-esteem measures), and ambivalent children showed more overtly negative descriptions of themselves. Similar results were obtained by Kaplan (1987), although in this study 6-year-olds classified as avoidant in infancy displayed considerable emotional vulnerability in response to imagined separations. Thus, by this age, individual differences in the quality of early attachment relationships are beginning to be translated into general models of attachment relations.

Consistent with this internalization process, considerable research has documented that early attachment classifications predict the quality of children's peer relationships through early childhood. (See Cohn, Patterson, & Christopoulos (1991) for a recent review of this literature.) For example, Sroufe (1983) found that children rated as securely attached at 12 months of age had better peer relations in preschool than children previously classified as insecure. This finding held across teacher and observer reports and across a range of indicators of peer competence (including popularity, aggression, empathy, and expression of positive feelings in peer relations). Cohn et al. (1991) also cite several unpublished studies showing that insecure attachment histories are associated with deficits in peer competence in school-aged children.

There is some evidence that parenting behaviors are influenced by parents' experiences within their own families of origin (see Belsky & Pensky, 1988; Ricks, 1985; Rutter, 1988). However, work within an attachment perspective has focused on how people's constructions of their childhood experiences or their working models of both themselves and others may influence future parenting behavior. Although Bowlby believed that working models are "tolerably accurate reflections" of actual childhood experiences (1973, p. 235), it is the content and structure of working models that are hypothesized to affect later close relationships—irrespective of actual childhood experiences.

Main grouped mothers according to their children's attachment classifications and examined differences in how they talked about their own childhood experiences with primary caretakers. She then used these differences in current representations of childhood experiences to define three parallel adult attachment groups and developed an interview method of assessing the adult styles (the Adult Attachment Interview; George, Kaplan, & Main, 1987). Allen and Hauser (1991) found that the observed quality of parent-child interactions in early adolescence predicted the quality of attachment representations 10 years later. Subsequent work has confirmed that parents' attachment representations are predictive of their infants' attachment patterns (e.g., Green-Eichberg, 1987; Main & Goldwyn, in press) and of the quality of the parent-child relationship beyond infancy (Crowell & Feldman, 1988; Main et al., 1985). Adult attachment representations have even been found to be predictive of infant outcomes when measured before the birth of the child (Benoit, Vidovic, & Roman, 1991; Fonagy et al., 1991; Ward & Carlson, 1991). For instance, Fonagy and colleagues found that 76% of mothers classified as autonomous (secure) prenatally had infants who were classified as secure in the Strange Situation 1 year later; in contrast, only 27% of mothers classified as insecure had infants classified as secure 1 year later. Using similar methods, Benoit reported striking evidence of concordance in attachment patterns across not just two, but three generations (maternal grandmothers, mothers, and infants) (Benoit et al., 1991).

Kobak and Sceery (1988) found evidence for the following hypothesized distinctions between Main's attachment groupings in terms of self and other representations:

> Individuals classified as Secure would represent the self as experiencing relatively little distress and others as being sources of support; those classified as Dismissive [corresponding to avoidant in childhood] would minimize acknowledgement of distress in self

representations while seeing others as not being supportive . . . and those classified as Preoccupied [corresponding to the childhood ambivalent group] would view the self as distressed while viewing others as supportive. (p. 138)

The fourth logical possibility of combinations of self and other representations—the self as distressed and others as unsupportive—was not addressed. This is particularly notable, given that Bowlby explicitly hypothesized that self and other models are likely to develop so as to be mutually confirming. Thus an unwanted child will come to both expect others to be uncaring and to feel essentially unlovable (Bowlby, 1977).

Attachment in Adult Relationships

Bowlby strongly maintains that the attachment system continues to operate throughout the life span and that how "an individual's attachment behavior becomes organized within his personality . . . [determines] the pattern of affectional bonds he makes during his life" (Bowlby, 1980, p. 41). Enduring romantic relationships generally are expected to be the most important attachment relationships in adult life. Not only are individual differences in attachment styles expected to be highlighted in romantic relationships, but such relationships also potentially may play a therapeutic role in moderating the effects of difficult early attachment relationships (e.g., Brown & Harris, 1978; Quinton, Rutter, & Liddle, 1984). Close nonromantic friends also may operate as attachment figures in adulthood (see Ainsworth, 1982, 1989). In fact, any adult relationships potentially could meet the criteria for evidence of an attachment component: (a) a desire for proximity with the attachment figure, especially under stressful conditions, (b) a sense of security derived from contact with the attachment figure, and (c) distress or protest when threatened with loss or separation from the attachment figure (see Weiss, 1982). Although there are important differences between childhood and adult attachment relationships (see Bartholomew, 1990; Hazan & Hutt, 1991), the underlying dynamics may be surprisingly similar (see also Shaver, Hazan, & Bradshaw, 1988).

Hazan and Shaver (1987) conceptualized romantic love as an attachment process and developed a self-report measure to differentiate adult analogues of the three infant attachment patterns. The *secure* style is characterized by ease of trusting and getting close to others; the *ambivalent* by a desire to merge with a partner, coupled with a fear of not being loved sufficiently; and the *avoidant* by discomfort in trusting and becoming close to others. As expected, individuals who chose a secure self-description reported more positive experiences and beliefs about love, and more favorable descriptions of their childhood relationships with parents than did insecure individuals. Ambivalent individuals reported especially high levels of obsessive preoccupation, desire for union, and the tendency to fall in love easily. Avoidant individuals reported the lowest trust and the most cynical beliefs about love. These results have been replicated and extended in a number of studies (e.g., Collins & Read, 1990; Feeney & Noller, 1990).

Hazan and Shaver's (1987) method of operationalizing adult attachment patterns has inspired a thriving new area of research that is moving in exciting directions. For instance, researchers have investigated attachment patterns in dating couples (Collins & Read, 1990; Davis & Kirkpatrick, 1991; Simpson, 1990), interactive behaviors of couples in the laboratory (Simpson, Rholes, & Nelligan, in press), the social-cognitive processes associated with attachment patterns (e.g., Collins, 1991), and the process of relinquishing parents as attachment figures (Hazan & Hutt, 1991). This framework has been used also to understand work satisfaction (Hazan & Shaver, 1990), religious beliefs (Kirkpatrick & Shaver, 1990, in press), and the fear of death (Mikulincer, Florian, & Tolmacz, 1990).

The work of Hazan and Shaver is important because it translates the childhood attachment paradigm into terms directly relevant to adult relationships. It differs in significant ways, however, from the previous adult attachment work by Main and colleagues. First, Main's work (and the Adult Attachment Interview in particular) focuses on family and parent-child relations, while Hazan's work focuses on romantic relations. Second, Main's assessment approach deals with *how* people have organized information about their childhood experiences and *how* this information is habitually processed, while Hazan assesses the *content* of people's conscious beliefs about their patterns in romantic relationships. Moreover, some of the most important factors in judging adult attachment patterns from an attachment interview (such as internal coherence, defensiveness, and idealization) may lead to systematic distortions in self-report attachment ratings. Finally, there are reasons to believe that the groupings yielded by the two approaches may differ in systematic ways. Most important, dismissing individuals as identified by Main look similar to secure individuals on self-report measures of distress and social competence. The dismissing style is, in part, defined in terms of defensively excluding from awareness negative feelings or attachment needs (or, in Bowlby's terms, "compulsive self-reliance") (see Cassidy & Kobak, 1988; Main et al., 1985). In contrast, avoidant individuals identified by Hazan's measure appear to consciously hold a negative view of themselves: They report low self-confidence and elevated levels of emotional extremes in relationships, self-doubts, and feelings of unacceptability to others (Feeney & Noller, 1990; Hazan & Shaver, 1987; Simpson, 1990). In fact, on a wide variety of measures, self-reported avoidant subjects typically report levels of distress comparable to those of ambivalent subjects and significantly more distress than secure subjects. Thus, although Main's interview approach to assessing representations of childhood relations and Hazan's self-report measure of styles of relating in romantic relationships were explicitly defined to correspond to child attachment classifications, these classifications may be conceptually quite different, and neither may be ideally suited to understanding the full range of variations in adult attachment relations.

To address these issues, I have proposed an expanded model of adult attachment patterns that builds on and integrates previous work applying an attachment perspective to adults (Bartholomew, 1990). The model was stimulated by a series of intensive interviews with young adults about their close relationships. During the course of these interviews, it became evident that the domains of family relations and peer relations should be assessed separately: Although similar patterns of beliefs and expectations were often evident across the two domains, in many cases they diverged considerably. It also became apparent that at least two distinct patterns of avoidance in adults can be identified (corresponding roughly to Main's dismissing style and Hazan's avoidant style) and that these two avoidant patterns are evident in both representations of family relations and peer relations. Finally I came to the conclusion that to understand adult attachment patterns, it is important to take into consideration both individuals' perceptions of themselves and their expectations of others. Thus two people can have similar perceptions of themselves but approach close relationships in very different ways; similarly two people can behave in similar ways but have very different phenomenal experiences and motivations for their behavior. I therefore looked to Bowlby's conceptual analysis of internal models of the self and other to provide a framework for examining adult attachment patterns.

Within this new framework, four prototypic attachment patterns can be defined in terms of the intersection of two underlying dimensions: positivity of models of the self and positivity of models of hypothetical others (see Figure 2.1). The degree of positivity of self models is associated with the degree of emotional dependence on others for self-validation; thus a *positive self-model* can be conceptualized as an internalized sense of self-worth that is not dependent on ongoing external validation. The *positivity of other model* reflects expectations of others' availability and supportiveness; positive other models thus facilitate actively seeking out intimacy and support in close relationships, and negative other models lead to avoidance of intimacy and support. This model departs from earlier work by differentiating two patterns marked by a hesitancy to become intimate with others: a *fearful* style characterized by a desire for social contact that is inhibited by fears of rejection and a *dismissing* style characterized by a defensive denial of the need or desire for intimate contact. This distinction reflects differing models of the self: People who fearfully avoid intimacy view themselves as undeserving of the love and support of others, and those who dismiss intimacy possess a positive model of the self that minimizes the subjective awareness of distress or social needs. These two avoidant patterns conceptually overlap with the avoidant style assessed by the Hazan self-report measure and the dismissing style assessed by Main's interview method, respectively. In contrast, those with a *preoccupied* style view themselves negatively but possess a positive model of others that motivates them to strive to find self-validation and fulfillment in intimate relationships. Finally those showing a *secure* pattern possess positive models of both themselves and others and, correspondingly, enjoy both personal autonomy and satisfying intimate relations with others. To summarize the model, the quality of early attachment relationships is hypothesized to lay the foundation of a sense of self and an orientation to others, and the intersection of these two dimensions yields varying approaches to close relationships.

The introduction of a fourth attachment pattern is consistent with recent work identifying a fourth distinct attachment pattern in infancy (Crittenden, 1988; Main & Solomon, 1990). Crittenden calls the fourth style "avoidant/ambivalent" because it combines elements of both insecure styles. Indirect evidence that this pattern may be parallel to the fearful adult pattern has been provided by Latty-Mann and Davis (1988) and Brennan, Shaver, and Tobey (in press).

Previous work has demonstrated that (a) the four patterns can be reliably assessed on the basis of semistructured interviews (the Peer Attachment Interview and Family Attachment Interview), (b) the resulting assessments predict individuals' self-concepts and interpersonal functioning (according to self-, peer-, and romantic partner-reports), (c) the model is applicable to both close peer relationships and representations of attachment experiences in the family, and (d) attachment patterns in these two domains and across self-reports and interview measures are moderately correlated (Bartholomew & Horowitz, 1991; Bartholomew & Scharfe, 1991). These findings have been replicated and extended by other researchers using both self-report and interview methods of assessment (e.g., Brennan et al., in press; Doumas, 1990;

MODEL OF SELF
(Dependence)

		Positive (Low)	Negative (High)
Positive (Low)		**SECURE** Comfortable with intimacy and autonomy	**PREOCCUPIED** Preoccupied with relationships
MODEL OF OTHER (Avoidance)			
Negative (High)		**DISMISSING** Dismissing of intimacy	**FEARFUL** Fearful of intimacy

Figure 2.1. Four Category Model of Adult Attachment

Fiala, 1991; O'Hearn & Davis, 1992). In addition, various studies independently have found that two dimensions underlie adult attachment patterns and that these two dimensions are consistent with the dimensions proposed by the four-category model (for a review, see Shaver & Hazan, in press). The relationship between Main's dismissing style and the dismissing style identified by the four-category model has not, as yet, been tested. However, Brennan et al. (in press) have confirmed that the avoidant style identified by Hazan's self-report measure largely overlaps with the fearful style.

Consistent with the hypothesis of continuity between childhood and adult attachment patterns, self-report measures of adult attachment have been correlated in theoretically consistent ways with self-reports of childhood parent-child relationships (e.g., Collins & Read, 1990; Hazan & Shaver, 1987). Through the use of a variety of other measures of relationship functioning, evidence also has accumulated of some continuity between childhood and adulthood patterns (for selective reviews see Belsky & Pensky, 1988; Ricks, 1985; and Rutter, 1988). None of this work, however, provides convincing evidence of continuity in specific attachment patterns over the life span or across generations, and, in many cases, the reported associations are weak. In contrast, Main's interview measure of family attachment representations has yielded a high concordance in attachment patterns across generations (e.g., Benoit et al., 1991; Fonagy et al., 1991). Although not conclusive, these findings are certainly suggestive of continuity in attachment patterns over the life span—at least as assessed by an interview measure of family attachment representations.

To explore these issues within the four-category model, ratings of family attachment representations (on the basis of a Family Attachment Interview) were correlated with both self-report and interview-based ratings of attachment in adult peer relationships (Bartholomew, 1989; Bartholomew & Horowitz, 1991). As expected, family attachment representations were more highly correlated with an interview-based measure of peer attachment patterns than a self-report measure: The average correlation between ratings of corresponding attachment patterns was .44 for interviews and .28 for self-reports. Points of divergence between the two sets of analyses point to limitations of relying exclusively on self-report measures of adult attachment. For example, the family preoccupied rating was highly correlated with the interview measure of preoccupied tendencies in peer relations ($r = .66$, $p < .01$), but was uncorrelated with the self-report preoccupied ratings ($r = .19$, ns). Moreover, the family preoccupied rating was positively correlated with self-reported security of attachment ($r = .32$, $p < .01$), suggesting defensiveness or self-presentational biases in self-report ratings. In contrast, the interview-based rating of preoccupied peer relations not only was correlated with ratings of family representations as expected but also was associated in predictable ways with specific dimensions of family representations. Thus preoccupation in peer relations was positively correlated with a common feature of preoccupied family representations—*role reversal,* or the tendency for children to look after the emotional needs of their parents at the expense of having their own needs met ($r = .31$ with mother and $r = .51$ with father). Thus initial results (particularly those based on interview-based attachment assessments) are consistent with the hypothesis of moderate correspondence across the family and peer domains.

In summary the four-category model is the first to provide a theoretical rationale for why four, rather than three, distinct attachment patterns are expected and the first to specify the expected *relations* among attachment styles. Within the present framework, subjects are rated for the *degree* to which they correspond to theoretically derived prototypes of each pattern. Individuals thereby are conceptualized as located in a two-dimensional space according to the relative positivity of their models of self and others. Such an approach is more sensitive to the complexity of individual differences than traditional grouping approaches. In addition, this model has several advantages for organizing previous work in adult attachment: (a) It is applicable to multiply relationship domains, (b) it can be considered in terms of styles or dimensions underlying attachment, and (c) it can be assessed on the basis of interviews or self-reports.

Adult Attachment and Relationship Competence

Adult attachment patterns summarize a wide variety of information relevant to the quality of adult relationships. For instance, the Peer Attachment Interview, designed to assess the four-category model, covers a cross section of close peer relationships (including friendships) and explores the subject's entire history of romantic relationships (Bartholomew & Horowitz, 1991). Based on the interview material, ratings are made of behavior in close relationships (e.g., support seeking, emotional expressiveness, self-disclosure, caregiving), emotional experiences in close relationships (jealousy, warmth, separation anxiety, self-confidence), general orientations to close relationships (trust, dependency), and characteristic relationship dynamics (mutuality, dominance). The interview ratings also assess subjects' ways of thinking about and organizing information about attachment (including internal consistency of the interview, defensiveness, and idealization of others). All of these factors are taken into consideration in assessing the attachment patterns, as well as consistencies across the different domains. For example, preoccupied individuals tend to be behaviorally extremely demanding of support and attention and emotionally hypersensitive and volatile. They also tend to be self-deprecating and excessively dependent on others' approval for self-validation and, at the same time, prone to idealize others.

Although self-report measures of adult attachment do not explicitly assess as many aspects of close relationships, both brief single-item measures (e.g., Hazan & Shaver, 1987) and dimensional measures of adult attachment (e.g., Collins & Read, 1990; Simpson, 1990) are moderately correlated with interview measures (see Bartholomew & Griffin, 1992). Moreover, the wide variety of relationship-related measures that have been found to be correlated with these self-report measures (including standard measures of relationship functioning, measures of beliefs about relationships, behavioral measures of relationship communication, and projective measures) suggest that they are capturing general styles of interaction in close relationships (e.g., Collins & Read, 1990; Feeney & Noller, 1990; Feeney, Noller, & Callan, 1991; Mikulincer et al., 1990; Simpson, 1990; Simpson et al., in press).

In this section, I selectively review research showing that adult attachment patterns are related to various facets of relationship competence. For the most part, this body of work indicates the usefulness of applying an attachment perspective to adult relationships and does not address the issue of continuity between childhood and adult patterns. In spite of the fact that platonic friendships may function as primary attachment relationships in adult life (e.g., Ainsworth, 1989), this work focuses primarily on adult romantic relationships and gives little attention to adult platonic relationships. This emphasis may stem from Hazan and Shaver's initial conceptualization of romantic love as an attachment process. However, at least within the four-category model, adult attachment patterns are as strongly associated with the quality of platonic friendships as with the quality of romantic relationships (Bartholomew & Horowitz, 1991; O'Hearn & Davis, 1992).

Interpersonal Problems

The varying interpersonal styles described by adult attachment patterns may or may not be considered problematic from the point of view of individuals or their social partners. Therefore, as an initial test of whether insecure attachment patterns in adults are associated with interpersonal difficulties, Bartholomew and Horowitz directly asked subjects to report on their interpersonal problems using the Inventory of Interpersonal Problems (IIP; Horowitz, Rosenberg, Baer, Ureno, & Villasenor, 1988). The IIP is designed to measure a broad cross section of interpersonal problems. The items measure specific problems, rather than styles or dispositions, (e.g., "It is hard for me to feel close to other people" and "I let other people take advantage of me too much").

A different profile of problems was found to be associated with each adult attachment pattern as assessed by attachment interviews focusing on peer relationships (Bartholomew & Horowitz, 1991). Secure individuals reported a relatively low mean level of problems in their relations with others, and, to the extent that they did experience problems, those problems were not distinctive in content. Consistent with prior findings suggesting that dismissing individuals deny experiencing subjective distress, those with a dismissing style also reported a low mean level of problems. The problems that were reported, however, strongly clustered around problems with becoming intimate with and feeling close to others. The two insecure styles defined by negative self-models—the fearful and preoccupied—were both associated with a higher mean endorsement of interpersonal problems. However, the profiles associated with these two styles were behaviorally distinct. The fearful tended to report problems related to feeling afraid around people, being unable to express their feelings in relationships, and lacking assertiveness in dealing with people. In contrast, the preoccupied tended to report problems with being overly dominant and demanding in relationships. Typical items that this group endorsed included "I try to change other people too much" and "I try to be the center of attention too much."

These profiles of problems have been validated by the reports of same-sex friends (Bartholomew & Horowitz, 1991) and by the reports of opposite-sex romantic partners (Bartholomew & Scharfe, 1991). In addition, ratings of family attachment representations (based on interviews) were related to reports of interpersonal problems (Bartholomew & Horowitz, 1991). Family attachment ratings were associated with the dimensions of dominance/submission and warmth/coldness underlying reports of interpersonal problems. The family ratings were associated especially strongly with the degree to which individuals experienced problems relating to being too cold and distant versus overly warm and giving in their social relations: The family ratings predicted 31% of the warmth dimension of interpersonal problems. Thus adult attachment representations in both the peer and family domains appear to be predictive of patterns of interpersonal difficulties.

Interpersonal Dependency

Consistent with the four-category model, the attachment styles defined as showing a negative self-model—the fearful and preoccupied—were both found to be associated with high interpersonal dependency (Bartholomew & Larsen, 1991). Parallel results were found by Sperling and Borgaro (1991) in a laboratory study of reciprocity of interpersonal feedback. Using a unidimensional scale of anxious romantic attachment that is expected to line up roughly along the self-model dimension, Sperling found that insecurely attached subjects were significantly more susceptible to feedback from an opposite-sex confederate than were secure subjects. Correlational studies also have documented a variety of characteristics that are expected to be associated with personal insecurity and overdependency: emotional extremes in relationships (Hazan & Shaver, 1987), low trust and susceptibility to experience negative feelings in relationships (Simpson, 1990), and low confidence in relationships (Feeney & Noller, 1990).

Although the negative consequences of excessive dependency are well documented (e.g., Barnett & Gotlib, 1988), the potential consequences of excessive independence have not been explored. Interestingly, however, the *dismissing style* was found to be associated with an elevated level of defensive autonomy or counterdependence: Individuals with this style tended to insist that they did not want or need the acceptance or support of others (Bartholomew & Larsen, 1991). These findings are reminiscent of Bowlby's (1980) description of compulsively self-reliant adults who maintain a detached or emotionally self-sufficient stance to defend against the awareness of unfulfilled attachment needs.

Relationship Communication

Individual differences in attachment patterns have implications for various aspects of communication in personal relationships—in particular, self-disclosure, regulation of feelings in relationships, support seeking and giving, and conflict resolution. Within the four-category model, openness of communication (operationalized as self-disclosure) is one of the defining features of the other-model dimension. Thus negative expectations of others lead both the fearful and the dismissing avoidant styles to inhibit self-disclosure with friends and romantic partners (Bartholomew & Horowitz, 1991; Bartholomew & Scharfe, 1991). This pattern of results has been replicated in a number of studies. Collins and Read (1990) found that a scale assessing comfort with, versus avoidance of, closeness was positively correlated with self-disclosure in dating relationships. Using a similar closeness scale, Feeney et al. (1991) found a positive correlation with marital disclosure as obtained from a 1-week diary measure (although this effect was found for men only). In an intensive study of self-disclosure and adult attachment, Mikulincer and Nachshon (1991) confirmed that the avoidant pattern of attachment (as assessed by Hazan's three-style measure), in contrast to the secure and ambivalent patterns, was associated with lower levels of disclosure and less positive responses to the disclosure of others. Interestingly, ambivalent subjects, in contrast to the secure, reported less flexibility in adjusting their levels of self-disclosure to the social situation and displayed less reciprocity in the content of their disclosure. Correspondingly we have found that preoccupied individuals tend to be indiscriminate and even intrusive in their self-disclosure (Bartholomew & Horowitz, 1991).

Adult attachment patterns can be conceptualized as distinct strategies of regulating negative affect within close relationships (see Cassidy & Kobak, 1988; Kobak & Sceery, 1988). A negative self-model is associated with heightened subjective distress and a tendency to focus on negative affect. Correspondingly Simpson (1990) found that continuous measures of both the avoidant (fearful) and ambivalent styles were associated with the tendency to experience negative affect within relationships. The valence of the other-model, in contrast, is predictive of the degree to which individuals express negative feelings and actively seek out proximity and support when distressed (Bartholomew & Horowitz, 1991). Those with negative other models have learned, presumably, that people are likely to ignore or reject their attempts to gain support. Thus the avoidant styles are negatively correlated with support seeking toward family members, friends, and romantic partners (Bartholomew, 1989; Bartholomew & Horowitz, 1991; Bartholomew & Scharfe, 1991; Kobak & Sceery, 1988). Similarly avoidant infants communicate less with their mothers when they are upset (Grossmann, Grossmann, & Schwan, 1986). Attachment theory is less helpful in predicting how the adult patterns are expected to differ in their capacities and inclinations to provide support; however, vicariously experienced distress also may lead to active avoidance on the part of avoidant individuals, resulting in less provision of support to social partners.

Simpson et al. (in press) found clear support for the importance of the avoidance dimension in predicting support seeking and giving. These authors studied the tendency of dating partners to seek out and provide support to one another when one partner was confronted with an anxiety-provoking situation. They found that women comfortable with closeness tended to seek more support as their level of anxiety increased, while avoidant women tended to seek less support with increasing anxiety. Similarly male partners comfortable with closeness gave more support as their partners' levels of anxiety increased, while avoidant men gave less support as their partners' levels of anxiety increased. Kobak and Hazan (1991) also found positive associations between security of attachment in the marital relationship and openness of disclosure and supportiveness of response in a couple-confiding task.

Individual differences in strategies of regulating negative affect are reflected also in styles of conflict resolution within relationships. Using a standard laboratory discussion of relationship problems, Kobak and Hazan (1991) demonstrated that security of attachment within the marital relationship was positively associated with more constructive approaches to problem solving as rated by observers. Feeney and colleagues (1991) also found that greater security of attachment was associated with more effective conflict resolution among newlyweds as assessed by both self-report and observational measures (see also Howes, Markman, & Lindahl, 1991; Senchak & Leonard, 1992). Individuals with a preoccupied attachment pattern appear to be at particular risk for maladaptive approaches to conflict. The combination of high distress and insecurity with an expressive, dominating interpersonal style may lead to an overly confrontive approach to conflict. Consistent with this profile, Levy and Davis (1988) found that ambivalent subjects were especially likely to endorse a dominating conflict style, and Feeney et al. (1991) found that anxious attachment was related to high levels of conflict in couples, as well as more coercive and destructive communication patterns.

Relationship Involvement and Satisfaction

The avoidance dimension underlying adult attachment patterns is systematically related to the degree of involvement in romantic relationships. In a study using Hazan's three-style self-report measure, avoidant subjects were less likely to report being in love than secure or ambivalent subjects (Feeney & Noller, 1990). In a study I conducted using the four-category model, both avoidant groups were less likely to be involved presently in a romantic relationship (approximately 26%, in contrast to 70% of the secure and preoccupied) (Bartholomew, 1989). From various interview and self-report measures included in the study, a number of reasons emerged as to why avoidant young adults may be at a disadvantage in forming romantic relationships. Both avoidant groups reported low sociability; they had relatively few friends and were not as popular among their peers as the secure and preoccupied. Fearful individuals carried the additional burden of extreme shyness and a hesitancy to pursue relationships out of a fear of rejection; dismissing individuals often reported lacking the motivation to actively pursue relationships. Parallel results were found for the length of previous relationships. In this college sample, the average length of previous relationships was about twice as long for secure and preoccupied subjects as for subjects in the two avoidant groups (Bartholomew, 1989). However, these results were only partially consistent with those of Hazan and Shaver's (1987) community sample: They found that both the ambivalent and avoidant groups reported shorter relationships than secure subjects.

Interestingly, differences in relationship lengths have not been reported in studies in which only romantically involved subjects were included (e.g., Collins & Read, 1990; Simpson, 1990). Moreover, in the only study to date examining attachment patterns in dating relationships over time, few reliable associations were found between attachment patterns and relationship stability over a 3-year period (Davis & Kirkpatrick, 1991). One notable exception was the tendency of ambivalent women (as self-classified on Hazan's measure) to have more stable relationships than secure or avoidant women. Although contrary to expectations, this result is not surprising, given the high dependency and dominating interpersonal style associated with the ambivalent pattern. This finding is hard to reconcile, however, with Hazan and Shaver's (1987) finding that preoccupied subjects reported shorter romantic relationships than secure subjects (using the same self-report measure). Thus, although the evidence suggests that attachment patterns may have more impact on the formation than the maintenance of relationships, further work in this area is clearly required.

In contrast to the longevity findings, several studies have examined and found evidence for the influence of attachment patterns on the quality of romantic relationships. Using a variety of measures of attachment and of dyadic adjustment (including satisfaction, commitment, trust, interdependence, problem intensity, and closeness), results have demonstrated consistently positive correlations between security of attachment and the quality of romantic relationships. Similar results have been found with dating relationships (e.g., Collins & Read, 1990; Davis & Kirkpatrick, 1991; Simpson, 1990) and with marital relationships (Feeney et al., 1991; Harrison-Greer, 1991; Howes et al., 1991; Senchak & Leonard, 1992). Self-reported security of attachment has even been found to be associated with optimism about the success of future dating relationships and marriage (Carnelley & Janoff-Bulman, 1992).

More specifically, patterns of correlations between attachment and relationship quality suggest that the adult attachment styles may have different implications for men and women. Most consistent has been the finding that for men, avoidance (whether measured by a dimensional measure or either avoidant style) predicts low relationship satisfaction for both members of a dyad, while for women anxious attachment (whether measured by a dimensional measure or the preoccupied/ambivalent style) predicts low relationship satisfaction for both members of a dyad (Collins & Read, 1990; Simpson, 1990; for partial support see Davis & Kirkpatrick, 1991; Harrison-Greer, 1991). To the degree that matching has been observed on attachment patterns, these matchings are also sex-linked. For instance, we have found that security of attachment in men is negatively correlated with the preoccupied rating of their female partners and that security of attachment in women is negatively correlated with avoidance in their male partners (Bartholomew & Scharfe, 1991; see also Collins & Read, 1990; Harrison-Greer, 1991; Simpson, 1990). These findings complement the satisfaction ratings: It appears that women are particularly unimpressed with avoidant partners and that more secure women are less likely to find themselves with avoidant men. Similarly men are especially dissatisfied with preoccupied partners, and more secure men are less likely to find themselves with preoccupied women.

Mechanisms of Continuity

An important next step is to identify the *mechanisms* by which adult attachment patterns are maintained. Attachment theory is consistent with a transactional model of social development in which individuals are both influenced by and actively construct their social environments (Sameroff & Chandler, 1975). In fact, it is precisely "because persons select and create later social environments that early relationships are viewed as having special importance" (Sroufe & Fleeson, 1986, p. 68). The degree to which early experiences predict later social functioning *independently* of continuity in the social environment is still a controversial and largely unexamined question (see Sroufe, Egeland, & Kreutzer, 1990, for a recent empirical study of this issue). But it seems reasonable to speculate that, over time, children gain more control over their social environments and, therefore, that their internal models of attachment relations become increasingly important in determining the quality of their relations outside the family. More specifically, working models are expected to be externalized and maintained through the choice of social environments and partners, habitual interaction patterns, and model-driven processing of socially relevant information.

Selective Affiliation

Selective affiliation, or the selection of social partners who are likely to confirm internal models, is expected to be important in maintaining adult attachment patterns (see Bartholomew, 1990). In fact, one of the most important distinctions between childhood and adult attachment relationships is that adults have much greater control over the people with whom they enter into and maintain personal relationships. For instance, individuals with a *dismissing style* may tend to choose preoccupied partners in order to validate their perceived need to maintain psychological distance–a preoccupied partner may, in fact, desire a pathological level of closeness with romantic partners. More generally, those who see themselves as undeserving of the love and acceptance of others are expected to have a greater than chance likelihood of entering into relationships with individuals who hold generally negative views of others. A striking example of selective affiliation at work has been presented by Swann and his colleagues: College students who had been randomly assigned roommates were more likely to wish to continue living with their roommates if the roommate held concordant views of their self-worth (Swann, Pelham, Hixon, & de la Ronde, 1991). Thus students with well-defined negative self-images preferred roommates who also thought poorly of them!

There is no evidence within an attachment perspective of selective affiliation in initial choice of relationship partners, but cross-sectional evidence is accumulating for nonrandom pairing of romantic partners based on attachment patterns. Collins and Read (1990) have reported positive correlations between romantic partners on scales related to security of attachment (also see Bartholomew & Scharfe, 1991; Harrison-Greer, 1991; Senchak & Leonard, 1992). As discussed previously, there is some evidence of specific sex-linked correlations of attachment patterns within couples: a negative correlation between male security and female anxiety and a negative correlation between female security and male avoidance. Findings also indicate a positive association between male avoidance and female anxious attachment (Bartholomew & Scharfe, 1991; Collins & Read, 1990; Davis & Kirkpatrick, 1991; Harrison-Greer, 1991). These results, taken as a whole, are consistent with selective affiliation in the attachment domain that is not reducible to a simple assortative mating (as demonstrated, for instance, by Buss, 1984, and Phillips, Fulker, Carey, & Nagoshi, 1988). However, longitudinal work is needed to examine how adult attachment patterns influence both the initial selection of relationship partners and the maintenance of relationships over time.

Interaction Patterns

Independent of initial partner choice, the interaction strategies associated with differing attachment styles may set in mo-tion self-fulfilling interpersonal patterns. For instance, the distancing expected of dismissing individuals may serve to fuel greater insecurity and dependency in their partners, leading to a self-perpetuating and mutually frustrating positive feedback loop. Although the interpersonal problems associated with each of the insecure patterns are suggestive of characteristic interaction patterns, little work has studied actual behavioral patterns. However, those studies that have looked at couple interaction in a laboratory setting have obtained very promising results. As previously discussed, (a) Simpson and colleagues (in press) found that the avoidance dimension of attachment was associated with deficits in seeking and giving support in an anxiety-provoking situation, (b) both Feeney and Howes found that the underlying dimensions of avoidance and anxiety were related to measures of couple communication and conflict strategies (Feeney et al., 1991; Howes et al., 1991), and (c) Kobak and Hazan (1991) documented associations between a Q-sort measure of security in the marital relationship and observed couple communication.

An important direction for future work is to assess the quality of interaction between subjects and strangers (or confederates) to examine whether attachment patterns are associated with interaction styles independent of partner choice and relationship histories. The one published study employing such a methodology found that adult attachment patterns do predict behavior in initial encounters with social partners: Avoidant attachment was associated with low disclosure and negative responses to disclosure by partners, and ambivalent attachment was associated with less flexibility of disclosure (Mikulincer & Nachshon, 1991). An important next step is to examine how interaction strategies associated with adult attachment patterns may elicit feedback from social partners that reinforces existing mental models and interaction patterns (see Swann, 1983, 1987).

Social Construal

A whole array of information-processing biases are available to guide the processing of social feedback to confirm internal models (see Swann, 1983, 1987). Internal models are expected to direct attention, organize and filter new information, and determine the accessibility of past experiences. Thereby, ambiguous stimuli—which, arguably, include virtually all social stimuli—tend to be assimilated into existing working models. Although a number of authors have discussed the applicability of information-processing biases to the understanding of working models of attachment (e.g., Bowlby, 1980; Main et al., 1985), little empirical work has been conducted in this area. A notable exception has been a series of studies by Collins (1991) showing that individuals explain relationship events in ways that are consistent with their models of attachment relations. She also has explored how the relationship between attachment style and behavior in close relationships may be mediated by explanations and emotions.

In the social environment, choice of social partners, style of interaction, and interpersonal construal are all closely intertwined. Thus individual differences in social construal may reflect real ongoing differences in experiences in close relationships. However, by controlling the social stimuli to which subjects respond, it is possible to isolate the expectations, construal biases, and interaction patterns that individuals bring to social situations. For example, Doumas (1990), working with the four-category model of adult attachment, demonstrated that subjects interpreted and emotionally responded to controlled social stimuli (films depicting separations and reunions) in ways consistent with their internal models of attachment. Standard experimental procedures also could be employed to study the conditions under which varying attachment representations are activated, how these representations guide processing and memory of relevant information, and how open they are to new information.

Caveats About Present Research

In spite of the recent explosion of research on adult attachment, surprisingly little attention has been given to specifying the nature of adult representations of attachment. The research varies widely in how these representations are conceptualized and assessed, with little recognition of the potential importance of these distinctions. Moreover, although assessments of adult attachment generally are assumed to reflect enduring attachment "styles," there is limited empirical basis for this assumption. Evidence of stability over time and evidence that attachment patterns are not entirely a reflection of current relationship dynamics are required.

Specificity of Attachment Representations

Adult attachment patterns have been defined variously in terms of intimate peer relations in general (e.g., Bartholomew & Horowitz, 1991), romantic relationships in general (e.g., Hazan & Shaver, 1987), a specific romantic relationship (e.g., Kobak & Hazan, 1991), and representations of family relations (e.g., Kobak & Sceery, 1988). Attachment patterns have been measured variously by dimensional or typological self-report measures (e.g., Collins & Read, 1990; Feeney & Noller, 1990), Q-sorts (e.g., Kobak & Hazan, 1991), and interviews (e.g., Kobak & Sceery, 1988). However, these distinctions have not been given sufficient attention in the field (cf. Shaver & Hazan, in press). For example, I am aware of no studies showing a correspondence between Hazan and Shaver's (1987) short self-report measure of romantic attachments and Main's intensive interview of representations of family relations (the Adult Attachment Interview), yet results yielded by these two measures are routinely cited together as if they describe the same patterns of attachment.

In my own work I have assessed representations of both familial and close peer relationships and have used multiple assessment methods (interviews, self-reports, and reports of significant others). Although the various domains and methods tend to converge, they are only moderately correlated and do not necessarily bear the same relations with outcome variables. For instance, interview-based ratings of peer and family attachment were found to predict interpersonal problems, but only peer attachment ratings made an independent contribution to the prediction of problems with dominance and submission (Bartholomew & Horowitz, 1991). Working with a somewhat different conceptualization of adult attachment, Sperling and colleagues have found that self-report attachment ratings of particular relationship types (with mother, father, friends, and sexual partners) are moderately correlated with one another but that mean endorsements of attachment patterns vary across relationship type (Sperling, Berman, & Fagen, 1991). Findings showing lack of concordance across different relationship domains (parental, romantic, and spiritual relationships) also have been reported by Kirkpatrick and Shaver (in press). Also suggestive of specificity in attachment representations are findings indicating that relationships with same- and opposite-sex parents may be differentially predictive of the quality of romantic relationships (e.g., Collins & Read, 1990; Jacobvitz, Fullinwider, & Loera, 1991). Clearly an important task for future work is to systematically compare attachment representations across relationship domains and methods of assessment.

Attachment Patterns as Individual or Relationship Characteristics: The Case of Selective Affiliation

A fundamental question in the study of adult attachment is the degree to which the identified attachment patterns are enduring dispositions that individuals bring to particular relationships or reflections of specific relationship dynamics or unique person-situation interactions (cf. Simpson, 1990). Observed correlations of attachment ratings within couples generally have been interpreted as indicating that individuals choose their romantic partners to complement their attachment patterns. Most of these findings, however, are based on self-report measures, and it is inherently difficult to interpret self-report ratings of attachment. For example, the finding that security in women is negatively correlated with avoidance in their male partners has at least four interpretations: (a) Secure women deliberately avoid becoming romantically involved with avoidant men (or avoidant men avoid becoming involved with secure women); (b) secure women are dissatisfied with avoidant partners and therefore tend to end such relationships, perhaps more so than women with other attachment patterns (or avoidant men tend to end relationships with secure women); (c) secure women, over time, encourage their male partners to become less avoidant, and/or avoidant males lead their partners to feel less secure; or (d) the attachment patterns of both partners are a reflection of the relationship dynamics that have developed within the particular relationship and do not bear any relation to enduring characteristics of either partner. Thus correlations between partners at one point in time may, at least in part, reflect the functioning of the current relationship rather than the operation of selective affiliation. Interestingly Simpson (1990) interprets a finding that the correlations between attachment patterns in dating couples are *low* as indicating that the ratings reflect dispositional tendencies rather than relationship dynamics. Other studies have found little or no evidence for selective affiliation (Cohn, Silver, Cowan, Cowan, & Pearson, 1991; Feeney et al., 1991; Howes et al., 1991).

The meaning of self-report attachment ratings is also called into question by the common finding that subjects in steady romantic relationships are very likely to rate themselves as secure on Hazan's self-report measure (Davis & Kirkpatrick, 1991: 75% secure; Howes et al., 1991: 90% secure; Kobak & Hazan, 1991: 76% secure; Senchak & Leonard, 1992: 82% secure). Our findings suggest that subjects in long-term romantic relationships inflate their ratings of security: In a sample of 158 such subjects, over 80% rated themselves as secure, although closer to 50% were judged to be primarily secure by expert coders on the basis of an interview (Bartholomew & Scharfe, 1991).

Interview ratings of attachment can help clarify the appropriate interpretation of these selective affiliation findings. Interview ratings are not as susceptible to influence by the current romantic relationship as self-report ratings because they cover a range of close relationships and also assess subjects' ways of thinking about and organizing information about attachment. We have found that self-report ratings are more strongly related to relationship satisfaction than interview ratings and that relationship satisfaction largely mediates observed correlations between partners' self-report ratings (Bartholomew & Scharfe, 1991). However, we also have found correlations between partner's interview-based attachment ratings that are consistent with previous research and that are not mediated by current relationship satisfaction. Of course, it still may be the case that the functioning of the current romantic relationship influences individuals' representations of their other close relationships and relationship histories.

Given that the quality of family attachment representations (as assessed by the Adult Attachment Interview) have been found to be surprisingly consistent across generations (e.g., Benoit et al., 1991), it is unlikely that family representations (at least as assessed by an interview method) are readily influenced by current relationships. Therefore partner matching on family attachment representations would provide the strongest evidence of selective affiliation operating in the attachment domain. With the exception of null results reported by Cohn, Silver, Cowan, Cowan, and Pearson (1991) (although the small sample size of 27 couples may have obscured potential relationships), I know of no findings that test selective affiliation with family attachment ratings. However Collins and Read's (1990) finding that retrospective descriptions of opposite-sex parents are associated with partners' self-report attachment ratings and Kobak's (1991) finding that interview-based family attachment ratings predict couple functioning over and above self-report ratings are suggestive that family attachment representations may play a role in selective affiliation.

Stability and Change

A basic premise of attachment theory is that internal representations of attachment formed during childhood and adolescence "tend to persist relatively unchanged into and throughout adult life" (Bowlby, 1977, p. 209). This stability is hypothesized to be based on an active process of construction and reconstruction; therefore, if people experience life events that are inconsistent with their existing models, changes in their models are expected. In particular, emotionally significant relationships that contradict earlier relationship patterns or major life transitions involving the adoption of new social roles may facilitate the reevaluation and potential reorganization of attachment representations (cf. Ricks, 1985). Thus, although attachment patterns are expected to have some traitlike stability, they also are expected to be sensitive to changes in the social environment. Several longitudinal studies have demonstrated temporal stability of attachment patterns during childhood (e.g., Main et al., 1985; Waters, 1978). Moreover, the stability of the caretaking environment appears to mediate the degree of stability of attachment patterns (e.g., Thompson, Lamb, & Estes, 1982).

In contrast to the childhood literature, little research has examined the stability of attachment patterns in adulthood. This gap is striking, given that childhood experiences are proposed to form the foundation of adult attachment styles and yet there is limited evidence of even short-term stability of these styles in adulthood. Moderate stability has been demonstrated over 1 or 2 months by using short self-report measures of attachment (Bartholomew, 1988; Collins & Read, 1990; Davis & Kirkpatrick, 1991). In addition, Hazan, Hutt, and Markus (1991) found approximately 78% stability in self-report attachment classifications over 1 year. Although promising, the inherent limitations of self-report measures call these results into question as sufficient evidence of stability. In particular, some individuals may be defensive and self-serving in their self-descriptions. For instance, it is striking that in Hazan's study the vast majority of reported changes in attachment patterns were from an insecure to secure style. This finding suggests that individuals become increasingly secure over time—a conclusion at odds with the proportions of insecure subjects observed in older samples (e.g., Hazan & Shaver, 1987). Alternatively at least some individuals who rated themselves as more secure at Time 2 may have entered important new relationships and their ratings may reflect the current state of their relationships rather than an enduring characteristic. This interpretation is consistent with Hazan's secondary finding that those subjects who changed were likely to have experienced relationships that were inconsistent with their prior pattern.

To date, only the stability of self-report attachment patterns focusing on romantic relationships has been investigated. It is therefore important for future research to determine the stability of interview-based attachment assessments and of family attachment patterns. Examination of relative patterns of stability and change across attachment domains also could shed light on the issue of specificity of attachment representations. For example, experiences with particular relevance to family or peer attachment patterns (e.g., leaving home for the first time or the breakup of a romantic relationship) may selectively influence attachment patterns in that domain.

In summary, attachment theory has proven exceptionally fruitful in understanding parent-child relationships, and initial work with adults suggests that it may prove equally fruitful in this new area of application. Research has demonstrated that individual differences in adult attachment patterns have implications for the formation and maintenance of satisfying adult relationships. In addition, a growing body of work is consistent with the hypothesis that early experiences in the family contribute to representational models that guide emotional reactions, interaction patterns, expectations, and processing biases in adult personal relationships. Although evidence showing direct links between childhood experiences and adult attachment patterns is still lacking, evidence does indicate that individuals' constructions of their childhood experiences may play a role in structuring the quality of their adult personal relationships.

However, there are pitfalls to this new line of research: Researchers have conceptualized and operationalized the attachment constructs in diverse ways without attending to the potential importance of these distinctions. Another crucial challenge for future work is to examine the theoretical assumptions underlying the notion of attachment "styles." Research needs to examine critically the degree of specificity of attachment patterns across domains and relationships and the processes through which attachment representations both guide the development of new relationships and accommodate to new experiences.

3

Parental Childhood Social Experiences and Their Effects on Children's Relationships

Martha Putallaz

Philip R. Costanzo

Tovah P. Klein

P eer relations researchers have become increasingly aware of the need to consider the role that parents play in their children's capacity to form satisfactory relationships with peers. Parents' interactional styles with their children (Baumrind, 1967; MacDonald & Parke, 1984; Putallaz, 1987), parental initiation and monitoring of peer activities (Bhavnagri & Parke, 1991; Finnie & Russell, 1988; Ladd & Golter, 1988), and parental social cognition (Mills & Rubin, 1990; Pettit et al., 1988) have all been found to relate to children's popularity and social competence among peers. Variations of a

AUTHORS' NOTE: We would like to thank Blair Sheppard for the helpful comments he provided on an earlier version of this chapter.

simple interactional model have been proposed in which the behaviors and cognitions of parents influence their children's social motivation, behavior, and cognition, which in turn affect the children's relationships with their peers (Parke, MacDonald, Beitel, & Bhavnagri, 1988; Putallaz & Heflin, 1990; Rubin, LeMare, & Lollis, 1990; Rubin & Sloman, 1984).

Far less is known, however, about the antecedents of the relevant parental behaviors. The purpose of this chapter is to expand the theoretical notions regarding parental influence on children's peer relationships to include at least one prior step in the process—the role that parents' childhood social experiences may play in the relationships that they develop with their children and the relationships that their children then develop with peers. It has long been presumed that the way parents construe their childhood experiences affects the way they treat their children. We explore this presumption, along with theories about possible modes of influence.

At least three issues have particular relevance for our purpose. First is the relation of childhood experiences of parental abuse to both the subsequent way these parents relate to their own children and the quality of their children's relationships with peers. Second is the remembered quality of the relationships that parents experienced with their own parents and the influences this has on their relationships with their children and on their children's subsequent peer relationships. Third is the parents' memories of their childhood peer relationships and the influence of these on their children's relationships. The separation of these areas in our review is not to imply their mutual exclusivity, but because the research has divided naturally in this manner for the most part. We conclude the chapter with an integration of these literatures and the proposal of an explanation of the role that parents play in the development of their children's social relationships. Although the definitions of *abuse* and categories of abuse differ across studies, the primary type of abuse considered in our review is physical child abuse.

Child Abuse

By far the most extreme, and perhaps the most readily identifiable, indicator of negative parent-child relationships is physical child abuse (although emotional abuse may be equally harmful, it is not as easily defined or identified, and much less is known about it). As such, abusive parent-child relationships can be highly informative about parenting patterns and the intergenerational transmission of social proclivities.

Child abuse is a serious and widespread problem. Estimates of the number of cases of child abuse annually range from 200,000 to 4 million in the United States alone, depending on the definition of *abuse* employed (Zigler & Hall, 1989). Yet despite its obvious importance, research identifying intergenerational processes or the dynamics of abuse, although expanding, remains relatively limited (see Cicchetti & Carlson, 1989, for a recent review). Interestingly the child abuse literature appears to be the earliest area of research identifying an empirical link between parents' childhood social experiences and their styles of parenting. Therefore study of the intergenerational transmission of abuse may not only help us understand how to prevent child abuse but also provide information regarding intergenerational transmission of patterns of parenting in general. Two types of studies mark the child abuse literature: *retrospective* (or *follow-back*) *studies* in which the childhoods of abusive parents are reviewed to identify potential predictors of abuse, and *prospective* (or *follow-forward*) *studies* in which parents at risk for abusing their children are identified prior to any incidence of abuse and are followed longitudinally to identify predictors of abuse. Information resulting from these different research approaches is reviewed, in turn, and then the relation between abusive parent-child relationships and children's peer relationships is considered.

Retrospective Studies. A parent's own experience of abuse as a child has long been associated with his or her abuse of offspring, beginning with the identification of the battered child syndrome (Fontana, 1968; Kempe, Silverman, Steele, Droegemueller, & Silver, 1962; Spinetta & Rigler, 1972). Such claims are well accepted and originally were established through the use of retrospective studies looking at the histories of parents identified as abusive. Melnick and Hurley (1969) found, among other factors, a high likelihood of emotional deprivation and abuse in the childhoods of abusive mothers. Steele and Pollock (1968) similarly found that, in a group of 60 abusive parents, all had themselves experienced abuse as children. Fontana (1968) also viewed abusive parents as suffering from their own abusive childhoods. Although a mechanism of transmission is not clearly spelled out in these studies, the authors' general conclusion is that children learn to love and nurture by being cared for by their parents. If they are not given such nurturance as children, they will be unable to properly nurture their own children. Consequently parents will re-create for their children what they themselves experienced in childhood. In addition, the models of aggressive behavior provided by abusive parents for their children serve to increase the likelihood of the intergenerational repetition of this abuse (Hertzberger, 1983). Social learning theory, then, in part, would explain the lessened ability of abused children to nurture their own children, as well as the increased incidence of continued abuse.

Researchers also have identified parental attitudes or personality traits related to abuse. Parents identified as abusive have been found to be highly demanding and to have premature expectations of their infants (Steele & Pollock, 1968), to be unable to empathize with their children (Melnick & Hurley, 1969), and to be unaware of the different stages of child development (Galdston, 1965). Further, abusive parents have been identified as angrier, more isolated, and more rigid than nonabusive parents (Milner & Wimberly, 1980; Spinetta, 1978).

The above studies have provided support for the psychiatric model, in which abusive parents are viewed as having some aberrant personal characteristic that leads them to abuse their children. Therefore researchers have focused on identifying the characteristics of maltreating parents (to the exclusion of process variables) that may distinguish them from nonmaltreating parents. This view contends that parents have a personality flaw that leads to their losing control, isolating themselves from others, distorting their children's abilities, and harboring anger from their own childhood experiences (for a review, see Wolfe, 1985). However, studies have not consistently shown a pattern of specific personality characteristics or traits that differentiates maltreating parents from nonmaltreating ones (Parke & Collmer, 1975; Wolfe, 1985). Further, researchers have moved from conceptualizations involving unidirectional influences to bidirectional ones (Bell, 1968; Belsky, 1980; Wolfe, 1985). Thus the parent and child are both seen as contributors to a dynamic process. Support for this contention comes from research identifying prematurity, handicapping conditions, and difficult temperament as factors putting children at risk for abuse (Belsky, 1980; Crittenden & Ainsworth, 1989; McCabe, 1984). The emphasis of researchers, then, has moved away from single variable, unidirectional influences of personality and has turned to interactive processes involving the parent, child, and, increasingly, sociological factors such as environmental stress. Thus the interaction between a parent's vulnerability to the stresses induced by both the child and the environment (e.g., unemployment, poverty) would be identified as contributors to parental maltreatment (Belsky, 1980; Wolfe, 1985).

Prospective Studies. Recently, despite great costs and complexity, researchers have begun to take a prospective, longitudinal approach to the study of child maltreatment. Typically these studies involve recruiting large samples of parents at risk for abuse due to, for example, their low socioeconomic status (e.g., Egeland, Jacobvitz, & Papatola, 1987; Egeland, Jacobvitz, & Sroufe, 1988; Pianta, Egeland, & Erickson, 1989) or the premature birth of their babies (e.g., Hunter & Kilstrom, 1979) and then following these families longitudinally to track incidence of abuse. Although retrospective studies have found substantial continuity of abuse (a nearly 100% rate of abuse in their own childhood characterizing abusive parents), prospective studies also reveal a second pattern, one of discontinuity, whereby some parents with an abusive history do not repeat this cycle with their own children (Cicchetti & Rizley, 1981; Egeland et al., 1988; Hunter & Kilstrom, 1979; Kaufman & Zigler, 1987).

Obviously the design of prospective studies does not result in a high number of abusive parents being studied. For example, Egeland et al. (1987) reported that 44 of the original 267 mothers in their sample had abused their children by the time of a 2-year follow-up (16.5%), while Hunter and Kilstrom (1979) found abuse had occurred in only 10 of their 255 families during the infants' first year (4%). Regardless, several findings have resulted consistently from these prospective studies of abuse. Similar to findings from retrospective abuse research is that evidence exists for intergenerational continuity of abuse for many, but not all, parents. Egeland et al. (1987) reported that by the time the children were 2 years of age, 70% of the mothers who had been abused as children were now abusing or providing only border-line care to (suspected of abusing) their own children. Of the 10 cases of abuse reported by Hunter and Kilstrom (1979), 9 occurred in families with a reported history of abuse, and in all 9 cases, the mothers reported a history of childhood abuse, whereas only 44% of the fathers did. It should be noted that these two major prospective research efforts inform us about abusive mothers, with little information regarding fathers, a topic discussed at greater length later in this review.

However, it is the results concerning the discontinuity of abuse from one generation to another that are perhaps the most intriguing. What enables parents who experienced parental abuse as children to escape repeating this abusive relationship with their own children? Two major factors appear to differentiate the nonrepeaters from the repeaters of abuse. The first factor is that mothers who described themselves as victims of childhood abuse but were not abusing their own children reported involvement in an emotionally supportive relationship with a nonabusing adult during childhood or with a therapist at any point in their lives (Egeland et al., 1988). Nonrepeaters were also more likely to be receiving emotional support currently from the father of the baby and/or other family members (Egeland et al., 1988; Hunter & Kilstrom, 1979).

The second factor is that nonrepeating parents were aware of their abuse and spoke of it in a coherent, integrated fashion with much emotion and detail and further verbalized how they wanted to raise their children. In contrast, the parents who abused their children spoke of their abusive history in vague generalities without emotion, were unable to recall specific experiences, and provided idealized descriptions of parents (Egeland et al., 1988; Hunter & Kilstrom, 1979). Further, they exhibited an apparent lack of understanding regarding how their own history might relate to the caretaking of their children (Egeland et al., 1987; Hunter & Kilstrom, 1979). Similar findings in a retrospective study of abusing and nonabusing parents by Trickett and Susman (1989) found that parents who had experienced harsh punishment as children but who were not abusing their own children were aware of their abusive past and viewed themselves as raising their children differently from how they were raised. Such results suggest that the parents' awareness of their abusive past and its accompanying affect and the way it could affect their relationship with their child was a second condition associated with discontinuity of childhood abuse.

Egeland and his colleagues, as well as other child abuse researchers, have conceptualized their results within the context of attachment theory. Attachment theory also serves as the primary conceptualization in the following section of this review (the influence of parents' remembered parent-child relationships on their own children's relationships). The reader is referred to Chapters 1 and 2 in this volume for a more detailed discussion of this theory than is contained in the following description.

Attachment Theory. Briefly, attachment theory is based on Bowlby's (1973, 1980, 1982) ethological-evolutionary conception of the attachment behavioral system, in which attachment is viewed as a basis for both protection from predators and exploration of the environment. The caregiver's sensitivity and responsiveness to the infant's cues and signals, and availability in times of distress affect the degree of trust and security the infant develops as a consequence of the attachment relationship.

According to Bretherton's (1985) discussion of Bowlby's (1973) concept, the child's internal working model of the attachment relationship is divided into complementary internal working models of the self and other. A rejecting attachment figure, then, would cause a child to develop an internal working model of that parent as rejecting and a complementary one of him- or herself as not worthy of love and comfort. Similarly an accepting attachment figure would cause a child to develop an internal working model of the parent as loving and of him- or herself as worthy of this love. Sroufe and Fleeson (1986) have proposed that, through dyadic interaction, the child would learn both of the roles characterizing the relationship. Thus abused children would internalize the roles of both the victim and the aggressor and would be able to reenact both roles at a later point. Relationships, therefore, are not only internalized by the individual but also are carried forward to new relationships (Sroufe & Fleeson, 1986).

Bowlby (1980) proposed that repeated experiences of rejection may lead to a deactivation of the attachment behavioral system and a defensive exclusion or distortion of attachment-relevant information from certain levels of processing, presumably to avoid the pain and anger associated with repeated rejection (see Chapter 2, this volume, for an extended discussion of this process). Indeed behavioral observations of young abused children have found them to be avoidant of their caregivers during dyadic interactions (Egeland & Sroufe, 1981; George & Main, 1979; Jacobson & Straker, 1982). Following from this, Main and Goldwyn (1984) posited that analogous cognitive processes also operate in adults who had experienced maltreatment as children. Just as the rejected infant avoids its mother, the rejected parent shifts attention away from attachment experiences and their accompanying affect in an effort to preserve a certain type of mental organization.

This conceptualization is in keeping with the findings reported earlier differentiating mothers who repeated their childhood abuse from those who did not. The repeaters spoke of their childhoods in vague and incoherent terms, unable to integrate their experiences into a cohesive recollection (Egeland et al., 1987; Egeland et al., 1988; Hunter & Kilstrom, 1979). They also spoke of their childhood memories without emotion, separating the cognition and affect, a notion referred to as *splitting* (Sullivan, 1953). This avoidant pattern may play a key role in the transmission of abuse. According to this viewpoint, the mothers who abused their children apparently split off their own victimization from an integrated view of their identities, while the nonabusive mothers spoke of their victimization more directly and coherently, integrating it into a more complete picture of their childhoods (Egeland, 1991).

Egeland (1991) recently speculated that precursors of the avoidant cognitive pattern identified in the mothers may be developing in the abused children whom he and his colleagues have been following longitudinally. The children (who are now entering adolescence) appear to differ from the nonabused children in their responses to projective test pictorial stimuli. The stories of abused children that included themes of anger and separation were tentative and fragmented and seemed to avoid or dismiss emotionally arousing information. In contrast, the stories of nonabused children included anger within a coherent framework of conflict and its resolution. The author interpreted the fragmentation displayed by the abused children as evidence of their attempts to avoid or dismiss information that was emotionally arousing, much like the splitting evidenced by their mothers.

Once established, these internal working models are posited to be quite resistant to change as they operate outside of conscious awareness and new information is assimilated into the existing schema (Bretherton, 1985; Main et al., 1985). The stability of working models would account for the strong intergenerational transmission of abuse. Although resistant to change, it is proposed that a cognitive-affective reworking of the "internal working model" of the self in relation to early parent-child relationships does take place in some rejected and/or maltreated individuals, resulting in a decrease in cognitive distortions and a lessening of the risk of repetition of abuse (Main & Goldwyn, 1984). Recovery of the factual events of childhood, along with the repressed painful affect associated with those memories, is presumed to be necessary for this reworking to occur (see Chapter 1, this volume, for further discussion). Fraiberg, Adelson, and Shapiro (1975) provided compelling case studies of two abusing mothers, who had themselves experienced child abuse, breaking the cycle of abuse following their ability to recall the facts and emotions surrounding their childhood victimization. During this process, these two mothers also experienced caring and emotionally supportive relationships with their therapists, one of the factors discussed previously as associated with breaking the cycle of abuse. Main and Goldwyn (1984) proposed that the reworking of a representational process may take place assisted by therapy or simply as the result of new environments and new relationships. The process of reworking, then, would account for the critical role of experiencing a supportive relationship in order to break the cycle of abuse, although the particular qualities of such a relationship remain unclear. Such relationships may serve a corrective or compensatory function for individuals whose primary relationships in their families of origin were so problematic (Belsky & Pensky, 1988).

Peer Relationships. In attachment theory, children who experience abusive relationships with their parents also would have difficulty in relationships with their peers. Specifically the reenactment of the victim or the aggressor roles learned from the parent-child relationship would be expected. Although research on abused children's peer relationships is limited, the evidence is consistent with these predictions. In contrast to their nonabused counterparts, abused children are less well liked by their peers (Haskett & Kistner, 1991) and evidence more aggressive or avoidant behavior (George & Main, 1979), more aggression especially in response to frustration (Herrenkohl & Herrenkohl, 1981), and a higher level of isolation and withdrawal (Jacobson & Straker, 1982) when interacting with their peers. The heightened aggression and isolated/avoidant behaviors shown by abused children are similar to behaviors found in abusive adults (Herrenkohl & Herrenkohl, 1981; Main & Goldwyn, 1984), which would also support a social learning explanation for these behaviors.

Perhaps most disturbing are the observed responses of abused children to the distress of other children (Klimes-Dougan & Kistner, 1990; Main & George, 1985). Abused toddlers responded to the distress of their peers with fear, threats, and angry gestures, at times mixing comforting and angry behaviors together (gentle patting escalating into hitting). In contrast, the nonabused toddlers tended to show prosocial behaviors, including sadness, empathy, and concern for the distressed children (Main & George, 1985). Abused preschoolers also were reported to be more likely than nonabused preschoolers to withdraw from or aggress against distressed peers. Additionally, abused children caused distress significantly more often than nonabused children (Klimes-Dougan & Kistner, 1990). Thus the experience of being abused as a child has implications for not only the later relationships these parents form with their children but also the relationships their children then develop with their peers.

Gender Effects. It is interesting to note the lack of importance assigned to the role of gender in the abuse literature. Given that results are probably influenced by gender of the parent, the child, or the grandparent who was the abuser, the minor role that gender has played in research to date is somewhat surprising. There are a few exceptions. As mentioned earlier, all cases of parental repeat abuse in the prospective study by Hunter and Kilstrom (1979) included a mother with a history of abuse, whether or not the father also reported this history (although, unfortunately, the gender of the abused child was not discussed). Further, these mothers were more likely than nonrepeater mothers to report being abused by their mothers. In the nonrepeating group, only 9 of the 40 reported abuse by their mothers, and 7 of these 9 had been removed from their mothers' care and raised by someone else. Essentially they appeared "saved" from their mothers' abuse. Thus the intergenerational cycle of abuse appears especially strong for daughters who experienced abusive relationships with their mothers, perhaps attributable to the strong identification process that marks this relationship (Chodorow, 1978).

Although Hunter and Kilstrom (1979) did not examine how the gender of the child related to the incidence of repeated abuse, Egeland et al. (1987) reported that it did not affect the continuity of abuse. However, an interesting finding emerged within a group of mothers who reported being both "emotionally supported" and nonabused as children. Within this group of mothers was a greater continuity of supportive parenting for mothers of girls and a greater likelihood of abusive incidents for mothers of boys. The authors suggest that this lack of continuity, especially for mothers of boys, may be due to the nature of the impoverished sample in general. Poverty itself includes great numbers of risk factors and stressors to which boys appear more vulnerable (Rutter, 1979). Consistent with this explanation, the emotionally supported parents who were not providing adequate care had higher life stress and anxiety scores than the emotionally supported mothers who were providing adequate care. Further, as Maccoby (1990) points out, boys tend to be more difficult to parent and raise than girls. Once again, however, it appears that mothers are more likely to repeat what they themselves experienced as children (in this case a supportive parental relationship) with their daughters than they are with their sons.

Thus, although few data exist regarding the role of gender in child abuse, the few reported findings suggest that gender is an important variable. Indeed, from an attachment theory viewpoint, gender would appear critical. Bretherton (1985), for one, has suggested that certain characteristics of an individual (which would include gender) might trigger the parent to reenact a particular role learned from his or her own attachment relationships. A father, for example, might behave harshly toward his son (a re-creation of his own father-son relationship) but act quite tenderly toward his wife (a reflection of his relationship with his mother). Future research is needed to clarify the role of gender in this process.

Remembered Parent-Child Relationships

As alluded to earlier, the focus on attachment theory provides a natural transition into the second literature to be reviewed regarding parents' memories of the quality of their own parent-child relationships. Main and Goldwyn (1984) do not view these two research areas as separate domains requiring disparate conceptualizations, but rather as experiences varying along a continuum from normal degrees of parental rejection to the extremes of experiencing parental abuse as a child. Thus abusive parents and children could be considered together with non-abusive samples with similar theoretical mechanisms applying to both groups. In fact, Bretherton (1985) suggests that experiencing parental rejection or neglect as a child may be even more damaging than being physically abused, as even negative attention from parents would be better than their psychological unavailability alone.

In support of their contention, Main and Goldwyn (1984) draw convincing parallels between the behavioral characteristics of those children experiencing parental abuse and those experiencing maternal rejection. In both instances, such children are likely to evidence (although in varying degrees) the development of unpredictable bouts of hostility, avoidance of persons (both adults and peers), infrequent friendly overtures, and little concern for others.

Thus the same conceptual model recently dominating the child abuse literature also currently serves as the primary theoretical driving force in this second area of research. Almost all research examining the influence of parents' remembered parent-child relationships on their own children's relationships is grounded in attachment theory. The primary work done in this domain is that of Main and her colleagues (e.g., Main et al., 1985). They examined the relation between children's attachment security at 12 months (with the mother), at 18 months (with the father), and at 6 years (with both parents) and the attachment security their parents remembered having with their own parents (measured when their children were 6 years old). Parents rated as secure in their own attachments with their parents (using the Adult Attachment Interview, Main & Goldwyn, 1984, which combines answers about both parents) tended to value attachment relationships and to view them as affecting personality development. They also discussed their parental relationships in a manner suggesting much reflection and a lack of idealization of their parents, similar to the parents described earlier who displayed the abuse discontinuity pattern. Parents rated as insecure in their attachments to their own parents not only lacked these qualities but also displayed one of the following three patterns. They (a) dismissed attachment relationships as unimportant, (b) seemed preoccupied with their current dependency on their parents and ability to please them, or (c) had not yet resolved the death of an attachment figure they lost during childhood.

Further, the parents' recollections of the security of their own attachment was related to the measures of their children's attachment security taken during infancy, with the relation being particularly strong for mothers. In addition, almost all of the behavioral indices of parent-child interaction related positively to the parents' recalled attachment security, with results again appearing stronger for mothers than fathers. This differential predictive strength was interpreted by Main et al. (1985) as an indication of the existence of a hierarchy of internal working models of attachment (Bowlby, 1982), with the mother most typically being ordered above the father in the hierarchy for the majority of children.

Again a pattern of discontinuity was also evident. Some parents who appeared to have had poor relationships with their parents were considered to be secure in their internal working models of relationships and had children who were quite secure in their attachments to them. As with the abusive mothers who had broken the cycle of abuse, they had coherent and integrated memories of their parental relationships, and some were described as having forgiven their parents (Main & Goldwyn, 1984) or as having experienced a period of rebelliousness during adolescence (Main et al., 1985). Again, invoking an attachment theory explanation of these results, the authors speculated that these parents had accomplished a cognitive-affective reworking of their internal models of relationships, thereby allowing a secure attachment relationship with their own children (Main et al., 1985).

Main's work has received corroboration from recent research, including two longitudinal studies conducted in Germany by Grossmann and her colleagues (Grossmann, Fremmer-Bombik, Rudolph, & Grossmann, 1988). They investigated the relation between children's behavioral interactions with and attachment security to their mothers (assessed at 12 months of age) and the security of the mothers' attachments to their own parents, again using the Adult Attachment Interview (administered when the children were 5-6 years old). Two major representations of attachment resulted from the mothers' attachment interviews. The first attachment representation, which valued attachment relationships and viewed them as important, was held by mothers who recalled at least one supportive figure during their childhood or who, despite the absence of such a figure, gave a balanced, thoughtful, and nondefensive description of their parents. The second attachment representation devalued attachment, and characterized mothers who presented an incoherent, idealized, detached, or defensive picture of their relationships with their parents.

Similar to those of Main et al. (1985), the data showed strong relations between the mothers' recalled attachment security with their own parents and their behavior with their infants, as well as their infants' security of attachment to them. The correspondence between maternal attachment representations and infant attachment was highly significant, as infant-mother attachment (secure vs. insecure) corresponded to maternal attachment representation (valued vs. devalued attachment) in 80% of the cases. Defensiveness when discussing their own attachment relationships was a significant differentiator between mothers of securely versus insecurely attached infants. Further, mothers who valued attachment interacted more sensitively and cooperatively with their infants than did mothers who devalued attachment.

Using an attachment framework to interpret their results, Grossmann et al. (1988) speculated that easy access to attachment-related memories and feelings in the mothers, whether positive or negative, seemed to promote sensitivity to their infants' signals and contingent responsiveness, which in turn enhanced the infants' communicative skills and tendency to rely on the mother when distressed. A blank or distorted memory seemed to lessen the ability of mothers to listen and feel sympathetic with their infants. Grossmann et al. (1988) speculated that these mothers pushed aside memories of their own distress by ignoring that of their infants. Thus, like the abused mothers who continued the cycle of abuse, their avoidance of their own remembered parental rejection was leading them to repeat the pattern of negative parenting with their own children.

Similar to previous research, Grossmann et al. (1988) identified a group of mothers who did not repeat the pattern of unsupportive parenting and instead established secure attachment relationships with their children. Although the process that allowed them to do so remains unclear, Grossmann et al. speculated that a period of rebellion during adolescence or a supportive husband or family member may have helped these mothers view their childhood and parents in a different light, thus contributing to a reworking of their internal working models of attachment. However, they did not speculate as to why some mothers who were found to have positive or nondefensive attachment representations had infants who were insecurely attached to them.

Further corroboration of the work of Main et al. (1985) comes from two studies reported by Ricks (1985), in which relations between mothers' memories of their childhood parental relationships (using the Mother-Father-Peer Scale developed by Epstein, 1983), their self-esteem, and their subsequent relationships and parenting style with their own children were examined. As predicted, mothers of securely attached infants had higher self-esteem scores and reported more positive recollections of childhood relationships with both their mothers and their fathers than did mothers of insecurely attached infants. The results concerning mothers' recollections of childhood acceptance by their own mothers were particularly strong.

It is important to note that such findings also have been obtained when mothers are observed interacting naturally with their children at home and not solely in laboratory settings such as those characterizing the work thus far. Biringen (1990) reported that recall of general parental acceptance by mothers (again using the Mother-Father-Peer Scale) correlated favorably with ratings of observed sensitivity to their infants' behavior, observed dyadic physical avoidance (warm and responsive interactions with their infants vs. cool and avoidant ones), the level of dyadic harmony between themselves and their infants, and their perceptions of their infants' responsiveness to them. Thus the results obtained previously in laboratory situations appear consistent with those obtained in a more natural home setting.

In a follow-up investigation reported by Ricks (1985), results indicated that ratings of the children's affective state during interactions with their mothers were related positively with the security of their attachment with their mothers and their mothers' observed display of support and pleasure with them. In terms of their mothers' recollections of their own parental relationships, mothers of insecurely attached infants were more defensive and more likely to idealize their parents than mothers of securely attached infants. As in the first of Rick's (1985) studies, mothers' remembered acceptance from their own mothers in childhood was the strongest predictor of child outcome. Further, the mothers of the insecurely attached infants who fared poorly as preschoolers also were likely to report the present unhappiness of their own mothers, the children's grandmothers.

As with earlier research, there was also evidence of discontinuity, with some mothers able to overcome their own negative childhood attachment experiences and establish secure relationships with their children. As in Main et al. (1985) and Grossmann et al. (1988), these mothers seemed to have successfully reworked childhood issues during adolescence or to have received strong support from their husbands and their husbands' families. They seemed to have forgiven their parents and established autonomous relationships with them. Applying Epstein's (1980) personality theory, Ricks (1985) posited that such relationships would involve experiences that disconfirmed earlier acquired models of self and other. For example, one mother of a securely attached child seemed to have abandoned a basic but maladaptive principle of her internal working of attachment—namely, "I must please mother"—and realized instead the impossibility of the task.

Belsky, Youngblade, and Pensky (1989) examined more specifically when a supportive relationship, such as that with a spouse, would be a factor in breaking the cycle of negative parenting. They found that the relation between child-rearing history and maternal affect varied as a function of marital quality. Specifically mothers who recalled their relationships with their parents (using the Rohner Parental Acceptance and Rejection Questionnaire, Rohner, 1960) as involving high rejection and low support displayed high negative affect when interacting with their children, but only under conditions of high marital negativity. In fact, Belsky et al. (1989) proposed that the observed irritable, punitive, and negative parental behavior seemed to be intergenerationally transmitted principally under conditions of poor marital quality. Considered together, these results suggested that a troubled marriage is an important condition of continuity with regard to problematic mothering and, inversely, that a good marriage can serve as a buffer against the intergenerational transmission of maternal negative affect.

These observations led Belsky et al. (1989) to consider what factors would enable a woman with a problematic child-rearing history to become involved in a supportive marriage that would buffer her from the intergenerational transmission process. Their data allowed them to examine two possible mediators of the link between child-rearing history and parenting: maternal physical attractiveness and maternal personality. Ratings of the mothers' physical attractiveness revealed that women with problematic child-rearing histories in poorer functioning marriages were disproportionately likely to be rated as unattractive, whereas those with comparable rearing histories in better marriages were disproportionately likely to be rated as attractive. In contrast, maternal personality (which included prenatal measures of ego strength, interpersonal affect, and self-esteem) revealed no evidence of its mediating role in the relation between child-rearing history and mothering.

Peer Relationships. As attachment theorists would predict, the quality of children's attachment to parents during infancy has been related to the quality of their later peer relationships (although the relation between grandparent-parent attachment and children's peer relationships has not been examined). Secure infants, for example, have been observed to relate better to unfamiliar adults (Main & Weston, 1981; Thompson & Lamb, 1983) and unfamiliar peers (Easterbrooks & Lamb, 1979; Lieberman, 1977; Pastor, 1981) than infants judged as insecure in their attachment. In fact, quality of infant attachment has been used successfully to predict social competence during the preschool years and beyond (Arend, Gove, & Sroufe, 1979; Booth et al., 1991; Cohn, 1990; LaFreniere & Sroufe, 1985; Waters, Wippman, & Sroufe, 1979). Even in a sample of preschoolers at risk for abuse from their mothers (Erickson et al., 1985), children who had been securely attached as infants appeared competent during interactions with peers, whereas children who had been classified as insecurely attached instead appeared to lack confidence and assertiveness in their dealings with peers. Other researchers (e.g., Bakeman & Brown, 1980; Clarke-Stewart, VanderStoep, & Killian, 1979) have not found such a relation, but that difference may be due to differences in assessment techniques (use of the Strange Situation). Thus the quality of the relationships that parents remember having had with their own parents may have implications for both the quality of the relationships they form with their children and the relationships their children develop with their peers.

Gender Effects. As was the case with the abuse literature, it is interesting to note the lack of attention given to the role of gender in this research. Most studies examined parents' memories of their parental relationships as a unit rather than considered each remembered relationship (with mother and father) separately. In the few that did separate these relationships, it appears that the impact of the mother-child relationship is especially strong. However, because only mothers were included in those studies, it is impossible to determine whether these results illustrate the importance of the remembered mother-child relationship or the importance of the same-sex parent-child relationship. Further, only one study considered the effect of fathers' remembered parental relationships along with those of mothers when examining the influence of these relationships on the quality of their children's relationships with them and with peers. Finally it appears that the quality of the relationships mothers develop with their children has a stronger influence on their children's outcomes than does the quality of the father-child relationship. However, no study examined how the gender of the child might impact these results. Combining the sexes together may have obscured the importance of fathers. Thus an important task for future researchers is to map the pathways of cross-generational effects on parents' behavior for boys and girls separately and in relation to their own mothers and fathers. Further, too little attention in general has been focused on the role of the child in influencing the process. Often the child comes across as the passive recipient of the parents' working models, as opposed to a participant in a dynamic process involving both parents and their children.

Other Issues. What is particularly striking is the consistency and similarity of the results from the abuse literature and those from the remembered parental relationships literature. Both reveal strong evidence of the potential for an intergenerational transmission of childhood relationship experiences. Both show a connection between repetition of negative parenting and a lack of a coherent, integrated memory of negative parent-child experiences. Further, both evidence a similar pattern of discontinuity under circumstances (e.g., a supportive marriage) facilitating a reworking of earlier negative childhood parental relationships. Finally both literatures also suffer from an overreliance on attachment theory as their overriding conceptual framework. An additional emphasis on more microanalytic behavioral exchanges and communication between parents and their children would be an important methodological addition.

Clearly the causes of intergenerational transmission require further empirical attention. Although difficult to obtain, prospective data on the influence of childhood relationships on eventual parental behavior and the quality of their children's relationships with peers are still lacking. Thus far, the link has been substantiated only retrospectively. Further, despite the association between parents' memories of their childhood relationships and their children's relationships with them and with peers, the validity of these memories is unclear. This issue also applies to parents' reports of childhood abuse. If recent work (cf. Ross, 1989) concerning the reconstructive nature of personal recall is considered, it is evident that the past is frequently "retrieved" in reference to the present. Indeed Ross indicates that the past frequently is distorted in service of present constructions. Yet, although the accuracy or reality of these memories remains in question, these recollections appear to tap meaningful parental perceptions.

Remembered Peer Relationships

The final part of this review involves an examination of the influence of parents' memories of their childhood relationships with peers, rather than with parents, on their children's relationships with peers. Use of the Mother-Father-Peer Scale in some of the earlier research has allowed a first, although murky, glimpse into this area. For example, Ricks (1985) found that the mothers of securely attached infants reported more positive recollections of childhood relationships with their peers than did mothers of insecurely attached infants. However, Biringen (1990) found that the mothers' recalled level of peer acceptance was not related to recalled parental acceptance or to any observed behavior with their infants, although it was related positively to maternal self-esteem and negatively to maternal anxiety. These analyses were secondary purposes of the above researchers, however, which may, in part, explain the mixed nature of the findings and the overall lack of attention paid to these results.

Two recent studies, however, were conducted with the primary purpose of considering the importance of parents' memories of their childhood peer relationships for their own children's peer relationships. In the first study (Putallaz et al., 1991), mothers of preschoolers (a low father participation rate prevented their data from being reported) were asked to recall a particular childhood experience characterizing their peer interactions and to rate their childhood social competence along several dimensions. Three types of parental childhood peer relationship memories were differentiated. The first group (a majority of mothers) recalled warm, positive memories of their childhood peer relationships, rated themselves as socially competent children, and associated positive affect with their childhoods. They described themselves as being nurturant with their children and viewed their children as being socially competent. The second group of mothers recalled negative childhood peer experiences, described themselves as socially incompetent children, and associated negative affect with their childhoods. They reported themselves to be lower in nurturance than the other two groups of mothers and viewed their children as the least socially competent. The third group of mothers recalled anxious/lonely peer experiences, described themselves as socially incompetent children, and associated negative affect with their childhoods. They described themselves as nurturant and attempted more to actively influence their children's social situation (having many intentions for their children, enrolling their children in many activities) than did the other mothers. Although they did not view their children as particularly socially competent, their children were rated as the most socially competent by the peers who interacted with them in the study, by their teachers, and by objective observers.

Using a socialization framework, Putallaz et al. (1991) offered two explanations to account for the higher social competence of the children of the anxious recollection mothers. First, in contrast to the other two groups of mothers, the anxious recollection mothers seemed to operate from an internal locus of control. Their anxious recollections tended to involve stories in which the mother was lonely or without friends due to her own social anxiety or inadequacy. Their subsequent parenting seemed to entail creating a sense of empowerment or social efficacy in their children so as to prevent them from falling victim to similar inaction and loneliness. The effort involved a close, warm relationship with their children, as well as active, intended behavior directed at making their children's worlds better than their own remembered childhoods.

In contrast, the other mothers tended to view the social world with an external locus of control, although differing in whether it was seen as a malevolent or benevolent world. Negative recollections involved stories in which other children were the source of rejection. These mothers did not report intentions to improve their children's lot in any active sense and described themselves as weak models of social relationships in terms of the nurturance they provided their children. It was speculated that the painful memories of rejection led this group to maintain distance in social relationships (including those with their children) as a way of protecting themselves from further rejection and pain, a notion similar to that espoused by attachment theorists. Such maternal behavior would not only provide a negative model for their children but also teach the children in their earliest interactions that social relationships are negative and nonnurturant. The optimistic external locus of control held by the positive recollection mothers may in a sense have led their children to be the victims of their mothers' success. Although describing themselves as nurturant with their children, they did not report active intentions and involvement in the social lives of their children. Having remembered a blissful childhood, these mothers might not realize the activity required on their parts in helping to create such bliss for their children.

A second explanation for the higher social competence of the children of anxious recollection mothers is that recollections are a reflection of the mothers' differential sensitivity. Mothers not only model behavior and actively create environments for their children but also communicate interpretations of the meaning of social behaviors and contexts. It may be that anxious recollection mothers, by virtue of their openness to social insecurity, provide their children with interpretive frames that help their children better understand the anxious, insecure behavior of peers. Hence they are likely to develop the capacity to be more "understanding" social partners and thus attract more desirable ratings from their peers and teachers. In short, mothers who are prone to social insecurity might be enhancing indirectly the social sensitivity of their children. Moreover, such sensitization is likely coupled with active problem solving. Thus mothers with anxious recollections may be making their children sensitive to uncomfortable situations and providing anticipatory coaching.

Given the lack of attention to gender in research, it is noteworthy that this pattern of results was influenced by gender of the child. In particular, anxious recollection mothers of girls evidenced child-rearing intentions focused on facilitating their children's avoidance of those negative experiences that they themselves recalled encountering as children. Anxious recollection mothers of boys, on the other hand, reported child-rearing intentions focused on facilitating their children's enhancement of those positive experiences that the mothers recalled having as children. Further, they reported behaviorally delivering on these intentions by affording a significantly higher investment of effort in their boys' organized social activities than any other group of mothers of either boys or girls.

Putallaz et al. (1991) concluded by proposing a gender moderated model of socialization, with the mother-child relationship holding different meanings for both the anxious recollection mothers and their children. These differential meanings were posited to flow from the sex-role-related experiences that accompany relationships and social interactions. From the mother's perspective, the daughter is viewed through the filter of a shared gender role. From the daughter's perspective, the mother serves as a salient mentor (although by no means the only one) for appropriate social behavior. With regard to boys, however, the mother's experiences as a female are instructive about the behavior of females but are not necessarily relevant to self. The mother, for her part, presumes that boys' experiences will be different from her own. Thus mothers' relationships with their boys, because of the gender-specific expectations in social interaction, may consist of a large number of complementary exchanges. The reported anxieties of mothers are likely to be met by their boys with enhanced support and understanding but from a different perspective. With girls, on the other hand, one would expect a greater number of similarity exchanges; that is, with the pull of same-sex identification, girls are likely to model the insecure social style of their mothers and to identify with her anxious feelings. Mothers, for their part, may be more likely to assume that their girls are "like them"; hence, they should avoid hurtful circumstances and be more socially cautious.

If this perspective has merit, it suggests a particularly potent influence of anxious, concerned mothers on their daughters. It is unfortunate that the potential influence of fathers could not be similarly examined in this study. Putallaz et al. (1991) further speculated that the components of social competence might differ for boys and girls. Girls with anxiety-prone mothers might become similarly anxiety prone and open about their insecurities and, as such, be particularly desirable social partners to other girls. On the other hand, boys with anxiety-prone mothers are likely to be placed in the position of understanding listener more frequently than other boys. Such interpersonal understanding of others' social vulnerabilities might render such boys particularly desirable social partners. Thus socially competent girls might be reared to be actively disclosing, while socially competent boys are reared to be active listeners.

In the second study of parents' remembered peer relationships (Cohen & Woody, 1991), mothers of third- through sixth-grade children rated their recalled childhoods as well as current social behavior (sociability, social withdrawal, and aggression) from items selected from the Revised Class Play (Masten, Morison, & Pellegrini, 1985). Results indicated that mothers who tended to view themselves as socially withdrawn or sociable, in childhood and/or currently, were more likely to perceive their children to exhibit similar behaviors. Further, mothers' peer experiences influenced how frequently they orchestrated (arranged and managed) their children's social lives. Mothers who considered themselves to be more socially withdrawn in childhood and/or who considered themselves to be sociable as adults had higher orchestration scores.

Cohen and Woody (1991) interpreted their results from an information-processing perspective. They proposed that mothers' reconstructions of their own peer experiences and values could be thought of as affective self-schemata, which would influence the way they attended to, perceived, interpreted, and responded to information. Their results also suggested that maternal experiences might have a proactive influence on their involvement behavior, independent of their specific cognitive appraisals of their children's behavior. Specifically mothers who considered themselves to be sociable as adults and/or who viewed themselves to be more socially withdrawn in childhood orchestrated more frequently. It is intuitive that more sociable adults would spend more time promoting their children's friendships. On the other hand, the higher levels of orchestration among mothers recalling being socially withdrawn as children suggest that they take measures to ensure that their children are not exposed to the same negative experiences that they were, a response similar to that of the anxious recollection mothers described by Putallaz et al. (1991).

An alternative explanation offered by Cohen and Woody (1991) is that the joint influence of mothers' childhood and current sociability determines their involvement as it captures their implicit theories about the potential for change versus stability in the characteristic of sociability across the life span. For example, mothers who recalled being socially withdrawn in childhood and who felt that they were able to change and become more social as adults may be guided by an implicit theory of sociability as an inherently unstable and malleable characteristic. This possibility implies that their efforts to orchestrate their children's social lives can have a positive impact on their children. Putallaz et al. (1991) proposed a similar relation between mothers' locus of control and the likelihood of maternal involvement in their children's social lives.

Parallels. Together, the peer recollection studies provide an interesting parallel to those of the remembered parent relationship research. Again there appear to be two types of mothers who remembered unsuccessful childhood peer relations. One set of mothers appears to be perpetuating their negative experience in their children through being poor social models and unconcerned about active involvement in their children's social relationships. The other set of mothers appears to have increased in their social skillfulness and seems to serve as the best developers of social competence in their children. The critical difference between these two sets of mothers is the internal model of social relationships they hold. Although the studies by Cohen and Woody (1991) and Putallaz et al. (1991) disagree on the specifics, they both appear to suggest that one set of mothers has come to believe that individuals are the locus of influence in their relationships and have chosen to actively influence their children's social lives. This notion of self as the source of successful relationships may be one product of the processing of abusive or poor parental relationships that permits parents to overcome their negative childhood social experiences.

A parallel also exists in the importance of gender in these findings. Mothers treat boys differently from girls. The focus of the findings is slightly different in the peer relationship research, however. It seems that mothers adopt complementary roles with boys, but they assume similarity with their daughters. The unfortunate consequence for girls is that mothers with anxious memories may be focusing on avoiding replication of their negative experiences for their daughters, while holding more positive intentions for their sons. History clouds their rearing of daughters more than their rearing of sons. Unfortunately there are no parallel data for fathers, something clearly requiring future research attention.

Concluding Remarks and Future Directions

The foregoing review of rather distinctive literatures in the broad domain of socialization suggests a number of tantalizing conclusions and implications:

1. Mental models of the nature of social relationships are intergenerationally communicated from parent to child.

2. These models, schemes, or scripts about social relationships manifest themselves in the very interpersonal behaviors that children engage in with their peers and with nonfamilial adults.

3. More intriguingly, these working models are carried through the life course. The frames for interpreting and engaging in intimate relations in later life are at least partly determined by the working models of parents and by intimate exchanges with them in early life.

4. Repetitive, intergenerationally communicated cycles of negative social behavior (e.g., abuse and interpersonal agonism) are not simple products of imitation or modeling, but are the distillates of the meaning-construction processes that social schemes enable. Thus parents do not simply abuse their children because

they have been abused by their own parents, but they continue the cycle of abuse because their past experiences as victims of it are transformed into agonistic ideologies about the nature of intimate social contact. As such, it is as important to understand how ideologies of social connection are communicated as it is to understand how the behavior of elders is modeled by their children. In fact, preventive approaches to phenomena such as abuse and child maltreatment may be best accomplished by interventions that seek to modify social schemes and belief systems of parents rather than by strict behavior change or "skill" intervention approaches. This intervention scenario is particularly pertinent if our notions of prevention extend to the intergenerational case. It is indeed plausible that agonistic working models of social relationships can persist across generations even if behavior itself is modified. This notion of the behavior-independent persistence of working models leads to the intriguing possibility that the abuse cycle could "skip" a generation.

5. Reported recollections of childhood social experiences might serve as an evocative index of social schemes and working models of social relationships. Indeed the role of memory processes in promoting the continuity of social definition and construction requires careful further inquiry. Memories themselves are constructions of the past, and those that are most available for retrieval should reflect the significant distillates of past social experience. It may well be that memories of social experience, particularly early social experience, can reveal the degree of continuity of attachment-derived social ideology (or the ubiquitously referred to "working model").

6. The impact of early intimate relations such as parent-infant attachment, though a powerful determinant of subsequent social outcome, should not in any way be regarded as an unmodifiable, preformed, or "experience-immune" set of structures. The nature of postnuclear reparative and buffering interactions and relationships needs further exploration. What experiences and social connections serve as antidotes to negative attachment experiences? What buffering experiences "break" intergenerational abuse cycles? Under what subsequent experiences do positive and connected working models go sour? As noted in this chapter,

follow-forward methodologies need to become a more frequent fixture in these literatures if issues of change and stability are to be explored appropriately. The lack of such longitudinally based explorations has led the field to imply that parent ideology, belief structure, and transmittable working models are overly consistent and monolithic in cast. Models of relationships are likely to be both context- and content-bound. Parents are neither loving nor permissive, nor hostile or controlling, in *all* of their transactions with their children. Children, for their part, are not uniformly irascible or calm, reflective or impulsive, but their behaviors and orientations vary as well. In short, although working models may have "central tendencies," they also, like any other human characteristic, possess variability. Indeed there may be instances in which with-parent variability may be more important than within-parent central tendency (e.g., in the case of the internalization of distinctive values; see Costanzo, 1991).

7. Finally, and perhaps most importantly, we must get beyond the issue of continuity versus discontinuity in attachment status or working models of relationships. In addition, we need rather pointed empirical studies that examine the processes by which models are both transmitted and modified. It is sometimes remarkable to consider how stable social-cognitive models are across the life course—so remarkable that it almost seems sufficient to confirm such stability. Nevertheless we will understand little about the conditions that give rise to this remarkable stability unless we probe the dynamics of interpersonal exchange in families. It is time to move beyond the step of descriptive accounts of relationship continuity to an examination of palpable causes for stability and instability.

Despite these tantalizing suggestions and promising directions for subsequent inquiry, our ability to offer an empirically based formulation linking broad issues of relationship formation, intergenerational transmission, and abuse-mediated social-developmental outcomes is impeded by the piecemeal nature of much of the evidence in these fields of inquiry. Although the research on these problems has had the virtue of taking up bold questions of interpersonal continuity, it has yet to generate bold,

overarching models to contextualize these questions. In particular, social, behavioral, and developmental scientists have not
offered an overarching and integrated perspective on the nature
and goals of socialization within which the events of early
intimate exchange and its products can be conceptually embed-
ded. We are now in need of a cogent formulation of socialization
that integrates its affective, interpersonal, and cognitive components. The recent upswing in interest in personal and intimate
relationships brings us to the brink of framing such a model.
Indeed the life-course continuity of personal, intimate, and social relationships cannot be sensibly considered without such a
model. In essence, to study emergent working models of social
relationships, social scientists require their own working model
of socialization.

A number of ideological forces have colluded to forestall the
development of an integrated perspective on socialization process during the past two decades. Two of the more prominent
inhibitors of such conceptual development are, ironically, two
of the most cogent advances in the study of social acquisition:

1. The discovery that processes of socialization are reciprocal
and bidirectional has afforded the study of social development
with a perspective that admits the study of the impact of phenomena such as child temperament, child constitutional endow-
ment, and child social response systems on the products of the
parent-child socialization bond. At the same time, the perspective of reciprocally determined parent-child socialization has
shrunk implicitly from acknowledging the great asymmetry in
the power relationship between parents and children in the
rearing process. As a by-product of this state of affairs, the field
of developmental psychology has been slow to explore the
processes of parent-to-child transmission of beliefs, attitudes,
values, and norms that are likely sequelae of disproportionate
parent socialization power. This slowness also has resulted in
the unfortunate sidestepping of considerations relating to the
goals of socialization on both the individual parent level and the
level of species-specific mandates of social adaptation.

2. The phenomenal growth in the application of cognitive perspectives to the study of social acquisition is another influence that has unwittingly forestalled the development of an integrated model of socialization. The study of social cognition has become a centerpiece of the search for appropriate frames of understanding for the developmental emergence of social phenomena. The pleasing conceptual generality of information-processing models of social perception, thought, and behavior has tended to lead to an unfortunate blurring of the distinction between nonsocial and social cognition. Although the knowledge acquisition processes in both domains undoubtedly share properties, the peculiar and unique components of social- and relationship-based cognitions and schemes are the ones most concordant with the effects of socialization; that is, social knowledge, working mental models of the social world, social schemata, and the like are almost entirely dependent on the process of meaning construction. Social events themselves have little meaning beyond the ideologies used by perceivers to construct them. For example, a "lie" could indeed be a "lie" to one perceiver and a kindness to another (e.g., telling a dishevelled friend how nice he or she looks on a particular day). The very meaning of social behaviors, including those involved in attachment relations, derives from the underlying meanings that humans attach to specific acts *and* the general frames they acquire for making sense of social reality. In essence, it is quite different to frame models of socialization that explore influences on the emergence of general *processes* of information integration, *and* to frame models involved with the emergence of internalized content and behavioral-norm-based guides for perceiving self and other in the social world. The former has been facilitated greatly by the upswing in social cognition theorizing; the latter has lagged considerably behind.

With the development of increasing interest in the dynamic properties of developing close relationships, it is now a propitious time to transcend the conceptual limitations ushered in by the above two important developments in the study of social behavior. To understand the degree to which developing orientations to social relationships and intimate exchange are mediated by socially transmitted familial influences, we must consider the asymmetric power of parents to affect their children's ideas, affects, identities, and interpersonal proclivities. We must understand also the *nature* of the messages and structures communicated in early intimate exchanges between parents and children. If the foregoing review has any merit, it should be clear to the reader that parents share not only their love, affection, hostility, nurturance, and neglect with their children but also their hopes, dreams, cognitions about social action, and social meaning with them. They do so wittingly by instruction and coaching and unwittingly by the direct modeling and enactment of their own implicit social beliefs. There is no sensible way to begin to approach these questions without a careful consideration of the general nature and species-relevant goals of socialization as a broad necessity of human collective life.

In this final section of these conclusions, we exhibit the temerity to provide a beginning model for linking the goals of socialization with the dynamics of intergenerational transmission of relationship proclivities. The search for the far-reaching connections between abuse cycles, attachment stabilities, and interpersonal communication of social ideology alluded to in this chapter require such a model.

Socialization is a requirement of group life. Individuals must live together in units for social as well as material survival. To do so, members of units must possess common orientations toward collective relationships and common understandings of the nature of social connection. Indeed the first and primary *goal* of socialization between generations is the communication of ideologies of *social connection*—that is, the communication of the conditions, rules, and meanings of belongingness and/or communal bonding. Parents possess an implicit awareness of this species-relevant goal and are further compelled to act on it by the inherent *dependency* of their children. In the process of ministering to them, the parent communicates an ideology of connection both in terms of meanings and affects. It allows the child to schematize social relations and to enact these schemes in their own emergent bonding with others. For example, abusive exchanges communicate to the child the "pain" of closeness, the price of connection, and the futility and instability of affection. A second goal of socialization seems almost antithetical to the first. We socialize our young to *individuate;* that is, to promote self-other communal connections, socialization must lend the child an image and definition of self as *distinct* from others. In the very same exchanges that communicate connection, models of individuation are communicated to children. We become members of a social collective when we acquire both the means to bond with others *and* the means to disconnect from others in ways that leave us whole entities.

Indeed the conditions established to explore attachment bonding via the Strange Situation give voice to this dualistic model of socialization. Securely attached infants and children are those who can separate and detach *without* fear of loss of connectedness. They are also those who can attach without experiencing the immediate need to *detach* because of the potential for de-individuation. Attachment operations, then, serve both of the major species specific goals of socialization in human collectives.

Accordingly, working models of attachment and close relationships should be divided into those schemes and principles that express *belief structures* relevant to individuation and those relevant to connectedness. The methodological implication of this formulation for researchers of intergenerational transmission is that the phenomena such as recalled parent childhood experiences should be codable into dimensions of connectedness and dimensions of individuation. It is these dimensions, then, that should be explored in their children. The differences in these working model notions could be related then to special population subgroups (the abused, the socially competent, the aggressive, etc.). Further, we need to know much more about *how* such dynamic models are communicated from parent to child. Research must develop to allow methods of observation that far exceed the limits of the attachment paradigm for this purpose.

It should be clear now that the formulation on socialization offered above is, on the one hand, quite preliminary and quite general. On the other hand, it is certainly not novel. The role of socialization in promoting connectedness and individuation in developing children has been a major theme of much of the work on the socialization of sex-typed norms. Beginning with the instrumental (individuated) and expressive (connected) distinction of Talcott Parsons concerning the culturally mediated social personae of males and females respectively, and following with Gilligan's (1982) profound distinction between the schematic moral principles of females (connection) versus males (individuated competence), this dualistic theme indeed has had a central place in the literature of social acquisition. What we add to this, however, is the idea that *both* components of socialized self-identity are requirements of optimal relationship formation in *both* males and females. The gender of the child, as well as the gender of the parent, may be a prime influence on the *balance* between these two socialization goals.

Nevertheless it is clear from the Putallaz et al. (1991) study relating parental memory and child competence that the anxious and vulnerable memories of mothers have their strongest relation to social competence in boys. Boys may receive many cultural messages promoting individual competence from various socialization influences (in a sense, these messages are "canalized" by these multiple sources). However, in the prime and significant cross-gender intimate relationships that boys have with their mothers, they have the opportunity to acquire expressive schemes related to social connection. If "complete" relationship development entails acquisition of both socialization components, then mothers who most strongly evidence (with safety) the components of vulnerability, social perspective, and self-social comparison will have boys whose working models of intimate social contact transcend canalized expectations.

By the same token, much more gender- and cross-gender-based work needs to be done on the socialization of intimacy in girls as well. What do fathers' social styles have to do with developing girls' working models? How do fathers and mothers provide their girls and boys with different balances of connectedness and individuation components of secure social identity? These are questions we must address. In the past we have treated gender as a fairly incidental cue in studies of attachment and in terms of broad theories of social acquisition. Is gender incidental in adult social relationships? If the reader's answer is no, then the scope of our research on the development of intimate relationships must expand to the complexities of gender-related interactional models. Indeed the Belsky et al. (1989) finding that a critical inhibiting factor in the repeated intergenerational cycle of abuse by mothers was their *physical attractiveness* may be an index of the importance of gender-relevant cues to social bonding. It may well be that because of the norm-related desirability of attractiveness in females, physically attractive females, even when "damaged" interpersonally by early agonistic and abusive interactions with parents, still promote *proximity seeking* from social others and therefore have a greater probability for encounters with corrective close relationships. We may find that "competence" in males serves the same intergenerational buffering function. In sum, characteristics that promote "surface" gender-role exemplification may offset the proximity and bonding-defeating effects of negative working models of social life.

These last examples simply underscore the importance of locating the kinds of socialization goals that are likely to become inhabitants of the cognitive and affective cores of developing working models. Both connection with separateness and separateness with connection constitute optimal balances promoting optimal models of social identity. Knowing who we are and how we fit with others is the essence of intimate relationship formation. Our research agenda should reflect the search for this essence whether we are exploring the social ravages of abuse, the beauty of parent-child attachment, or the nature of later life romance. Although the child is the father of the man and the mother of the woman, the influences that form that child's social self-identification are the grandparents of it all.

4

Parental Ideas as Influences on Children's Social Competence

Rosemary S. L. Mills

Kenneth H. Rubin

S *ocial competence* refers to the ability to function effectively in interpersonal transactions, in which the term "effective" means outcomes that are successful from the perspectives of all social partners (Rubin & Rose-Krasnor, in press). As such, it encompasses skills and abilities relating to all aspects of interpersonal problem solving, from the self-regulation of emotions aroused in social interaction, to the negotiation of solutions to interpersonal conflicts. Both conventional wisdom and formal psychological theory hold that the attainment of social competence is one of the most important developmental tasks, both as an end in itself and as an inner resource that spurs social and emotional development (see Hartup, 1983, for a review). Adding support to this idea are data indicating that social difficulties in childhood not only are symptomatic of current distress but also represent risk factors for subsequent social and emotional maladjustment (e.g., Parker & Asher, 1987; Rubin, Hymel, Mills, & Rose-Krasnor, 1991). Given its obvious significance in development, it is critical to explore the origins of social competence.

The family represents a reasonable starting point. Children grow up in families, often with two parents and one or more siblings. It is likely that children's parents and siblings influence their development. In addition, families are subject to societal and cultural influences (Belsky, 1984; Bronfenbrenner, 1979). These ecological forces most likely influence parental beliefs, socialization strategies, and the quality of parent-child relationships. In turn, these familial factors influence the way children learn to relate to and interact with other people.

Support for this idea can be found in studies linking parental behaviors with various indices of social competence. Popular children have mothers who appear to be less demanding, more agreeable, and more positive than mothers of less popular children (Putallaz, 1987). Popular preschoolers are more likely than unpopular children to have mothers who provide opportunities for their children to interact with peers and who monitor indirectly their children's peer interactions (Ladd & Golter, 1988; Parke et al., 1988). They are also more likely to have parents who use explanations and give praise when interacting with their children in a teaching context (Roopnarine & Adams, 1987). It also has been found that the frequency of preschoolers' negative peer-directed behaviors is inversely related to the frequency of mothers' positive interactions with their children at home (Stevenson-Hinde, Hinde, & Simpson, 1986). Also the frequency of children's hostile behaviors with peers is associated with the degree to which mothers disconfirm and attempt to control their children without providing them with appropriate rationales for their authoritarian actions (Attili, 1989).

Unless they are merely coincidental, these links between parenting and peer relations reflect not only the parent's influence on the child but also the child's influence on the parent. Although it is difficult, if not impossible, to disentangle the respective influences of parent and child, directions of influence can be inferred from evidence concerning the processes involved.

Of course, making inferences requires conceptions that not only identify antecedents and outcomes but also provide a detailed explication of the processes that link them (Duck, 1990). In this chapter we consider processes through which parental ideas may influence social competence in children.

Parental ideas encompass cognitions, representations, beliefs, inferences, and perceptions relevant to caregiving situations (Goodnow, 1988; Goodnow & Collins, 1990). It is assumed that (a) these ideas have multiple interrelated sources, including the personal experience of caregiving transactions, external pressures on coping resources, direct experience with children and parenting, and cultural values and norms about children and child rearing, (b) they are highly charged with emotion, and (c) they guide parents' behavior in caregiving situations. We begin by describing the way parental ideas may influence children's social development. We then describe the evidence linking parental ideas to social competence outcomes in children.

The Role of Parents
in the Development of Social Competence

According to Hartup (1985), the parent-child relationship serves at least three functions in the child's development of social competence. First, parent-child interaction is the context in which many competencies necessary for social interaction begin to develop. This relationship furnishes the child with many of the skills needed to conduct relationships with other people, such as language skills and the ability to control impulses. Second, the parent-child relationship constitutes emotional and cognitive resources that allow the child to explore his or her social and nonsocial environments. It is a safety net permitting the child to take the risk of venturing forth and a source of help in problem solving. Third, the early parent-child relationship is a forerunner of other relationships. It is in this relationship that the child begins to form expectations and assumptions about interactions with other people and to develop strategies for protecting the self and attaining personal goals.

In keeping with this analysis of the parent-child relationship, current views of the parents' role in the development of social competence hold parents to be both providers of emotional security and teachers of social skills (Putallaz & Heflin, 1990; Rubin et al., 1991).

Parental Sensitivity, Felt Security, and Social Competence

Most toddlers and preschoolers develop secure relationships with their parents (Ainsworth et al., 1978). These relationships are thought to be caused and maintained, in part, by sensitive and responsive parenting involving prompt, consistent, and appropriate responses to the child. The sensitive and responsive parent is willing and able to perceive the child's signals, to consider the child's perspective, and to respond promptly and appropriately according to the child's needs. Although such a parent may, from time to time, become irritated by the child's behavior, he or she accepts and respects the child and does not harbor resentment.

The quality of parent-child interaction largely determines the nature of the expectations and assumptions, or internal working models, that the child forms about caregiving transactions (Bowlby, 1973). These working representations guide the child's behavior toward the parent and generalize to other relationships. In a secure relationship, the child believes that the parent is available and responsive to his or her needs for protection, nurturance, and physical care and forms a complementary belief that the self is competent and worthy of response. These working representations generalize to include other relationships. A child with a sense of security is sufficiently free of stress and is trusting and self-confident enough to explore the social environment. This exploration leads to interaction with peers and to play experiences that promote the development of social skills (Rubin et al., 1991; Rubin & Rose-Krasnor, 1986).

Further, the sensitive and responsive parent effectively nurtures these skills. The sensitive parent is emotionally available, is highly attuned to and respectful of the child's perspective, and is able to anticipate the child's behaviors, the consequences of these behaviors, and the outcomes of his or her own actions. As a result, the parent trusts in the child's competence, respects the child's autonomy, and encourages independent development of social problem-solving skills. Rather than directly tell the child what to do, the parent provokes the child to think through and solve interpersonal dilemmas at levels just beyond what the child can handle on his or her own (e.g., Vygotsky, 1978) and uses "distancing" strategies (Sigel, 1982) that get the child to consider alternative problem solutions and to anticipate their potential consequences (e.g., "What are all of the things you can do in order to . . .?").

Some children experience insensitive and unresponsive caregiving. Their parents are emotionally unavailable or inconsistent in their responses and not attuned to their children's needs and capacities. These children develop insecure relationships with their parents and form internal working models of attachment that hold the social world to be a comfortless and unpredictable place. These representations lead to the development of defensive coping strategies.

More specifically, according to Bowlby (1973), attachment behavior that is not met with comfort or support arouses anger and anxiety. A baby whose parent has been inaccessible and unresponsive is frequently angry because the parent's unresponsiveness is painful and frustrating. At the same time, because of uncertainty about the parent's response, the infant is apprehensive and readily upset by stressful situations. To protect against these intolerable emotions, the infant develops defensive strategies.

These strategies involve excluding from conscious processing any information that, when processed in the past, aroused anger and anxiety (Bowlby, 1980; Case, 1991). In situations that could arouse these emotions, the infant excludes from processing any messages that might activate the emotions. Thus the infant blocks conscious awareness and the processing of thoughts, feelings, and desires related to its need for the parent. This blockage of the information-processing system leads to deactivation of the behavioral system mediating attachment behavior, such that attachment-related thoughts and emotions are blocked from expression, as well as from conscious processing.

When stressful situations arouse the infant's need for contact with the parent, different coping strategies are activated, depending on the nature of the infant's expectations and assumptions about the parent (Bowlby, 1973; Chapters 1 and 2, this volume). Given the variety of ways that parents treat their children, there are likely to be many working models of attachment. Ainsworth and her colleagues (Ainsworth et al., 1978) suggest that an important dimension on which these working models may vary is the infant's certainty about being rejected by the parent. When the infant fully expects to be rebuffed (presumably because the parent has consistently been rejecting in the past), the infant blocks awareness of attachment needs and the anger associated with the rejection of these needs. In the Strange Situation assessment procedure, this appears to be the strategy used by babies who avoid the mother during reunion episodes, maintain exploratory behavior throughout all episodes, and seem more friendly with the stranger than with the mother (avoidant attachment pattern). When the infant is apprehensive but not wholly certain about being rebuffed (presumably because the parent sometimes has been comforting), the infant feels ambivalent about the parent and becomes preoccupied with seeking the parent's love and acceptance. In the Strange Situation, this defensive coping style is attributed to babies who mingle avoidant and contact-seeking behaviors during reunion episodes, inhibit exploration throughout all episodes, and show fear of the stranger (ambivalent attachment pattern). These patterns of behavior, and others identified subsequently (e.g., Main & Solomon, 1986), deviate from the normative style of coping, which consists of heightened proximity and contact seeking in reunion episodes with little or no resistance or avoidance, and inhibited exploration specifically during separation from the mother (secure attachment pattern).

Bowlby (1973) proposed that the expectations and assumptions that infants build up about others, and the coping strategies associated with them, are internalized and carried forward into subsequent relationships. It has been proposed that, in their subsequent peer relationships, avoidant children are guided by expectations of rejection and consequently perceive peers as hostile and tend to strike out aggressively, whereas ambivalent children are guided by fear of rejection and attempt to avoid it through passive, dependent behavior and withdrawal (Renken, Egeland, Marvinney, Mangelsdorf, & Sroufe, 1989). It follows that these defensive styles of behavior with peers may interfere with opportunities to gain access to disconfirming information; thus children may prevent themselves from adapting their representations of relationships.

Avoidant and ambivalent children are hindered further in their development of social competence by the fact that their parents are poor teachers of social skills. Insensitive and unresponsive parents are emotionally unavailable, poorly attuned to social situations, and unable to anticipate others' behaviors, the consequences of these behaviors, or the outcomes of their own actions. Consequently they may fail to notice when their children are having difficulties in the peer culture. If they do recognize their children's difficulties, they may be more preoccupied with their own than with their children's needs, and they may respond in ways that serve their own needs rather than those of their children. As a result, they are likely to be ineffective teachers of social problem-solving skills (Rubin et al., 1991).

There appears to be some conceptual justification, then, for thinking that parents play a role in their children's development of social competence. In essence, the way children relate to their peers is thought to depend on the quality of their internal working models of attachment (cf. Chapters 1 and 2, this volume) and the effectiveness of their parents' teaching methods (cf. Chapters 5 and 6, this volume), both of which depend on the degree to which their parents are sensitive and responsive caregivers. It is thought that parents who are sensitive and responsive to their children provide them with a sense of emotional security and support that permits them to explore the social world and avail themselves of opportunities to learn how to relate to others. Parents are also effective teachers of social skills, and this effectiveness further facilitates their children's development of social competence. Insensitive and unresponsive parents promote insecurity and the development of maladaptive defensive strategies in their children, which carry over into subsequent peer relationships and interfere with opportunities to learn social skills. Of further detriment to their children's development of social competence is the ineffective way these parents teach their children social skills.

This perspective seems to have some encouraging empirical support. It is well established that the quality of caregiving is related to individual differences in attachment quality and that secure infants subsequently fare better than insecure infants on indices of social competence (e.g., Sroufe & Fleeson, 1986). Efforts to improve the prediction of peer difficulties from felt insecurity are focusing on the possibility that different types of peer difficulties may be predictable from different types of insecurity (e.g., Jacobson & Wille, 1986; Renken et al., 1989) and that certain ecological factors may contribute as well (e.g., Booth et al., 1991).

There is also some general evidence that parental sensitivity is related to social competence. In early and middle childhood, aspects of sensitive parenting such as setting clear expectations, exerting control rationally, communicating openly, and providing warmth and support are associated with social competence (Maccoby & Martin, 1983). Aggressive children appear to have parents who are hostile and rejecting (Olweus, 1980; Patterson, 1982). Socially withdrawn children seem to have parents who control through guilt-induction, do not respect their children's autonomy, and may vacillate between neglect and negative attention (Hetherington & Martin, 1986). But these general links have not satisfied the need to understand how parents contribute to the internal working models of relationships that presumably guide their children's behavior toward peers.

We have suggested that the way parents behave in caregiving situations depends on how they process information in these situations and that this processing, in turn, depends on certain "setting conditions" (Rubin & Mills, 1992). These setting conditions include socioecological factors (e.g., economic resources, employment conditions, living conditions), personal and social resources (e.g., psychological resources, availability of social support), and beliefs about children and child rearing (e.g., beliefs about what causes development, how parents can promote development, what characteristics are important). Further, the setting conditions interact with each other. For example, mothers with low socioeconomic status choose more power- assertive strategies for dealing with their children's displays of unskilled social behaviors than other mothers and believe less in children's ability to learn social skills autonomously, particularly when their sense of social support is low (Mills & Rubin, 1990, 1992).

How do these setting conditions influence the way parents interact with their children? We focus on parents' psychological resources—specifically their internal working representations of relationships—and consider how they influence parents' behavior in caregiving situations. Parents' working models of relationships constitute one of the most important psychological resources that they bring to their parenting role. Recent efforts to examine parents' own working representations of relationships, and the way they may guide parents' caregiving behavior, may lend some insight into the processes involved.

Parental Representations of Relationships and Parental Sensitivity

According to Bowlby (1988), internal working models of attachment are composed of complementary models of both care-seeking and caregiving, which guide the appraisal of current attachment and caregiving situations. These working models and their defensive components influence parents' manner of *processing* information relevant to attachment and caregiving, as well as the *content* of their attachment and caregiving ideas (ideas about themselves as caregivers, the child as an individual needing care, and the relation between them) (e.g., Bretherton, Biringen, Ridgeway, Maslin, & Sherman, 1989; George & Solomon, 1989; Main et al., 1985).

More specifically, Bowlby (1980) postulated that working representations and the defenses associated with them have a number of consequences for information processing. Secure parents are able to process information and emotion relevant to attachment relationships. As a result, their processing of affective messages fits, rather than distorts, reality, and they are able to engage in free and open affective communication. For parents who are cognitively "disconnected," on the other hand, there are a number of information-processing consequences. The blocking of attachment-relevant affect leads to diversion of attention away from interpersonal events to self-involvement, to distorted perceptions and attributions about interpersonal events, to inhibition of emotional responses to interpersonal events, and to displacement of emotional responses away from the person eliciting them and toward someone else (Bowlby, 1980).

The effects of attachment representations on information processing are thought to contribute to parents' ability to incorporate information about child, self, and situation into their thinking and behavior in caregiving situations (e.g., Bretherton et al., 1989; George & Solomon, 1989). The more parents are able to process affective information, the more involved and attentive they may be as caregivers, the less distortion there may be in their inferences about their children's behaviors, and the better able they may be to adapt their ideas to new information. The more they are emotionally and cognitively disconnected, on the other hand, the less engaged they may be as caregivers, the more often they may misidentify the causes of their child's behavior, the more prone they may be to displace emotional reactions onto their child, and the more rigid they may be when faced with new or discrepant information. These effects on information processing in caregiving situations, in turn, may influence the parents' emotional availability and responsiveness to affective messages (Bretherton, 1990; Grossmann & Grossmann, 1991) and, through this, the child's felt security.

Thus parents' representations of their own attachment histories are believed to influence their caregiving ideas, the quality of their caregiving behavior, and their children's felt security (see Chapter 3, this volume). It follows from this set of links that some association should exist between parents' caregiving ideas and their children's social competence. In the next section, we consider whether any evidence supports this association.

Caregiving Ideas and Indices
of Children's Social Competence

Researchers have examined the relations between children's social competence and parents' ideas about the importance of social competence, how social skills are learned, why unskilled behaviors occur, and how to correct children's unskilled behaviors.

Ideas About the Importance of Social Competence

It appears that some level of parental involvement in organizing and managing children's social contacts is associated with positive peer relations (e.g., Ladd & Golter, 1988; Parke et al., 1988; Russell & Finnie, 1990). Moreover, the more important that parents think it is for their children to be socially competent, the more likely they are to be involved in promoting it. Thus Cohen (1989) found that the more mothers valued and felt responsible for their children's sociability, the more they tended to be involved in promoting their children's peer relationships.

Not surprisingly, then, it has been found that mothers who considered the development of social skills to be very important had children who were more likely than other children to demonstrate social competence in the classroom (Rubin, Mills, & Rose-Krasnor, 1989). These children initiated peer play, used appropriate requests to attain their goals, and were successful in achieving their goals. Mothers who did not believe so strongly in the importance of social skills had children who demonstrated less social competence than other children. These children frequently attempted to control the behavior of others, cried to achieve their goals, and showed indications of being hyperactive and distractible. It may be that parental involvement in promoting the development of social competence is mediated by strong beliefs in the importance of social skills. When a socially competent child demonstrates poor social performance, parents who place a relatively high value on social competence are likely to be the most involved and responsive. Over time, such involvement may be positively reinforced by the child's acquisition of social skills.

Ideas About How Social Skills Are Learned

Parental sensitivity presumes a recognition that children play an active role in their own learning by exploring, experimenting, and learning independently. Mothers who believe in such learning express a preference for indirect teaching strategies (e.g., asking questions, making suggestions, giving explanations) over directive strategies (e.g., issuing imperatives, giving directions) and also behave less directively (Skinner, 1985). Because indirect strategies are more sensitive to a child's capacity for active learning than directive strategies, indirect teaching strategies should be associated with social competence in children, and power-assertive strategies should be associated with social difficulties.

In research verifying this expectation (Rubin et al., 1989), it was found that mothers who indicated they would use indirect strategies to help their children learn social skills (e.g., arranging opportunities for peer play) had preschool children who, in the classroom, were competently assertive and prosocial in meeting their social goals. Mothers who said they would use power-assertive strategies (e.g., direct teaching, punishment) had youngsters who were unassertive, fearful, anxious, and adult-oriented.

Ideas About Unskilled Social Behaviors

Parental sensitivity is believed to depend on parents' ability to interpret their children's behaviors appropriately, constructively, and without excessive distortion. Parents generally view their children optimistically, dismissing their negative behavior as transitory and situationally caused, and attributing their positive behavior to inherent traits (Dix & Grusec, 1985; Goodnow, Knight, & Cashmore, 1985). Parents who think their children are to blame for their negative behaviors tend to feel negative about these behaviors and endorse the use of force in dealing with them (e.g., Dix & Lochman, 1990; Dix, Ruble, & Zambarano, 1989).

Optimistic parental interpretations of child behaviors appear to be associated with social competence in children. Mothers with socially competent preschool children believe that social skills and the lack thereof are caused by factors *external* to their children, such as parental teaching and the provision of opportunities for peer play, whereas mothers whose children do not demonstrate social competence believe that the development of social competence is caused by factors *internal* to the child (e.g., "just born that way," "too insecure") (Rubin et al., 1989). Because external attributions focus on causes that parents can do something about, these attributions may be conducive to constructive ways of teaching children social skills. Internal attributions, on the other hand, may be conducive to ineffective teaching.

Summary

From the limited evidence available to date, it can be concluded that parents who believe social competence is important, who recognize their children's need and capacity for autonomous learning, and who think external factors are responsible when difficulties occur tend to be involved, sensitive, and responsive in their behavior and tend to have children who demonstrate social competence.

These associations can be interpreted in the light of the mutual influences that occur between child and parent. Parents who want their children to be socially competent, who recognize their needs and capacities, and who view their social difficulties constructively are likely to be involved and effective in helping them become socially competent. At the same time, parents are likely to recognize the value of social competence when they see it in their children, and children who demonstrate social competence will be veridically perceived as both competent and capable of learning independently. Thus the data are consistent with a scenario involving reciprocal influence processes in which both constructive beliefs on the part of the parent and characteristics in the child that are conducive to such beliefs play a role.

Because parents' ideas about the importance of social competence, the way social skills are learned, and the reasons for children's peer difficulties all appear to be related to children's social competence, it may be that certain *patterns* of ideas, rather than particular ideas in isolation, are associated with social competence. Do children with social difficulties have parents whose caregiving ideas reflect working representations of relationships suggestive of insecurity? Do children with different *kinds* of difficulties in their peer relationships have parents who can be distinguished on the basis of their caregiving ideas? We turn to these questions next.

Caregiving Ideas and the Quality of Peer Relationships in Childhood

Beginning in early childhood, a significant proportion of children begin to manifest disturbances in their peer relationships (Cicchetti & Toth, 1991). The two major forms of peer disturbance that have been studied to date are aggression and social withdrawal (Pepler & Rubin, 1991; Rubin & Asendorpf, 1993).

In this section we consider whether certain patterns of parental ideas tend to foster these types of peer difficulties. We also consider whether these patterns change with the age of the child. Parents' perceptions of their children's behaviors change somewhat as their children grow older (e.g., McNally, Eisenberg, & Harris, 1991; Mills & Rubin, 1992). We found that, as their children enter middle childhood, mothers typically develop a stronger belief in the importance of active, independent learning of social skills; become less inclined to attribute aggression and withdrawal to age-related factors; become more negative about aggression in girls and less negative about it in boys; and increasingly favor low-power strategies for dealing with unskilled social behaviors, such as asking the child to explain his or her behavior (Mills & Rubin, 1992). Given the tendency for caregiving ideas to change somewhat as children grow older, patterns of caregiving ideas associated with children's social difficulties may also change.

Caregiving Ideas and Peer Relationships in Early Childhood

In our research we found that mothers of 4-year-old children identified as aggressive, socially withdrawn, or average in social competence differed in their caregiving ideas (Rubin & Mills, 1990). The mothers of the withdrawn children placed more importance on teaching social skills directively than did mothers of average children and were more likely to choose highly directive strategies for dealing with peer difficulties (aggressive and socially withdrawn behaviors). They were angrier and more disappointed, guilty, and embarrassed about these peer difficulties than other mothers, and they were more inclined to blame them on traits in their children.

These findings may partly reflect a difference between mothers of withdrawn and average children in their caregiving representations. The difference is suggestive of overinvolvement in mothers of withdrawn children. Specifically, these mothers' emphasis on control, their tendency to make trait attributions, and their more pronounced anger, disappointment, guilt, and embarrassment suggest that these mothers may not distinguish clearly between themselves and their children and may be prone to negative perceptions of both.

To speculate further, mothers of withdrawn children may have somewhat ambivalent caregiving representations involving anxious preoccupation with their children, and this ambivalence may foster in their children the development of an anxious withdrawn style of relating to peers. In caregiving situations these mothers may be anxious and readily upset by events that strain the parent-child relationship; they may direct blame diffusely to both self and child when upsetting events occur; they may be unable to recognize clearly and respect their children's autonomy; and they may attempt to be highly controlling. Given the reciprocal nature of the parent-child relationship, this overinvolvement may be partly a result of the nature of the child's behavior. The difficulty of dealing with passive, withdrawn behavior (Bugental & Shennum, 1984) may be such that it tends to lead to overinvolvement.

The mothers of aggressive children gave a different impression. These mothers did not believe in active, independent learning as strongly as mothers of average children, yet in dealing with both aggressive and withdrawn behavior, they were more inclined than the other mothers to choose very indirect strategies or to say they would not respond at all. They were also more inclined to attribute their children's aggressiveness to age (e.g., "He's only 4"). This pattern of information processing suggests that these mothers were attempting to avoid dealing with their children's aggressive tendencies by attributing the behavior to a temporary condition. This finding leads us to wonder whether these mothers have an avoidant style of attachment that may cause them, in caregiving situations, to block the processing of information relevant to attachment and caregiving, to neutralize their affective reactions to their children, and to choose socialization strategies that minimize their involvement. It also leads us to wonder whether this style of caregiving may foster the development of an aggressive stance toward peers.

These are, of course, highly tentative interpretations of the data. Moreover, as we suggest below, they may apply only to the period of early childhood.

Caregiving Ideas and Peer Relationships in Middle Childhood

In a study completed recently, we examined the beliefs of mothers of 5- and 9-year-old children identified as socially withdrawn, aggressive, or average in social competence. The mothers could not be distinguished from one another on the basis of their beliefs about how early children show skills in making friends and sharing possessions, how important these skills are, how stable they are, or how parents can promote them. But they could be distinguished on the basis of their attributions about why children acquire or fail to acquire social skills, their beliefs about the influence parents can have when their children have difficulties, and their causal attributions about, affective reactions to, and choices of strategies for correcting aggressive and socially withdrawn behavior.

For example, mothers of 5- and 9-year-old withdrawn children considered it more difficult for a parent to change the cause of a child's difficulty making friends than did mothers of average children. Also they were less likely than mothers of average children to say they would respond to displays of social withdrawal. Interestingly they were also more likely than mothers of average children to attribute unskilled behaviors to traits in their children, yet they reported much less pronounced affective reactions to these behaviors (less disappointment, disgust, embarrassment, and sadness about aggression, and less disappointment, sadness, guilt, surprise, and puzzlement about withdrawal). This pattern of findings suggests that, in middle childhood, mothers of withdrawn children blame unskilled behaviors on traits in their children and view them pessimistically, yet seem to be lacking any affective reaction. On the whole, the impression these mothers give is one of detachment.

Mothers of aggressive children differed from those of average children in several respects. Mothers of aggressive children of only age 5 were more likely than mothers of average children to attribute success in attaining friendship initiation and sharing skills to indirect external causes (e.g., opportunity to learn, exposure to positive models). Mothers of aggressive children of both ages 5 and 9 were more likely to blame unskilled behaviors (aggression and withdrawal) on traits in their children, and they were less surprised and puzzled about these behaviors than mothers of average children. These findings suggest that mothers of aggressive children in middle childhood perceive their children somewhat negatively.

Summary

Mothers of withdrawn and aggressive children can be distinguished from those of average children on the basis of their ideas about caregiving. Further, the ideas that distinguish them seem to differ, depending on the age of the children. It is possible that, between early and middle childhood, mothers of withdrawn children shift from overreacting to underreacting to their children's social difficulties, while mothers of aggressive children become more negative in their perceptions of their children. These changes may be precipitated by age-related changes in the meaning of children's behaviors. By the time their children reach school age, mothers of withdrawn children may think their influence on their children is minimal, while mothers of aggressive children may be less inclined to attribute their children's aggressiveness to a passing phase.

We hasten to note, however, that the data from early and middle childhood are cross-sectional, as well as being from different studies and different samples. Therefore it is impossible to say whether the findings reflect changes in mothers or differences between the samples.

Conclusions

Our purpose in this chapter has been to examine the impact that parental ideas may have on the development of children's social competence with peers. Social competence may be, in part, a product of parents' internal working models of attachment caregiving, which influence parents' caregiving ideas and their processing of information in caregiving situations. The more blocked is parents' processing of affective information, the less is their ability to notice, freely communicate about, and appropriately respond to their own and their children's emotions in caregiving situations. These effects may interfere with parental sensitivity, promote the development of felt insecurity in the child, and foster the development of peer relational difficulties.

We described some encouraging empirical evidence for this pathway from parents' caregiving ideas to their children's social competence. Mothers who believe social competence is important, who recognize their child's need and capacity for autonomous learning, and who think external factors are responsible when difficulties occur, tend to have children who demonstrate social competence. In addition, there are distinct patterns of information processing in mothers whose children evidence different types of peer difficulties (aggression and social withdrawal), particularly in early childhood.

As yet, however, there is no evidence that caregiving ideas play a causal role in children's development of peer competence. Such evidence requires that the influence of the parent on the child be disentangled from the influence of the child on the parent. Although this disentanglement may be impossible to accomplish, convergent evidence may permit inferences to be drawn about the influence of parental ideas on children's social competence. Toward this end, parents' ideas and children's social competence should be traced longitudinally. If it were found that parental ideas at Time 1 significantly predicted peer competence at Time 2, even after concurrent and stability correlations were taken into account, there would be some support for the belief that parental ideas have a causal effect on social competence.

In the light of the limitations of this approach (e.g., Rogosa, 1978), however, additional convergent evidence for a causal relation between caregiving ideas and children's social competence with peers must come from data establishing other links in the pathway leading from parental attachment representations to children's social competence. One of these links is the one we have postulated between the quality of parental attachment representations and patterns of parental information processing in caregiving situations. We found distinct patterns of information processing in mothers, but whether the patterns reflect mothers' attachment caregiving representations is impossible to say. It has yet to be determined whether associations exist between parental attachment representations and patterns of information processing in caregiving situations, whether they are moderated by other setting conditions, and whether they change as the child grows older, the parent changes, and the parent-child relationship develops.

Finally, another link that needs to be studied is the one between patterns of parental information processing in caregiving situations and the quality of children's attachment representations. How do patterns of information processing in parents influence the development of felt security or insecurity in children? Information about the patterns of affective communication associated with different patterns of parental information processing may shed light on the way parents' caregiving ideas influence their children's attachment representations.

5

Substance and Style: Understanding the Ways in Which Parents Teach Children About Social Relationships

Gregory S. Pettit

Jacquelyn Mize

Children are bombarded constantly with social communications from their parents about how best to get along with other people and what reasonably can be expected from other people in social situations. Consider the following scene, witnessed by one of the authors: Two mothers lead their 3-year-olds (both of whom look somewhat bewildered and are clutching their mothers' hands) into the classroom on the children's first day of nursery school. The mother of the first child, busily chatting with another mother, urges her son to join some children already at play in the sandbox. When he hesitates,

AUTHORS' NOTE: Preparation of this chapter was supported, in part, by Grant No. 42498 from the National Institute of Mental Health and by Project 747 from the Alabama Agricultural Experiment Station.

she tells him just to be nice and to share and that the others will let him play. The son makes an attempt to join the play but soon returns to mother, whimpering that the others would not let him play. The mother admonishes him for not trying hard enough and then pushes him back toward the group, reminding him to "be nice." The second mother, meanwhile, carefully watches a child filling a large toy truck with sand. Stooping down, she directs her daughter's attention to the sandbox and asks her to notice what the child there is doing. Together they walk to the sandbox as the mother mentions that the other child might need some help filling up the truck. When the other child says no, the mother tells her daughter that it is okay, that the other child probably just wanted to be alone for a while, and that maybe they can play together later.

What messages were communicated to the children about the world of social relationships? Through what channels were these messages conveyed? Were some sources of social communication more potent than others? How might the son reconcile the apparent contradictions in the messages being communicated across different channels? These questions serve as core organizing themes for the discussion of social relationship learning that follows.

This chapter is divided into four major sections. In the first section we briefly summarize existing research linking parent-child relationship style with children's emerging social-behavioral orientations. The term *style* is used here to refer to how parents interact with their children, irrespective of content. We restrict our review to investigations conducted in the past 5 years or so, an especially fertile period of inquiry in this area. Although we emphasize parental contributions and suggest a parenting-to-child-outcomes chain of influence, we recognize that children play important roles in determining their own course of socialization (see Lytton, 1990). Where appropriate, we address issues of presumed causality and bidirectionality.

In the second section we summarize findings from studies specifically designed to examine the strategies that parents use in teaching children social skills and in structuring opportunities for contact with peers. The terms *substance, coaching,* and *content* are used in the current context to describe the explicit messages or informational content of such parent-child encounters. These studies have been important in showing that parents do, in fact, take an active role in this arena and that both the amount and quality of teaching and structuring contribute to children's peer relations skills. Nonetheless, research in this area has been somewhat vague with regard to what might be called the *natural ecology of explicit teaching;* that is, little information exists on what parents spontaneously say to their children about relationships, at what ages, and with what effects. Moreover, it is not yet clear whether children seek out parents or other family members for information on how to acquire friends or resolve conflicts. This ambiguity may be due to the fact that such occurrences are difficult to observe directly and that parental recollections of such occurrences (as might be summarized in a daily log) may not yield the kinds of information that process analyses of parental teaching require.

In the third section of the chapter we provide a brief description of a recent empirical investigation aimed at overcoming some of the limitations highlighted in the first two sections. This study employs a carefully considered set of laboratory procedures and allows for the disentangling of substance and style components of parental teaching. Preliminary findings suggest that what parents say is as important as how they say it, when assisting their children in peer relations.

In the final section of the chapter we offer a conceptual model that integrates past research findings, identifies existing lacunae, and provides direction for the next generation of studies. This model stresses the interdependencies among the different modes of social transmission (e.g., that the effectiveness of direct instruction may be constrained by the overall quality of the parent-child relationship). We conclude the chapter with a discussion of the implications of our model (and our own empirical findings) for preventive interventions with children at risk for peer relationship problems.

Stylistic Qualities of Parenting
and Their Relation to Children's Competence With Peers

A large body of literature has documented relations between parenting styles and children's social orientations with siblings and peers (see reviews by Cohn, Patterson, & Christopoulos, 1991; Pettit & Harrist, 1993). Research in this area typically has focused on parental disciplinary style, affective qualities of the parent-child relationship, and/or interactional synchrony/asynchrony between parents and their children.

Findings from several recent interview-based studies underscore the importance of parental disciplinary styles for children's developing competence with peers. Hart et al. (1990) asked mothers of elementary school-aged children to respond to stories depicting hypothetical conflict situations and then coded the responses in terms of induction versus power assertion. Maternal power assertion predicted low levels of peer acceptance, on the basis of sociometric ratings. In a subsequent study, Hart, DeWolf, Wozniak, and Burts (1992) assessed both mothers' and fathers' responses to hypothetical conflict situations similar to those used in the previous study, again coding the responses along an inductive-power assertive continuum. Although findings were qualified somewhat by gender and age effects, parents of prosocial and popular preschoolers were more likely to state they would use inductive styles, whereas parents of antisocial and unpopular preschoolers were more likely to use power assertive teaching strategies. Similar findings were reported by Pettit et al. (1988), who assessed mothers' disciplinary practices through the use of hypothetical stories and a semistructured interview. Peer competence, indexed by peer and teacher ratings, was associated with low levels of mothers' restrictive discipline. Weiss, Dodge, Bates, and Pettit (1992), using a variation of the Pettit et al. (1988) interview format, found a significant relation between mothers' harsh discipline of their children at age 4 and their children's aggression toward peers (a composite measure based on peer, teacher, and observer assessments) at kindergarten.

This relation continued to be significant even after the impact of several child biological and family ecological factors had been statistically removed.

Results from observational studies further attest to the importance of parental disciplinary effectiveness in children's subsequent development of competence with peers. Dishion (1990) examined the relations among grade school boys' antisocial behavior, academic skill deficit, sociometric status, and parental discipline. The discipline construct was represented by observer summary ratings (e.g., lack of evenhandedness) and molecular behaviors (e.g., parental nattering). Antisocial behavior was assessed in terms of parent, child, and teacher reports; academic success was estimated on the basis of achievement test scores. Compared with other boys, socially rejected boys had parents who were significantly more likely to engage in inept disciplinary practices. The relation between discipline and peer relations outcomes was statistically mediated by the boys' antisocial behavior and academic problems; that is, low levels of parental management skill were associated with higher levels of antisocial behavior and lower levels of academic performance, which in turn were associated with higher levels of peer rejection. According to Dishion (1990), extreme exposure to inept and aversive parental discipline eventually "trains" the child to use aversive behavior to gain control over a disorganized, unpleasant family environment. These behavioral tendencies may solidify into an antisocial disposition that is displayed across many social settings, including those containing peers.

Several investigators have begun to examine affective qualities of parenting as predictors of children's peer acceptance and social behavior. In an early study of this type, MacDonald and Parke (1984) videotaped mothers and fathers in their homes, interacting with their preschool-aged children. Attributes of these interactions then were coded, and measures derived from them were correlated with the children's behavior with peers, as rated by teachers and as observed in a laboratory playroom. Parental verbal stimulation and affectively positive play qualities were associated with children's competence with peers. In a subsequent study of preschool-aged boys, MacDonald (1987) coded parent-child interaction during two brief laboratory play sessions. Interactional qualities then were related to the boys' sociometric status. Parents of popular boys engaged them in high levels of physical play, and the boys displayed positive affect during these encounters. Rejected boys more often were overstimulated, and their interactions with their parents were more poorly coordinated. Parents of neglected boys engaged them in less physical play; these boys were generally passive in responding to their parents.

Putallaz (1987) examined mother-child relationship style as related to first-grade children's sociometric status and social behavior with peers. Mothers were observed interacting with their children in a research trailer as they played a word-naming game; the children were observed interacting with a peer in the same setting, with a variety of toys present to stimulate social play. Children who had received higher sociometric ratings from their first-grade classmates had mothers who focused on feelings and displayed high rates of agreeable behavior and low rates of disagreeable, demanding behavior. Positive, agreeable mothers also had children who engaged in comparatively high rates of agreeable behavior with peers. These findings suggest that children may acquire affective dispositions similar to those displayed by their mothers.

Interactional synchrony recently has emerged as an important alternative framework for interpreting variations in children's early social experience (Pettit & Harrist, 1993). Although substantial differences exist in the ways synchrony-related concepts have been operationalized, the overarching consideration that ties the varied perspectives together is an emphasis on contingent and predictable interchanges in family relations. Research examining the association between interactional synchrony and children's psychosocial adjustment derives from two distinct fields of inquiry. Attachment theorists and mother-infant researchers (e.g., Ainsworth et al., 1978; Smith & Pederson, 1988) have stressed the importance of an affectively positive and synchronous mother-infant relationship style for children's optimal social adaptation (including a secure attachment). This line of work is perhaps best illustrated by recent findings reported by Isabella and

Belsky (1991). These researchers built on their own and others'
prior work to examine mother-infant interactional precursors of
infant attachment security. A set of mother and infant behaviors
observed in the home were scored for their co-occurrence and
were scaled a priori into categories judged characteristic of
synchronous or asynchronous interactional exchanges. Infant
attachment security was evaluated later in the Ainsworth Strange
Situation when the infants were 12 months of age. As predicted,
securely attached infants had previously experienced dyadic
interactions that were positively synchronous (harmonious and
sensitively connected). In contrast, the earlier dyadic interactions of insecure-avoidant infants were characterized by asynchrony—specifically, the presence of insensitive, intrusive
maternal behaviors—whereas the earlier dyadic pattern observed
among insecure-resistant infants was one of maternal inconsistency or underinvolvement. Isabella and Belsky (1991) speculate
that, on the one hand, synchronous interactions promote positive social adaptation because the presence of a predictable
social partner leads to efficacious self-appraisals. Asynchrony, on
the other hand, may contribute to maladaptation (an angry,
externalizing social orientation or a fearful, internalizing one),
depending on whether it is manifested as understimulation or
overstimulation. These findings are intriguing and suggest that
emergent styles of relating to others (including peers) have their
roots in early parent-child interaction.

Researchers working within a social-learning framework also
have been concerned with the role of family interactional syn-
chrony/asynchrony in children's behavioral adjustment. Patterson's
(1982) pioneering research has documented the ever-escalating
cycles of hostility characteristic of the interactions between
aggressive children and their parents. In the present framework,
these coercive cycles are conceptualized as instances of affectively negative synchrony—that is, the synchronization of aversive behaviors between family members. Patterson suggests that
once a parent and child are entrapped in a coercive exchange,
the coercion itself is reinforced, regardless of the outcome of the
struggle. Wahler and Dumas (1986) have argued that the key to
understanding the basis for these aversive interactions lies in an

examination of what immediately precedes the coercive bouts. These researchers have reported home observational data on multistressed mother-child dyads that reveal high levels of indiscriminate parenting (near-random dispensing of positive and negative parental attention) except during extended coercive (synchronous) episodes. Wahler and Dumas have hypothesized that these children were misbehaving to reduce maternal indiscriminate attention; that is, the children appeared to find participation in a coercive exchange to be less aversive than parental unpredictability.

Drawing from findings in the mother-infant literature and the child-clinical literature, Pettit and his colleagues (Pettit et al., 1991; Pettit & Sinclair, 1991) recently sought to explicate the social-behavioral sequelae of synchrony-related styles of family interaction. Pettit et al. (1991) observed 30 prekindergarten-aged children and their families in their homes; ratings of the children's social behavior subsequently were obtained from their kindergarten teachers. Interactional episodes were coded in terms of the frequencies of responsive listening (a proxy measure for positive synchrony), protracted coercive exchanges (negative synchrony), and parental intrusiveness. Teacher-rated competence was associated most strongly with responsiveness and teacher-rated aggression with coerciveness. These findings were replicated and extended with a larger sample of 165 children and their families (including the original 30 subject families) (Pettit & Sinclair, 1991). Not only did the responsiveness/competence and coerciveness/aggression associations continue to hold, but in this larger sample, asynchrony (defined as a combination of parental intrusiveness and unresponsiveness) also significantly predicted children's social withdrawal.

In a more detailed examination of the link between interactional synchrony and children's social behavior, Harrist (1991) recoded each of the interactional episodes originally analyzed by Pettit et al. (1991). Her coding system was designed explicitly to capture the most critical aspects of synchrony/asynchrony previously identified in the literature (dyadic engagement, affectivity, behavioral interconnectedness, and parental appropriateness). These components were used to operationally define *parent-child positive synchrony* (affectively positive, connected,

and appropriate exchanges), *negative synchrony* (affectively negative and connected exchanges), and *asynchrony* (disconnected
and/or inappropriate exchanges). The three indices of synchrony
then were related to children's social behavior at school, as rated
by peers and teachers and as observed on the playground. Consistent with predictions, positively synchronous family interactions
forecasted later competent behavior with peers, whereas negatively synchronous interactions predicted later aggression and
social withdrawal.

The literature reviewed above provides support for the link
between stylistic qualities of family interaction and children's
later social-behavioral competence with peers. Socially competent children are more likely to have experienced consistent and
inductive discipline, emotional warmth and support, and harmonious interactions with their parents. Less competent children,
especially socially rejected and aggressive children, are more
likely to have experienced punitive, power assertive discipline,
rejection, and disharmonious interactions with their parents. What
do children learn through warm and synchronous versus harsh and
disharmonious relationships that carries over into their interactions with peers? To date, explanations for the linkage between
family experience and children's subsequent behavioral orientations have centered on children's acquisition of social information-
processing patterns (Dodge, Bates, & Pettit, 1990), on internal
working models of relationships (Bretherton, Ridgeway, & Cassidy,
1990), on practice in the encoding and decoding of emotional
signals (Parke et al., 1988), on modeling and behavioral internalization (Putallaz, 1987), and on learning in response to reinforcement contingencies (Patterson, 1982; Wahler & Dumas, 1986).
These explanatory mechanisms are not mutually exclusive, but
likely operate in conjunction with one another, depending on
the nature of the interactional experience, to produce in children a general style and approach to relationships. It also is likely
that different mechanisms are operative at different stages of
development (e.g., internal working models in infancy, social information processing patterns in early childhood; see Pettit, 1992).

On close scrutiny, two key limitations of this literature become apparent. First, although parent-child data have been obtained in a wide range of settings, insufficient attention has been devoted to how these setting differences may affect the obtained samples of behavior. When families are asked to engage their children in physical play (MacDonald, 1987; MacDonald & Parke, 1984), for example, the resulting individual differences, while predictive of peer competence, may nonetheless provide little information on whether families spontaneously engage their children in such ways. Rather it may be that parents of competent children simply are better at following the researcher's instructions and/or are more cognizant of socially appropriate (or desirable) ways of playing with their children. What is missing from much of the current literature, then, is a thorough accounting of whether and how variations in assessment context—in both laboratory and home settings—influence parents' and children's social interchanges.

Another limitation of the existing literature is its myopic focus on single and isolated socialization strategies. Some studies might be concerned with affective qualities, some with disciplinary effectiveness, and yet others with behavioral predictability. It probably is erroneous to draw strong inferences about specific parental influences even where such inferences might be warranted (e.g., in the case of longitudinal research), unless multiple stylistic qualities have been assessed and contrasted. To do this, it will be necessary to evaluate systematically the relative impact of a range of important interactional processes (e.g., discipline style, positive involvement) on a variety of socialization outcomes. It is noteworthy that the magnitude of relations between parenting style and children's competence is typically rather modest. It may be the case that warm maternal involvement (or any other stylistic quality) simply is not sufficient to produce optimal levels of peer competence in children. Rather, children also may need explicit parental guidance and supervision to acquire social skills. This possibility is examined in the next section.

The Substance of Parental Teaching:
Explicit Structuring and Coaching

How might parents actively take part in the provision of peer interaction opportunities and in the promotion of specific social skills? The findings from several recent descriptive and predictive studies suggest a number of possibilities. To determine whether mothers' direct involvement facilitated peer play, Parke and Bhavnagri (1989) observed pairs of mothers and their 24-month-old children in a laboratory playroom under two experimental conditions. In the first condition, the children played together and the mothers were instructed not to assist or involve themselves in the peer play. In the second condition, one of the mothers was told to "help the children play together." As expected, children's play was rated as more competent (e.g., more cooperative) in the mother-facilitation condition than in the no-involvement condition. The strategies most strongly associated with competent peer play were mothers' overall ability to express affect and their overall supervisory skill (e.g., ability to sustain interaction). In a subsequent study, Bhavnagri and Parke (1991) extended the experimental paradigm by including mothers and fathers, a wider age range of children, and a sequencing of the supervised and unsupervised conditions that was designed to rule out alternative explanations (e.g., child fatigue) of the previously found differences among conditions. As in the earlier study, children's play was rated as more competent in the supervised conditions than in the parent-uninvolved conditions; this finding held only for younger preschoolers, however. Mothers and fathers were rated as equally skilled in supervising/facilitating play, but mothers subsequently reported (during a semistructured interview) that they were more likely than fathers to actually perform in a supervisory role at home.

Whereas Parke and Bhavnagri (1989; Bhavnagri & Parke, 1991) did not examine the relations between parents' supervision and children's competence outside the laboratory setting, recent studies by Ladd (Ladd & Golter, 1988; Ladd & Hart, 1991) and by Russell (Finnie & Russell, 1988; Russell & Finnie, 1990) did establish this link. Ladd and Golter (1988) sought to gather descriptive information on parents' naturally occurring tendencies to initiate (create opportunities) and monitor (via direct or indirect supervision) their preschoolers' peer contacts. Parents were trained to keep detailed daily logs regarding their children's nonschool peer contacts, noting type of initiation (e.g., suggested by parent or requested by child) and whether the contact had been monitored directly or indirectly. The majority of the children's contacts were monitored indirectly by parents; very few contacts were completely unmonitored. Parents who actively arranged contacts and who indirectly supervised these contacts had children that were better liked by their peers. Children of parents who relied on indirect monitoring were less hostile toward peers, according to teachers. Ladd and Golter (1988) offer two possible explanations for the associations between parental management and peer status. First, they note that parents who rely extensively on direct forms of supervision may interfere with their children's development of important social skills, such as initiating and maintaining interaction (see Mize & Ladd, 1990). Alternatively it may be that parents' management styles are a reflection of their children's competence, whereby low levels of skillfulness with peers, as perceived by parents, elicit more direct, hands-on supervision. This issue was addressed in a subsequent study (Ladd & Hart, 1991) in which parent initiation (coded as low, moderate, or high) and child competence with peers were each assessed at two points in time. Parents in the moderately involved group were more likely to actively involve their preschool children in arranging contacts than were parents in the other two groups. Boys of moderately involved parents displayed significant gains in peer status over time. For girls, however, such gains were evidenced only when parents were uninvolved (when parents initiated comparatively fewer contacts than did the girls). These findings suggest that, at least for boys, parental over- and underinvolvement may limit children's opportunities for acquiring social skills.

In contrast with the Ladd studies, which were aimed primarily at describing general qualities of parental supervision, two sets of studies by Russell were concerned with the specific informational content communicated by mothers to their preschool children during initial play encounters with unfamiliar peers. In the first study (Finnie & Russell, 1988), groups of high and low social status preschoolers (based on a teacher ranking) were observed with their mothers in a laboratory playroom where two children of intermediate social status (unfamiliar to the target child) were engaged in play. Each mother was told that the children were to "play together as well as possible" and that she was to "give as much or as little help" as needed. An observer was present in the room at all times; audiotapes were made of all verbal transactions. Mothers of low-status children were significantly more likely to avoid the supervisory role entirely and to engage in less skillful supervision than mothers of high-status children. These latter mothers tended to use more active and skillful strategies (e.g., by making relevant group-oriented statements). Later these same mothers were asked to respond to several hypothetical situations (e.g., initiating friendship, resolving conflict) to assess their knowledge of supervisory strategies. Mothers of high-status children were more likely to suggest positive and assertive strategies and were less likely to suggest avoidance strategies than were mothers of low-status children. Finnie and Russell (1988) interpret these findings as suggesting that children may acquire their social skills, in part, as a function of modeling, direct instruction, and verbal prompting.

In a follow-up study, Russell and Finnie (1990) again examined what mothers did to assist their preschool children in entering play, as well as what mothers said to their children immediately prior to the play (preparatory instructions). As before, mothers of high- and low-status children (the latter subdivided into "rejected" and "neglected" groups, based on teacher rankings) were observed in a laboratory playroom with two unfamiliar, intermediate-status children of the same age and gender. For the first 5 minutes of the session, the mother and child were seated away from the peer dyad, which was already engaged in play. Each mother was told that this period was to be used to offer suggestions that might be useful to her child in joining play. At the end of the instruction period, the mother was told that it was time for her child to join in play with the other children, with the goal that the children play together as "successfully as possible." Mothers of high-status children were more likely to make group-oriented statements during both the instruction period and the play period than were mothers of low-status children. Mothers of low-status children were more likely to disrupt play by taking charge than were mothers of high-status children. Few differences were found between mothers of low-status rejected and neglected children, perhaps because of the nonstandard procedure used to identify these children (use of teacher rankings rather than sociometric data).

It is clear that many parents actively participate in organizing and structuring peer activities for their young children. Evidence that parents (especially mothers) consider these practices to be important and engage in them with some regularity comes from several interview and questionnaire studies. Cohen and Woody (1991), for example, report that mothers' most frequently occurring types of involvement (occurring nearly every day) were "orchestrating" (e.g., specific attempts to arrange and manage their children's peer activities) and monitoring (distal supervision). Bhavnagri and Parke (1991) and Ladd and Hart (1991) also found that mothers and fathers report that they actively participate in the supervision and monitoring of their children's peer play in both the home and neighborhood settings, with level of participation varying as a function of child age and gender.

Differences in the frequency, intensity, and quality of parental involvement, as assessed in interview and laboratory studies, appear to be important as predictors of children's actual competence with peers. In general, children's success with peers is associated with moderate levels of parental structuring and organizing, sensitive inclusion of the child in the decision making, and explicit coaching and advice giving that focus on the use of group-oriented, nondisruptive play strategies. Of course, the direction of effect cannot be determined from these findings because it may be the case that competent children elicit these forms of management strategies from parents. However, the short-term longitudinal findings of Ladd and Hart (1991), whereby prior management strategies predicted gains in children's peer status, are suggestive of a parent-to-child chain of influence.

Research in this area has made significant contributions to our understanding of parents' roles in the socialization of interpersonally competent children. Nonetheless, gaps in our knowledge remain to be filled. A key issue is whether parental structuring and coaching are themselves critical determinants of children's subsequent competence with peers, or whether these management styles are merely epiphenomenal to a more general type of competent parenting. As Patterson and Yoerger (1991) argue, insufficient attention has been devoted to the identification of parenting qualities that are outcome-specific. In other words, in the absence of independent assessments of other components of effective parenting (e.g., relationship style, teaching strategies), there is no way of determining the unique contribution of activities management and coaching in the development of interpersonal competence.

The current literature also is limited in what it can tell us about parents' natural inclinations (as opposed to experimenter-elicited tendencies) to assist their children in peer relations. From Bhavnagri and Parke (1991) and Russell and Finnie (1990), we know that parents will engage actively in facilitating peer play *when asked to do so.* However, as yet no observational data indicate how often and under what circumstances parents engage in such behavior in their everyday lives or what transpires during these episodes. Moreover, it is not yet clear that children behave in accordance with their parents' advice. It is notable that neither of the two Russell investigations (Finnie & Russell, 1988; Russell & Finnie, 1990) included an assessment of the children's behavior in the peer entry situation. Consequently the extent to which children attend to the content of their parents' coaching and translate it into behavioral performance cannot be determined. It is plausible that children's responsiveness to parental guidance is a reliable individual difference, determined in part by the quality of the parent-child relationship and the child's developmental status.

Finally it must be recognized that only a limited number of assessment contexts have been employed in the study of parents' structuring and coaching. For example, Ladd and Hart (1991) restricted their measurement of parental involvement to that occurring within parent-described peer "contacts." This restriction necessarily excludes other situations in which parents may provide guidance and advice to their children (e.g., on hearing of a child's complaints about a peer conflict after the fact). This single-setting focus also is evident in observational studies. Typically in such studies a parent and child are observed together in a laboratory playroom containing one or more unfamiliar peers (Bhavnagri & Parke, 1991; Russell & Finnie, 1990). The critical question is whether the task is best suited for eliciting the kinds of behaviors of interest. As a way of illustrating this issue, consider a child who is experiencing social adjustment problems with peers because of an inability to constructively work out conflicts. The source of this child's social problems may be quite different from that of a child who is insecure about initiating interactions with other children. To study the ways the children's mothers assist them in these two disparate situations, it would be desirable to have tasks that were designed explicitly for these purposes. Decisions regarding the types of task to be employed need not be made arbitrarily; there are at least two possible sources of guidance: (a) The researcher can rely on existing findings from the study of peer social difficulties (e.g., see Dodge et al., 1986) and assume that situations that create the potential for such difficulties will be best suited for studying mothers' coaching and (b) the researcher can adopt a more direct approach and try to identify the situations that parents report as being especially problematic (e.g., through the Family Challenges Survey; Pettit, Cullen, Brown, & Sinclair, n.d.). To clarify the contributions of explicit structuring and coaching to children's social competence, investigations are needed that take into account the ways variations in context may affect the amount, quality, and need for parental guidance and that examine multiple channels of socialization and their relative contributions to children's social competence.

Multiple Pathways in the Socialization
of Peer Competence: An Observational Study
of Mothers and Their Preschool-Aged Children

We recently developed and pilot-tested a multisegmented laboratory protocol that we believe will enable an empirical examination of two distinct pathways by which mothers transmit messages to their children about social relationships. In this procedure mothers have an opportunity both to supervise children's play in a naturalistic context and to coach their children through a series of videotaped social problem vignettes. In addition to measures of the quality of mothers' supervision during peer play and the content of coaching during the videotaped dilemmas, a separate set of measures describing stylistic qualities of mother-child interaction is obtained for each session. These measures were selected to provide estimates of overall relationship quality, as well as relationship-enhancing maternal behavior. Of particular interest is the degree of overlap between each type of measure and the extent to which they independently predict children's competence with peers.

A number of noteworthy features were included to help overcome some of the limitations highlighted in the previously reviewed literature. The study employs a carefully considered set of social situations that have been identified by teachers (McFadyen-Ketchum, 1991) and by parents (Pettit et al., n.d.) as highly relevant for preschool-aged children and their peers. Mothers' coaching of social behaviors was observed both in an unstructured setting, in which mothers simply were told to behave as they normally would at home, and in an experimenter-elicited setting, in which mothers were instructed to discuss hypothetical social problems depicted in videotaped vignettes. Mothers' teaching in a cognitive task was assessed separately from social coaching. This latter assessment was included because we conceptualize parenting competence as situationally specific, at least to some extent; that is, a parent may be skilled at teaching cognitive concepts but lack knowledge, skill, or motivation to help a child with social problems. To test this possibility, we compared mothers' ability to supervise and coach in social situations with their skill in helping their children solve a puzzle task. Finally we examined the behavior of the target children and the unfamiliar peers to determine whether mothers' coaching had any bearing on the quality of peer play.

We hypothesized that stylistic qualities of the mother-child relationship and mothers' direct coaching of social content would make independent contributions to the prediction of children's social competence with peers. This hypothesis is based on the earlier reviewed findings indicating that parent-child relationship style and parental guidance and coaching are associated with the quality of children's peer relationships. We also hypothesized that the statistical interaction of parent-child relationship style and coaching content would make an additional contribution to the prediction of children's social skills. The conceptual basis of this hypothesis is that a minimal level of parent-child positive synchrony may be necessary before a child can benefit from (or is willing to be responsive to) even good advice. We also tested the hypothesis that relationship style and coaching content are interchangeable or redundant in the prediction of child social skill.

Data were collected for 50 preschool-aged children enrolled in three classrooms at the Auburn University Child Study Center. To provide some assurance that the children who would participate in the mother-child interaction tasks were representative of the range of social competence levels of children in the center, we conducted sociometric screening in each class. This screening led to the identification of 10 moderately high-status children (4 boys) and 13 moderately low-status children (9 boys). For the purposes of this study, *high-status children* were defined as those who met the dual criteria of having standardized social preference scores (positive minus negative sociometric nominations) at least 1 *sd* above the class mean and sociometric ratings at least .3 *sd* above their class mean. *Low status* was defined as having a social preference score at least 1 *sd* below the class mean and a rating score of $-.3$ *sd* or lower. Mothers of children who met these criteria were invited to participate with their children in the mother-child interaction tasks. Children who did not meet these criteria were classified as average status and served as play partners during the mother-child interaction assessment.

Each of the 23 mother-child pairs who took part in the laboratory assessment phase of the study was videotaped from behind a one-way mirror in a series of three mother-child interaction contexts. In the first segment (natural coaching), a mother was asked to stay in a comfortably furnished room (containing a sofa, tables, toys, and magazines) with her child and an average status child of the same gender. The mother was told that she should act as she would were the two children playing together at her home for the first time. After 5 minutes an attractive hand-held computer game was introduced into the room, providing an opportunity for the mother to promote sharing or turn taking, should she so desire. During the second segment (prompted coaching), the mother was asked to help her child interpret and determine an appropriate response to a series of 12 peer-interaction dilemmas presented on videotape (from Dodge, Bates, & Pettit, 1990). Each vignette portrayed an elementary-aged child who experiences rejection by a peer or peers whose intentions are either benign (e.g., accidental), hostile, or ambiguous (e.g., child approaches two peers and asks to join them, but the peers offer no response). Specifically each mother was told to "make sure your child understands what happened and why it happened, and what he/she should do next, if he/she were the child in the story." In an attempt to elicit from mothers the style of coaching each would most naturally use, the specific technique (e.g., didactic or discussion) was left up to the individual mother. In the third interaction context (cognitive task), the mother was told that her child was to try to copy (with other blocks) a pattern made of 1-inch cubes (from the WISC-R) and that she could give the child as much or as little help as she wished.

Videorecords of each laboratory segment were coded separately by trained graduate-level research assistants who were blind to the children's status. Detailed rating scales were developed to assess critical dimensions of parent-child relationship style and important aspects of the thematic content mothers provided in their discussions. Where feasible, sets of conceptually and empirically related codes were summed to form composite measures in order to increase reliability of measurement and to reduce the number of variables for analyses. We focus here on the subsets of codes that appear to be best suited for distinguishing among mother-child relationship style, coaching content, and quality of maternal teaching of a cognitive task.

To assess relationship-enhancing style, mothers' behavior during the natural coaching segment was rated on 5-point Likert-type scales for enthusiasm, sensitivity, and inductive teaching style. These ratings were moderately highly correlated and were summed to form a measure called *positive parenting* (alpha = .86). A global rating of mother-child *interactional synchrony* constituted the measure of overall relationship quality and reflected the extent to which mother and child were responsive to one another's cues and engaged in smooth and reciprocal behavioral exchanges. A single item indexed the quality of supervision that mothers provided children during peer play. High ratings for *supervision* indicated the provision of appropriate guidance in sensitive and positive ways; hence supervision contains elements of both style and content.

Ratings tapping coaching content as assessed during prompted coaching were drawn from our review of the research on supervision of children's play, as well as from our own pilot work. For each of the 12 videotaped vignettes, observers rated the extent to which mothers (a) emphasized a positive interpretation of the outcomes (does mother suggest child adopt a resilient, bounce-back attitude, for instance finding other peers with whom to play, or does she focus on a negative, sad, or angry reaction to the event?), (b) encouraged constructive strategies for responding to the event (does mother focus child's attention on a positive strategy or encourage or accept an aggressive or withdrawing strategy?), and (c) stressed the value or fun of peer interaction (does mother focus on pleasure of playing with peers or suggest that child would be better off playing alone?). Each of these items was scored on a 3-point scale in which the highest rating, a 3, indicated a clear expression of the positive end of the continuum (e.g., playing with peers is fun), a 2 indicated no expression or a neutral message, and a 1 indicated expression of the negative end of the continuum (e.g., you don't really want to play with peers). Internal consistencies across the 12 vignettes for each of the three items were moderately high (alpha = .77, .82, and .75 for positive interpretations, constructive strategies, and value of peer interaction, respectively), and so scores for all 12 vignettes were summed to form three composite content scores. These three content codes then were summed to form a score called *maternal coaching skill* (alpha = .76).

Codes for cognitive teaching strategies were taken from studies that employed similar tasks (e.g., Moore, 1986) and reflected aspects of teaching found to be associated with higher levels of cognitive skills. Ratings were made on 5-point Likert-type scales for each of the following items: (a) the extent to which the mother focused on the child's successes during the block task, (b) the extent to which the mother provided the child with hints as opposed to specific directions, and (c) the extent to which the mother used the task as an opportunity for encouraging problem-solving skills (as opposed to focusing on finishing the task "correctly"). These ratings were moderately to highly correlated (*rs* = .36 to .75) and so were summed to form a single measure of the quality of maternal teaching (alpha = .88).

A second coder recoded 25% of the videotapes for reliability purposes. Interrater agreement for all 5-point scales (within 1 scale point) for the natural coaching and cognitive teaching tasks averaged .89 (range = .67 to 1.0). Exact agreement for the three coaching content ratings averaged .71 (range = .69 to .74). In the light of these modest levels of interrater agreement, considerable caution should be exercised in the interpretation of findings. We currently are fine-tuning the rating scales to ensure that the phenomena they are intended to represent are more clearly distinguishable.

Two teachers in each classroom (the head teacher and assistant teacher) completed a modified version of the Teacher's Checklist of Peer Relationships (Dodge & Somberg, 1987), consisting of 12 items rated on 5-point Likert-type scales, 5 of which pertain to the child's social competence and peer acceptance, and 7 of which describe children's social attentiveness and social problem-solving skills (e.g., "understanding others' feelings") (Pettit & Harrist, 1993). Ratings provided by the two teachers were moderately highly correlated (rs = .70 and .66) and so were averaged to give more reliable estimates of child social competence (alphas = .90 and .88 for competence and attentiveness, respectively). The two scales were highly correlated (r = .74) and so were summed to create a measure of *teacher-rated social skillfulness.*

The quality of children's interaction with the peer during natural coaching was assessed by summing 5-point Likert-type ratings for the child's interest in playing with the peer (seeks out the peer) and the quality of peer play (the extent of sustained positive play). These items were highly correlated (r = .86) and so were summed to form a measure of *play quality.* Interrater agreement (exact) averaged .75 across the two items, with 100% agreement within 1 scale point.

To evaluate the relations among maternal behavior measures, we first examined the correlations among maternal variables within the naturalistic coaching context (see Table 5.1). Not unexpectedly, the two maternal style variables—positive parenting and mother-child synchrony—were significantly correlated, and both were significantly related to quality of play supervision. The correlation between supervision and the style variables may reflect the fact that high-quality supervision of peer play was facilitated by a sensitive and inductive approach. Correlations between maternal coaching skill and the maternal style and supervision measures were positive but nonsignificant. These findings suggest that the explicit advice that parents give children about social relationships can be distinguished from the style of the parent-child relationship. Moreover, a positive, synchronous parent-child relationship does not necessarily predict the provision of appropriate guidance regarding peer relations.

To address the issue of whether parental teaching competence is domain-specific, we examined relations among mothers' behaviors across the different contexts. As can be seen in Table 5.1, the only significant correlation indicated that quality of teaching in the cognitive task was significantly related to positive parenting style in natural coaching. This result may be due to the fact that high ratings for teaching quality in the cognitive task were earned for positivity, sensitivity to the child's needs,

Table 5.1. Intercorrelations Among Mother and Child Behavior in the Three Laboratory Contexts and Children's Classroom Behavior

	Children's Social Competence		Mothers' Behavior			
	Teacher-rated skillfulness	Play quality in NC	Supervision	Positive	Synchrony	Coaching
Children's Social Competence						
Teacher-rated skillfulness						
Play quality in NC	.44*					
Mothers' Behavior						
Supervision in NC	.18	.51*				
Positive in NC	.38*	.23	.60**			
Synchrony in NC	.57**	.42*	.64**	.85**		
Coaching in PC	.50**	.42*	.31+	.22	.36+	
Quality of teaching in CT	.15	-.19	.07	.46*	.26	.03

NOTE: NC = Natural Coaching; PC = Prompted Coaching; CT = Cognitive Task.
+p < .10; *p < .05; **p < .01.

and use of reasoning to help the child solve the problem, qualities that overlap, in part, with the constituents of positive parenting. It is also possible that stylistic qualities of mother-child interaction are generally consistent across contexts. More germane for our research questions, no relationship was found between maternal coaching skill and quality of teaching in the cognitive task. Thus, although stylistic qualities of parent-child interaction may be somewhat consistent across several contexts, expertise in teaching about content in one domain (e.g., cognitive tasks) does not necessarily predict the ability to teach about other domains.

We next examined the predictability of children's social competence (in the classroom and with the unfamiliar peer) from measures of mothers' relationship style and coaching content (see Table 5.1). Relationship style and coaching content were associated with both measures of child social competence, but in general they were slightly more strongly related to teacher-rated social skillfulness than to competence as assessed in the brief free play period. The only exception to this pattern was the moderately strong correlation between quality of supervision and child play quality during the peer-play session. This pattern may be the result of a halo effect (the tendency to rate mothers' supervision quality as high if children were playing cooperatively), but it also may reflect the impact of mothers' efforts to facilitate positive peer play.

To further explore the nature of the statistical association between the maternal measures and child social competence, we employed multiple regression strategies with teacher-rated social skillfulness as the criterion variable and the four mother-child interaction measures that were correlated with social competence (positive parenting, synchrony, and supervision in natural coaching, and maternal coaching skill in prompted coaching) as independent variables. The overall multiple correlation was significant ($p = .03$), with the four predictors accounting for 46% of the variance in classroom social competence. Only two of these predictors—synchrony ($B = .74, p = .05$) and maternal coaching skill ($B = .49, p = .07$)—made significant (or near significant) contributions to the prediction of teacher-rated social competence. Therefore these two variables were selected for further examination.

We next performed two hierarchical regression analyses to address the question of whether the statistical interaction of style (synchrony) and coaching skill is incrementally predictive of competence. In the first equation, designed to test the hypothesis that a synchronous parent-child relationship style alone is predictive of peer social competence, we entered synchrony, then coaching skill, and then the multiplicative interaction of synchrony and coaching skill. Together these variables explained 49% of the variance in teacher-rated social skillfulness (p = .008). Synchrony accounted for 29% of the variance (p = .01), coaching skill contributed an additional 11% (p = .08), and the interaction of synchrony and coaching added 9% (p = .10). To establish the magnitude of the nonredundant, unique contributions of style and coaching to the prediction of classroom competence, a second hierarchical regression was performed in which coaching skill was entered first, followed by synchrony and the interaction term. Coaching accounted for 25% of the variance in teacher-rated skillfulness (p = .02), synchrony accounted for an additional 15% of the variance (p = .05), and the interaction of coaching and synchrony again contributed 9% of the variance.

It would appear, then, that both mother-child interactional synchrony and the skillfulness of mothers' coaching about social relationships contribute to the prediction of children's social competence. Given the low correlation between the two parenting qualities, it seems reasonable to assume that they represent two separate "paths" by which children may acquire competence. These data are consistent with the report by Barocas et al. (1991) that maternal affect during a cognitive teaching task was relatively independent of teaching strategy but that both predicted children's attentional skills and verbal IQ. Alternatively it may be that children who are more skilled in peer relations elicit higher quality coaching and/or are more likely to engage their mothers in reciprocal, synchronous exchanges. Longitudinal and experimental/intervention studies (discussed below) will be required to tease out possible directions of effect.

The findings that the statistical interaction of relationship style and coaching skill also contributes (albeit marginally so) to the prediction of social competence is intriguing and suggests that children who have highly synchronous relationships with their mothers and who have mothers skilled in coaching social skills may be especially likely to be rated as competent in their peer relations. Conversely children who experience asynchronous interactions with their mothers and who have mothers deficient in coaching social skills may be the least socially competent children in their classrooms. Additional analyses, with a larger sample of subjects, will be required to fully address these possibilities.

A Model for the Socialization of Peer Competence

We suggested that parent-child interaction is the prime context for the development of early social skills and social-cognitive processes. We proposed, moreover that within this context, lessons about social relationships are conveyed through multiple modes or channels of communication. Although several modes of transmission are possible, we were concerned particularly with the implicit messages conveyed through parent-child relationship style and the messages explicit in the information that parents provide in their efforts to guide or direct children's interactions with peers. Our review of the literature highlighted evidence that both style and informational content contribute to the prediction of children's social competence but failed to resolve issues regarding the nature of the predictive relationships; that is, still lacking from the research literature are independent assessments of multiple components of parenting that would permit a determination of whether parental coaching and style make independent contributions to the development of children's social competence, or whether they are redundant, perhaps reflecting elements of more general parenting competence.

Our preliminary data support our notion that content and style are separate, nonredundant contributors to the development of children's peer competence. Specifically our analyses suggest that style and content are not mere proxy indices of general parenting ability, but rather reflect distinct dimensions of parenting. Children appear to benefit both from participation in a positive, synchronous relationship and from being recipients of direct guidance and advice regarding social relationships. At the same time, these data suggest that parental teaching skill is at least somewhat domain-specific; that is, a parent may be skilled at teaching about content in one domain, such as cognitive skills, yet not be able to provide good advice on handling problems with peers.

The results of our investigation also afford some evidence of the natural ecology of parental coaching and indicate that parents are active in providing children with guidance in peer relationships, at least in the laboratory assessment context. All but two of the mothers in our sample made some overt attempt to help their children become involved in play with the peer, to enhance the quality of peer play, or to help the children negotiate conflict during natural coaching. Of course, these data do not speak to the issue of whether and how mothers provide guidance in more naturalistic settings. To study this issue more directly, researchers might employ techniques, such as direct observation and parent diaries, that have been used to study parent leave-taking behavior in preschool (Bradbard, Endsley, & Mize, 1991; Melson & Kim, 1990). Procedures used in the study of very young children's reactions to the distress of others (Zahn-Waxler, Radke-Yarrow, & King, 1979) might also prove useful. In the Zahn-Waxler et al. study, each mother was asked to describe via audiotape all instances over a 9-month period in which her child observed another person in distress. Mothers of children who responded most altruistically to these events communicated the content of the behavior they expected of the children, they provided a rationale for their expectation, and they reinforced the message with appropriately strong affect.

If both style and coaching do influence children's acquisition of social skills, through which mechanisms might the process occur? That is, what exactly do children learn through each mode of transmission? It is possible that the two modes contribute to different (but perhaps overlapping) aspects of competence and that different mechanisms account for these links. Empirical support for these hypotheses requires investigations of various modes of parental transmission as they relate to specific mechanisms and outcomes. In lieu of relevant data, we offer a model that focuses on how variations in parenting style (especially what we have referred to as *interactional synchrony*) and coaching skill might reasonably be expected to be associated with basic behavioral differences and the underlying components of social competence that differentiate socially skilled from less skilled young children. This model is speculative and is proposed as an heuristic for further research in this area. The general outline of the model is depicted in Figure 5.1.

A growing body of research portrays children with good peer relationships as behaving in ways that are not only generally positive (as opposed to hostile, withdrawn, or overly aggressive) but also relevant and responsive to peers' ongoing activities (Asher, 1983; Pettit & Harrist, 1993). Successful entry into ongoing play groups is predicted by low levels of disagreement and high levels of positive behavioral synchrony (Dodge et al., 1986), and conversations of well-liked preschoolers are interconnected and coordinated with those of peers (Black & Hazen, 1990). The behavior of low-status children, in contrast, often is not well coordinated with that of peers, in that they are more likely to respond noncontingently (Black & Hazen, 1990) and to make statements that are irrelevant to the peer group's interests (Putallaz, 1983).

The ability to achieve positive, synchronous peer interaction appears to hinge on a set of social cognitive processes that may serve as guides for or place constraints on the behaviors that children are likely to perform (Ladd & Mize, 1983). Three types of processes would seem to be particularly relevant in the current context. Socially competent children, compared to less skilled children, have repertoires of social knowledge that are richer and more relevant to the social problem (Pettit et al., 1988), are "friendlier" (Mize & Ladd, 1988), and are more effective (Asher & Renshaw, 1981). Second, competent children are more skilled at attending to and discriminating relevant social cues (Dodge et al., 1986; Putallaz, 1983). Third, socially competent children tend to make accurate and constructive attributions for behavior, whereas a tendency to make self-defeating or inappropriate attributions for behavior characterizes the social

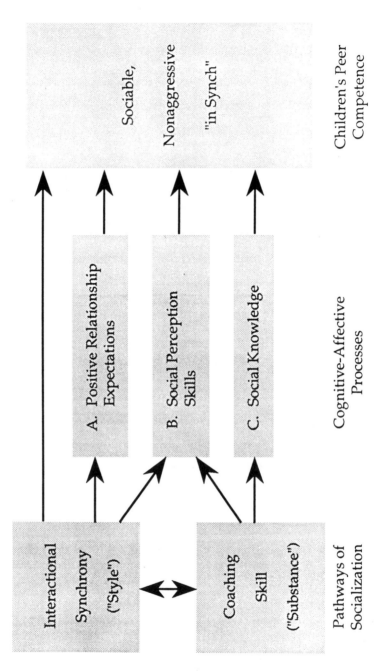

Figure 5.1. Proposed Model for the Socialization of Peer Competence

cognitive processes of some children who have peer relationship difficulties.

How, then, might parenting style and coaching skill affect the social cognitive processes that guide children's peer interaction? Is it the case that social cognitive factors mediate the relation between these parenting qualities and children's behavioral competence? As shown in Figure 5.1, early parent-child interaction probably provides the key context for learning and practicing the fundamental relationship skills of turn taking and reciprocity and hence may contribute directly to a child's behavioral style with peers. A warm, synchronous style of interaction also may contribute to a child's general approach to and expectations for relationships, including a proclivity to view relationships with others as rewarding and a tendency to engage others in generally positive ways. Participation in positively synchronous relationships additionally may contribute to a child's attentiveness and sensitivity to social cues; such a contribution may, in turn, allow the child to coordinate his or her behavior with that of another. This interpersonal sensitivity may arise out of having many opportunities to practice and being rewarded for attempts to "read" the cues of the caregiver and mesh one's behavior with that of a sensitive interactive partner. Children involved in asynchronous parent-child relationships, in contrast, may fail to develop skills for reading social cues, may learn that social relationships are unpredictable, and may withdraw or respond with hostility to protect the self from further unrewarding relationships. Thus parent-child interactional synchrony may have both direct and indirect (mediated) links with children's behavioral competence (see Figure 5.1).

A "good" (highly synchronous) relationship style, however, may not by itself be adequate for providing children with the requisite skills for meeting many of the challenges of peer interaction. For instance, how is one to interpret a rebuff by a playmate? How does one defend one's property without alienating a friend? How does one make friends in a new neighborhood? We suggest that a warm, synchronous parent-child relationship makes a significant, perhaps even necessary, contribution to the development of social competence with peers but that style alone is insufficient for the development of optimal levels of social skillfulness. Children also need guidance in how to interpret and respond to the many perplexing issues that arise in the day-to-day world of peer relationships. In this regard, some parents regularly may reinforce social perception skills by encouraging children to attend to social cues as guides for behavior (e.g., other-oriented induction), while other parents justify behavioral expectations by reliance on prohibitions, threats, or general principles (cf. Hoffman & Saltzstein, 1967). It also is likely that parental discussions about peer relationships affect the size and quality of children's repertoires of social strategy information, as well as the attributions that children make about social behavior. The relation between parental coaching and children's behavioral competence is, therefore, likely to be mediated by the children's social knowledge and social perception skills, as illustrated in Figure 5.1.

Parenting style and content typically may operate conjointly, such that children who are participants in warm, synchronous relationships with caretakers and who receive explicit guidance on handling peer relationship issues are especially competent with peers. It is conceivable, however, that some minimal level of interactional synchrony is necessary for children to benefit from parental coaching. Children involved in a hostile relationship with a parent may not be able to benefit from even good advice offered by that parent regarding peer interaction. The power of a coercive relationship to convey messages about the value of manipulation and aggression may overwhelm any explicit information the parent may try to impart about social skills and cooperation.

Moreover, it is likely that there are developmental changes in the relative importance of the channels of influence that we have proposed. For instance, participation in a positively synchronous relationship likely lays the foundation for a child's overall approach to social relationships during infancy, but continues to be important throughout childhood. Coaching of social skills probably becomes especially critical during the early preschool years as children have their first peer experiences. The explanations that parents provide about others' behavior may become increasingly relevant as children experience more complex relationships. Parental encouragement to attend to social cues and to be guided by concern for others, we suggest, makes important contributions to children's social sensitivity and social competence from toddlerhood through adolescence.

Assessing the adequacy of this or any similar model is a multistep process requiring correlational and longitudinal research. The most powerful test of a model of parental socialization, however, will come from experimental interventions in which various aspects of parenting behavior are manipulated and the effects of parenting changes on children's social competence and underlying social cognitive processes are assessed. In spite of (or perhaps because of) a general acceptance of the important role that parents play in shaping children's social competence, efforts to involve parents as trainers or adjuncts to social skill training are rare (Budd, 1985). Moreover, most parent-based interventions have very small sample sizes or poorly validated measures, and none are based on the current state of knowledge about children's social skills and social cognitive processes. Nonetheless an examination of existing models may shed light on possible directions for future efforts.

The existing parent-based interventions can be categorized as targeting one of the two pathways we have hypothesized as being important in the transmission of social skills. The largest body of literature focuses on changing parents' ways of interacting with the child by teaching them to intervene early in oppositional behavior, to reward compliance and other positive behavior, and to ignore or punish undesirable behavior (e.g., Patterson, 1982). Even though many of the children in such interventions probably have peer relationship difficulties (Dishion, 1990), few of these programs have targeted children's social skills. In the model we have proposed, the peer relationship skills of some participants might be expected to benefit (indirectly) as a result of this form of intervention through its effects on parent-child relationship style; that is, as parent-child interaction becomes more positive and synchronous and as children learn to use more positive and less coercive tactics to obtain desired outcomes, they may be able to generalize these lessons to other contexts.

However, the limitations of this assumption are highlighted by
the results of an effort to train parents to enhance the sibling-
interaction and play skills of four handicapped children (Powell,
Salzberg, Rule, Levy, & Itzkowitz, 1983). Although parents completed behavior management training, their efforts had no effect
on the children's play until the parents were given specific
formal instruction in how to promote play skills. This study
suggests that increasing the effectiveness of parental discipline
may be insufficient if one goal of intervention is to improve
children's peer relationships.

A second, smaller, group of parent-based interventions focuses on training parents to teach their children social problem-
solving skills or peer interaction skills. The best known of these
programs, developed by Spivak and Shure (Shure, 1981), trained
mothers to use formal (scripted) and informal dialogues to
increase children's ability to think of alternative solutions to
problems and to evaluate consequences of the solutions. Participant children evidenced gains in the number of relevant strategies they could generate and were rated as better adjusted at the
end of the intervention. A recent study by Budd and Itzkowitz
(1990) is the only effort we are aware of that has targeted
specifically parental teaching of peer relationship skills. Parents participated in a series of four educational sessions focusing on children's social skills and ways parents teach children
social skills. Participants' knowledge of social skills and their
perceptions of their own children's skillfulness increased
from pretest to posttest. However, because no independent
assessment of changes in children's behavior was obtained, it is
impossible to evaluate the general utility of this parent-based
intervention.

The data we have reported have implications for the design of
parent-based interventions. Results of intervention efforts, in
turn, will shed more light on the channels through which parents influence children's social competence. Specifically our
data suggest that impaired social skill development may arise
from the accumulation of insufficiently synchronous parent-
child interaction and inadequate coaching of social skills. If it is
the cumulative impact of the messages conveyed through differ-

ent modes of influence that determine children's social competence, then intervention aimed at either channel may have beneficial effects on children's social adjustment. If, on the other hand, the pathways are functionally interdependent, then intervention aimed both at parent-child relationship style and at parental coaching may be necessary to improve children's social functioning. Empirical examination of these possibilities would provide the most persuasive evidence regarding the actions and interactions of channels of influence we have proposed.

Little is known currently about how early family experiences are transformed into individual differences in children's social functioning with peers, but accumulating evidence suggests that young children develop social skills in the context of adult-mediated experience. In this chapter we have proposed that parents "teach" children about interpersonal relationships tacitly through their style of interacting with their children and explicitly through their verbal communications regarding social relationships. We have speculated that the messages conveyed through these two channels affect separate, but perhaps overlapping, aspects of children's social competence. Data from our pilot study support the contention that parent-child synchrony and parent coaching of social skills make independent contributions to children's social competence with peers. Questions remain, however, concerning the natural ecology of parental efforts to teach children these skills and the social cognitive processes that mediate the link between parenting and children's behavior with peers. Future research should be directed at refining methods of assessing parent-child relationship style and coaching content and at extending these assessments into home and school settings, with the aim of describing the topography of naturally occurring coaching. At the same time, it will be important to contrast similarities and differences between mothers and fathers and to examine the ways parents may complement one another in teaching their children social skills. Finally, to illuminate the possible mechanisms of transmission, research must evaluate the effect of parenting style and coaching on children's social knowledge, social perception skills, and general approaches to relationships.

Direct Parental Influences on Young Children's Peer Relations

Gary W. Ladd

Karen D. Le Sieur

Susan M. Profilet

Much of the knowledge we have acquired about children's social development has been generated by researchers interested in either family-child relations or child-peer relations. Only recently have researchers begun to search for linkages between these two domains and thus to incorporate elements of both the family and peer systems into their investigations of children's learning about relationships. Evidence of this focus can be found in many recent investigations and in the theories and models that investigators are developing to guide their work.

Current perspectives on linkages between the family and peer systems owe a substantial debt to ecological systems theory (Bronfenbrenner, 1979, 1986). Within this perspective, social systems such as the family and the peer culture are not viewed as isolated from each other, but rather as enmeshed within a larger network of social systems including the personal network, neighborhood, community, and larger culture (Belsky, 1984; Parke & Tinsley, 1984; Tinsley & Parke, 1984).

Investigators who study linkages between the family and peer systems tend to view them as bidirectional pathways—that is, as processes through which one system exerts influence on another and vice versa. Families, for example, may actively attempt to influence children's peer relations, while the converse also may be true (Ladd, 1991). Moreover, positive as well as negative effects may be transmitted along these pathways, as in families who encourage children to develop prosocial behaviors or where children's adverse peer experiences cause parents to create overly protective or restrictive policies toward playmates.

In this chapter we consider pathways that are consistent with a "family effects" interpretation—that is, research designed to understand how specific family or parenting processes affect the development of children's peer interactions and relationships. Viewed in this manner, pathways include both the processes through which parents influence their children and the resulting child outcomes that may mediate or influence the child's social experiences with peers.

Investigators' attempts to define potential pathways and to investigate the mechanisms that may influence children's competence and success in peer relations are at an early stage. Parke and colleagues (Parke et al., 1987) have proposed that families influence children's peer relations through either indirect or direct pathways. *Indirect pathways* include family processes that impinge on the child but that have little or no bearing on the child's access, interactions, or relationships with peers. Included among these are features associated with the family environment and parent-child relationship, including attachment, abuse, child-rearing styles, discipline, marital relations, and parental pathology (see Cicchetti, Lynch, Shonk, & Manly, 1992; Cooper & Cooper, in press; Zahn-Waxler, Denham, & Ianotti, 1992).

Direct pathways, which constitute the focus of this chapter, are defined as strategies that parents employ to "manage" their children's access to peers and to promote their social skills and relationships in this context. Examples of direct influences include parents' efforts to involve children in peer-oriented settings, to arrange play contacts, to choose or influence play partners, and to plan or supervise children's peer activities and interactions (see Ladd, Profilet, & Hart, 1992; Lollis, Ross, & Tate, 1992).

Direct Parental Influences

It has been proposed that children's relationships and interactions with family members provide them with a broad range of opportunities to develop basic social competencies (Asher, Renshaw, & Hymel, 1982; Putallaz & Heflin, 1990). Those who study direct pathways extend this assumption by proposing that parents also seek to control and influence their child's experiences with agemates, often by intentionally or unintentionally "managing" the child's peer environment, interactions, and relationships (see Ladd et al., 1992). The degree to which parents manage and structure the child's peer relations, and the form and effects of their involvement often vary greatly from family to family (Ladd & Hart, 1992).

In the newly emerging literature on family-peer relations, research on the parents' contribution as "manager" of children's early peer relations has become an increasingly important topic. Thus far, researchers interested in studying direct parental influences have concentrated on gathering descriptive data and on examining the relation between targeted parental behaviors and child social-behavioral outcomes. This growing body of literature, however, encompasses a variety of investigational paradigms, methods, and samples. Investigators have, for example, conducted studies in both laboratory and field settings and have attempted to assess specific forms of parental influence across a variety of family members and age groups of children.

Moreover, several forms of parental management, each representing distinct pathways or "direct" modes of influence, have been articulated in recent theories (Ladd, 1991; Ladd et al., 1992; Lollis et al., 1992). Ladd and Coleman (in press) classify these forms of management into four categories: parent as designer, as mediator, as supervisor, and as consultant. In the next several sections, we review the conceptual and empirical status of each of these potential pathways.

Parent as Designer

Parents act as designers when they actively choose or seek to influence the child's social ecology, including the neighborhood, preschool, or other environments that will bring children into contact with peers. For example, in choosing a neighborhood, parents may evaluate factors such as density of the child population, accessibility of agemates, and the overall landscape and terrain (e.g., is it safe and easily navigated by the child, are there sidewalks and playgrounds, are surrounding houses nearby or distant).

Parents also may influence the nature of children's social lives by sending them to child care or preschool. By enrolling children in these settings, parents provide access to a "ready-made" peer group and a context in which they are encouraged to interact, get along, and make friends with peers. However, differences in preschool environments and curricula may affect the extent to which children profit from their social experiences at school (see Vandell, Henderson, & Wilson, 1988). Therefore parents' choice of preschool may have an important impact on the nature of children's early peer experiences and relationships and, ultimately, the types of social skills that children develop during this period.

Another way that parents act as designers of early social environments is by involving children in other types of community settings where peers are present (see Ladd & Price, 1987). Parents who take their children to parks, libraries, pools, or other child-focused community activities (e.g., art, exercise, sports, Scouts programs) are supplying a context in which the children are encouraged to meet, interact, and form relationships with peers.

Choice of Neighborhood. Parents may choose a neighborhood for a variety of reasons, including financial needs, accessibility to schools, type of community, quality of life, proximity to the workplace, and social opportunities for themselves and their children. Regardless of their reasons, however, the neighborhoods where parents choose to live will likely affect their children's opportunities for peer interaction. For the young child, who lacks both the mobility and school contacts available to the older child, the structure of the neighborhood may have an important impact on the availability of playmates and play contexts (Rubin & Sloman, 1984).

Because the neighborhood presents a wide array of social opportunities (Garbarino & Gilliam, 1980), it can be considered one of the most important contexts for the socialization of young children. According to Moore and Young (1978), children spend much of their time involved in peer activities within the confines of the neighborhood; opportunities for interaction may occur on playgrounds, on sidewalks, in school yards, in vacant lots, and within and around each other's homes. Children appear to have greater access to peers, and larger social networks, when their neighborhoods have large child populations and are characterized by features such as short distances between homes and the presence of sidewalks and playgrounds (Berg & Medrich, 1980; Medrich, Roizen, Rubin, & Buckley, 1982).

Not all children live in neighborhoods that possess these advantages, however. The physical isolation or inaccessibility of some homes may create barriers for peer contact and may restrict children's social mobility (Berg & Medrich, 1980; Medrich et al., 1982). Child populations may be less dense in rural, as opposed to urban, environments (van Vliet, 1981). The advantages of urban environments may be mitigated, however, if the neighborhood is a dangerous one: Dangerous neighborhoods have been shown to limit children's peer contacts (Cochran & Riley, 1988). The topography of the neighborhood also may influence peer contact; research indicates that flat locations provide more opportunities for peer contacts than do hilly locations (Berg & Medrich, 1980; Medrich et al., 1982).

Evidence also suggests that physical proximity influences the quality of children's peer relationships. It appears that when the child population of a neighborhood is less dense, or proximate, the quality of children's peer relationships may be affected. Studies by Medrich and colleagues (Berg & Medrich, 1980; Medrich et al., 1982) suggest that, in low-density neighborhoods, children's social networks and friendships tend to be sparser and more formal, perhaps due to the fact that play arrangements become less spontaneous for the child and more involved and time-consuming for the parent.

Data from studies with elementary-age children reveal that children who named each other as friends were more likely to live in close proximity to each other than were nonfriends (Gallagher, 1958; Segoe, 1939). These studies are contradicted, however, by others that show little or no relation between proximity and friendship (DeVault, 1957; Potashin, 1946). However, there is some indication that age may be a factor in the relation between proximity and friendship. DeVault (1957) found that younger children tend to live closer to mutual friends than do older children.

Preschool/Child Care. Little is known about why parents choose to send their children to preschool or day care. It seems likely, however, that parents are motivated by a variety of intrinsic needs or goals, including the desire to promote school readiness and to provide intellectual or social stimulation, foster peer friendships, obtain convenient child care, and increase children's independence (Rubin & Sloman, 1984). Despite parents' reasons for involving children in preschool or day care, most appear to value the social aspect of early schooling (Renscorla, 1989).

Evidence for the social benefits of early school attendance can be found in several studies. In preschool and day-care settings, children's involvement and sociability with peers has been shown to increase over time. Among toddlers who regularly attend preschool, the proportion of child-peer interactions tends to increase, while that of teacher-child interactions decreases (Finkelstein, Dent, Gallacher, & Ramey, 1978). In fact, research by Howes (1988) indicates that child-peer interactions emerge at very early ages in preschool settings, such that complementary and reciprocal play often emerge by age 1, and social pretend play by age 2.

Howes's research (1983, 1988) also indicates that preschool/ day-care settings may allow children to develop lasting friendships. Moreover, children's participation in stable friendships was related to the development of more complex and sophisticated forms of social interactions and play. Children who lost friendships, in contrast (due to a child leaving the preschool), tended to become less socially skilled and less accepted by peers.

The duration and stability of children's preschool experiences also may impact their social development and competence. In research conducted with male toddlers in teacher-supported play groups, more sophisticated forms of play were observed as children became more familiar with their peers; this behavior was not true among boys who spent less time together (Mueller & Brenner, 1977). Similarly Howes (1988) found that time spent in child care was positively associated with the sophistication of children's social skills. Children who began preschool earlier had less difficulty with peers than did those who entered later (as rated by teachers).

The importance of preschool as a source for the acquisition of social skills and enduring relationships also is illustrated in recent studies of adjustment to grade school. Ladd and Price (1987) studied 4- and 5-year-olds who were making the transition from preschool to kindergarten; the researchers found that children's prosocial behavior in preschool (e.g., cooperative play and social conversation) predicted their peer acceptance in kindergarten. Results from a second study (Ladd, 1990) revealed that children who maintained friendships over the transition from preschool to kindergarten tended to develop more favorable attitudes toward school.

The degree to which children benefit from the social provisions of preschool may depend, in part, on the quality of the program or setting chosen by the parent. Studies of day-care quality show that children enrolled in high-quality day care (Vandell et al., 1988) often evidence higher levels of positive, friendly social interactions and lower levels of nonsocial behavior. Also teachers tended to perceive children who were enrolled in high-quality day care as having higher levels of school adjustment.

Community Activities. Many community settings and activities also may serve as staging areas for the development of early social competence, and parents may play an important role in facilitating children's access to these resources. Often communities provide both structured and unstructured activities that serve as settings for peer interaction. Little research is available on the effects of structured activities (e.g., Little League, Scouts, 4-H) on preschoolers, possibly because they are generally less available or are considered to be less appropriate for this age group. Some data are available, however, on unstructured activities such as those that occur in parks, playgrounds, libraries, and the neighborhood swimming pool.

Unstructured activities present children with the opportunity for informal peer contact and, therefore, represent settings in which they are often free to construct their own play activities and interactions. Bryant (1985), in a study of neighborhood/ community supports for children, found that involvement in unstructured community activities was predictive of perspective-taking skills, especially among older children (age 10 versus age 7). One interpretation of this finding, advanced by Bryant, is that children's efforts to construct their own activities in this context led to greater autonomy, control, mastery, and, ultimately, better perspective-taking skills.

Evidence attesting to the positive effects of unstructured community peer activities also has been reported in research by Ladd and Price (1987). In this study, which was designed to examine factors affecting children's transition from preschool to kindergarten, Ladd and Price asked parents to report the number of unstructured peer activities their children participated in (e.g., church school, going to a swimming pool or library) on a regular basis. They found that whereas children who were exposed to a narrower range of peer contexts in the community were more anxious at the beginning of kindergarten, those who had experienced a broader range of contacts displayed lower levels of anxiety and fewer absences.

Summary and Conclusions. At present, most of the research that is relevant to the role of parent as designer has been conducted for another purpose—for example, to investigate the effects of early child-rearing contexts (e.g., preschool) on children's peer opportunities, interactions, and relationships. Little or no research has been conducted that directly examines parents' efforts to control or manipulate children's access to specific peer contexts.

Thus, although parents probably vary in the degree to which they try to influence or "design" children's social environments, we know very little about individual differences in this domain. Even less is known about how parents' attempts to manage early peer environments might affect the development of children's social competence.

It does seem clear, however, that contexts such as neighborhoods, preschools, and community settings play a central role in the development of children's early peer relationships and social skills. Available evidence suggests that the character of these settings determines, in large part, both the opportunities that children have to meet and interact with peers and the types of relationships they develop (e.g., Berg & Medrich, 1980; Medrich et al., 1982). Children appear to have more peer contacts and closer peer relationships in settings that afford convenient, attractive, and safe play locations. Sustained proximity to playmates, as might occur in some types of neighborhoods and school settings, appears to be an important prerequisite for long-term or lasting peer relationships (e.g., DeVault, 1957; Howes, 1988).

Clearly more research is needed to understand the strategies that parents use to structure or design early social environments, and the potential effects this role has on children's social development. At the descriptive level, it would be helpful to know more about the types of social settings that are available to young children in different locales and socioeconomic strata (e.g., urban vs. rural, higher vs. lower SES neighborhoods, family vs. center-based child care) and the extent to which parents differ in their use of available environmental resources. Beyond this, it also will be important to understand why parents design and use early social environments differently (e.g., bases for their choice of neighborhoods, schools, community activities). Further attention also should be focused on the means through which children gain access to these settings (how families create access to early peer settings and regulate children's participation in these contexts) and the types of experiences they encounter in them (e.g., mechanisms within settings that foster peer competence).

Parent as Mediator

Parents who act as mediators do more than facilitate their child's access to particular social settings. Rather, as mediators, parents seek to influence the child's play opportunities and relationships with specific peers.

A variety of parental management activities are subsumed under this role, including helping children find potential playmates, initiating and arranging play opportunities, and regulating children's choice of play partners (Bhavnagri, 1987; Ladd & Coleman, in press; Ladd & Golter, 1988). Thus parents may not only influence children's choice of playmates but also exert control over their play activities—that is, the who, what, where, and when of the child's peer engagements.

As a step toward building the child's social network, parents may help their child find potential playmates—the "who" function of the mediator role. This help may take the form of encouraging the child to identify potential playmates in the neighborhood or school or arranging for the child to get together with familiar peers (e.g., children of the family's friends). Parents also may choose playmates on the basis of their observations of their child's interactions with peers in informal contexts (e.g., at the pool, in the neighborhood). Once a playmate network has been established, parents may continue to regulate the child's choice of play partners by controlling the frequency of contact with particular peers. These decisions may be predicated on factors such as the parents' perceptions of their child's social needs and characteristics, their view of particular playmates or playmate characteristics, and family policies or values.

The "where," "when," and "what" of the mediating role are reflected in parents' attempts to influence the parameters of specific child-peer play encounters. Parents may not only help their child to schedule play bouts but also have an important say in determining where the child will play, what he or she will do, and when the interaction will take place. Parents who help a child arrange these facets of peer contacts may do so not only as a means of promoting safe and productive play opportunities but also as a way of teaching the child how to initiate and maintain social relationships.

Initiating Peer Contacts. Ladd and Golter (1988) studied parents' efforts to initiate nonschool (in-home) play contacts with their preschoolers, using a telephone-log methodology. Data on parents' initiations and preschoolers' informal (nonschool) peer relations were gathered when the children were in preschool, and measures of children's classroom peer relations were obtained after they had entered kindergarten.

The investigators found that approximately half (49%) of the sampled parents had initiated one or more peer contacts. Children of parents who did initiate peer contacts were more likely to have a wider range of nonschool playmates and a larger number of consistent playmates in this context. Second, boys of parents who were classified as initiators also tended to develop higher levels of classroom peer acceptance after the transition to kindergarten. Interestingly no such trends were observed for girls, a lack suggesting that this type of early socialization support may benefit boys more than girls.

In another study conducted with younger children, Ladd, Hart, Wadsworth, and Golter (1988) assessed parents' efforts to manage their children's peer relations prior to preschool entrance. Data was gathered on such functions as the extent to which parents arranged children's peer contacts and purchased toys that could be used for social purposes (e.g., interacting with peers). The results indicated that parents who had higher levels of involvement in these mediating roles tended to have children who spent more time playing in peers' homes. Apparently young children's social ties and experiences are more likely to extend beyond their homes and families when parents engage in these forms of mediation.

Further evidence of the importance of parental mediation is reported by Krappman (1986) in a study of German grade school-age children and their families. Krappman assessed parents' efforts to arrange and organize children's peer relations and found that parents who were active in this role tended to have children who developed closer and more harmonious ties with peers.

Recent studies also suggest that the degree to which parents engage in various mediational roles may depend, in part, on the age of the child. Bhavnagri & Parke (1991) found that parents of younger preschoolers were more likely to arrange peer-play opportunities than were parents of older preschoolers. Specifically parent-initiated peer contacts were more common among mothers of 2-year-olds than among mothers of 3- to 6-year-olds, and older children tended to arrange more of their own play contacts.

Play groups. Another way that parents may mediate young children's social experiences with peers is by sponsoring or involving them in informal play groups. The group-oriented dynamics and activities that children experience in this context may help prepare them for the demands of larger peer environments, such as classrooms and playgrounds. At present some evidence suggests that children's play group experience is related to their social competence. Using home interviews, Liebermann (1977) combined assessments of preschoolers' experiences with peers in group and dyadic settings and found that the resulting index was positively associated with children's competence in laboratory-based observations of their social behaviors. Children with greater peer experience tended to display more sophisticated forms of verbal behavior.

Early play group experience also was assessed by Ladd et al. (1988) in a study of young children's transition to preschool. Results indicated that the benefits of early play group experience depended on the age of the child. Among older children (41-55 months), involvement in a larger number of play groups was positively associated with several measures of school adjustment, including their ability to adjust to classroom routines. The reverse was found for younger children (23-40 months), suggesting that extensive group-oriented experiences with peers may be less adaptive for younger, as opposed to older, preschoolers.

Summary and Conclusions. Although these investigations provide some insight into relations that may exist between parental mediation and children's social competence, the existing evidence is largely descriptive and correlational in nature. In addition, because investigators have been concerned primarily with the presence rather than the process of mediation, we know very little about the precursors of parents' mediational activities or the strategies and contexts they employ to create informal play opportunities for children.

It is evident, however, that parents' mediational activities are related to the amount of social contact children experience with peers and the quality of their peer relations (Bhavnagri & Parke, 1991; Ladd & Golter, 1988; Ladd & Hart, 1992). Specifically studies of parental mediation indicate that the children of parents who initiated peer contacts had a wider range of nonschool playmates and a larger number of consistent playmates (Ladd & Golter, 1988; Ladd & Hart, 1992). It appears, however, that the effects of parent initiations may be gender-related—for boys, parent initiation was positively correlated with peer acceptance in preschool settings, but no such relationship emerged for girls.

Parents' decisions to mediate children's peer contact through the use of play groups also may have important consequences for children's development. Participation in play groups may provide children with the skills needed to function in larger peer environments (e.g., the classroom or playground). The effectiveness of play groups as a socializing agent, however, may be related to the age of the child. Preliminary findings suggest that play group participation is positively associated with classroom adjustment for older, but not for younger, preschool children (Ladd et al., 1988).

Although parental mediation appears to enhance children's opportunities for peer contact, further research is needed to clarify the potential impact of these activities on children's social skills and peer relationships. At the descriptive level, it would be helpful to know why some parents choose to mediate peer contacts but others do not, and why parents employ different types of mediational strategies. In assessing developmental differences in parental mediation, it will be necessary to include an evaluation of the role that children play in the initiation of peer contact. We are, for example, only beginning to understand how parental initiations change as a function of the age of the child and children's initiations (Bhavnagri & Parke, 1991; Ladd & Hart, 1992). The presence of gender-related differences in parental mediation, as well as in child outcomes, suggests that gender also should be an important factor in future investigations of the mediator role.

Unfortunately, because research on parental mediation has been correlational in design, we know very little about the effects of mediation on child outcomes. As such, it will be important for investigators to consider cause-effect relationships, such as the impact of parental mediation on children's social competence and peer relations and on children's ability to initiate their own peer contacts.

Parent as Supervisor

Parents act as supervisors when they oversee and regulate children's ongoing interactions with peers. According to Lollis et al. (1992), most forms of parental supervision can be classified into one of two major types—termed *directive* and *interactive* intervention—each of which may serve different functions in the context of the child's play or peer interactions.

Directive interventions refer to the styles of supervision in which the parent does not become an active participant in the child's play, but rather operates as an observer or facilitator of the activity. It has been hypothesized that directive interventions tend to be reactive in nature, based on situational determinants, and temporally linked to the events that parents are trying to influence (Lollis et al., 1992). Parents' use of this form of intervention may be determined by their assessments of the play situation, the children's behaviors, and the potential effectiveness of prior supervisory behaviors. The primary functions of this type of supervision may be to support or enhance the child's interactive skills, to discourage or redirect objectionable behaviors, to resolve conflicts, and to gain short-term compliance from the child during peer interactions (Kuczynski, 1984; Zahn-Waxler et al., 1979).

Parents who engage in *interactive interventions,* in contrast, supervise children's peer interactions from within the play context, often as participants in the play activity. As members of the activity, parents may attempt to impact the direction or flow of play, to shape the course of child-peer interactions, to prompt specific behaviors, and so on. Parents also may use this style of supervision to establish synchrony or reciprocity in children's interactions, to maintain children's interest in peers or play, and to prevent conflicts or disruptions before they occur (Lollis et al., 1992).

It has been hypothesized that directive and interactive parental supervisory strategies, and the benefits they provide, vary depending on the age of the child (Bhavnagri, 1987; Bhavnagri & Parke, 1985, 1991; Lollis et al., 1992). According to this logic, parents of younger preschoolers are more likely to employ interactive interventions (Lollis et al., 1992) in which they structure and participate in children's peer interactions and play situations. Parents of older preschoolers, in contrast, are more likely to employ management styles that are less controlling and participatory (directive interventions); for example, parents may listen to children's play from another room and intervene only when problems and difficulties arise (e.g., conflicts).

A third form of parental supervision, *monitoring,* may be used by the parent when play occurs in a location outside of the parent's immediate influence (e.g., in another room, in the neighborhood, at a neighbor's house). Parents act as monitors when they regulate peer interactions through a knowledge of the children's play activities and whereabouts. *Monitoring* differs from the two forms of supervision defined above because it refers to activities that are primarily cognitive in nature and has seldom been assessed with families of young children. Most researchers have defined *monitoring* as parents' knowledge and awareness of children's whereabouts, activities, and social companions.

Interactive Intervention. Research conducted on interactive intervention indicates that this supervisory style may have the effect of increasing the child's level of social competence, though findings are mixed regarding the longevity of the effect. Five major studies, which constitute the primary investigations to date, share two common features: They are lab-based and focus on the effects of maternal interactive intervention on children's interactions with unfamiliar peers.

In the first of two of these studies conducted by Bhavnagri and Parke (1985), the effect of maternal intervention on toddler's social competence was assessed during four play intervals spanning a total of 30 minutes. During the first 5-minute interval, mothers were instructed to allow the child and peer to play without maternal intervention. During the next two 10-minute intervals, first the child's and then the peer's mother was given responsibility for intervening in the play context. For the final 5-minute interval, mothers again were instructed not to interfere with children's peer interactions. During all four intervals, children's behavior was rated on four global indices: social skill, play, affect, and social competence.

Bhavnagri and Parke (1985) found that children exhibited higher levels of social competence within the maternal intervention intervals than they did during the intervals where intervention was absent. During maternal intervention, children displayed more advanced social skills, including turn taking and longer play bouts. Further analysis revealed, however, that facilitative effects of maternal intervention may be temporary. The gains that children displayed in conjunction with maternal support returned to baseline during the final nonintervention interval. An additional significant finding was that the social competence of mothers' intervention strategies was positively correlated with the skillfulness of the children's behaviors. This finding suggests that it is less the presence of the mother and more the skill of the intervention that may be responsible for the gains that children achieved.

Bhavnagri and Parke's most recent study (1991) was designed to explore potential differences in maternal and paternal intervention skill, as well as to address potential methodological flaws in the structure of their play sequence. In this study the ABBA (nonintervention, intervention, intervention, nonintervention) sequence used in the first two studies was altered to become an ABABA (nonintervention, intervention, nonintervention, intervention, nonintervention) sequence. An additional nonintervention interval, placed in the middle of the sequence, was used to provide an assessment of child-peer interaction that was not confounded by events corresponding to the first and last nonintervention segment (novelty vs. fatigue or diminished interest in play).

The sample for this study included 70 preschoolers who were grouped into younger (2 years 2 months to 3 years 6 months) and older (3 years 7 months to 5 years 11 months) age groups. Results indicated that the interventions performed by both mothers and fathers were equally effective and yielded the same increases in children's social competence that were found in the first study. Bhavnagri and Parke's findings also supported the hypothesis that interactive intervention may benefit younger preschoolers more than older preschoolers. On the basis of analyses designed to compare younger (age 2 to 3½ years) and older (age 3½ to 6 years) age groups, they found that younger children benefited most from maintained support during the interaction intervals. Older children, in contrast, were capable of maintaining interactions on their own and needed assistance only with initiating play activities. These results suggest that striking changes may occur in the benefits that children accrue from parental interventions during the course of early childhood.

The effects of different types of maternal intervention (directive and interactive) on the social competence of young children also have been investigated in a recent study by Lollis (1990). Toddlers (aged 15-18 months) were paired with unfamiliar peers for a 12-minute play session. Half of the mothers were asked to respond to the child-peer interaction in a manner characteristic of their behavior, but not to intervene directly in the play session. The other half of the mothers were told to interact extensively in the play session. Both sets of mothers intervened as instructed by the researcher for the first 8 minutes of the session. At the end of this interval, both sets of mothers departed and children's behavior was assessed in the absence of maternal intervention.

Lollis (1990) found that although extensive maternal interaction included more unsolicited direction about both social skills and play activities, there was little difference in the quality of play between either intervention group prior to maternal departure. When child and peer interacted without maternal intervention, however, those children who had received extensive interactive maternal attention were more likely to spend time in dyadic play and expressed less negative affect. This finding suggests that, among toddlers, interactive intervention is more effective than directive intervention at increasing social competence and the quality of play.

Research conducted by Nash (1989) provides additional insight into the age effects for interactive intervention. In a study of toddlers (aged 14 months), significant differences were found in the effectiveness of physical (interactive) versus verbal (directive) interventions. During three successive 10-minute play intervals, mothers were instructed to encourage child-peer interaction during the first and last intervals and to remain uninvolved during the middle interval. In general, when maternal intervention of either type occurred, child-peer interactions were more frequent and of longer duration. Interventions were more successful if they were physical (object-oriented) and interactive versus if they were verbal (directive).

In summary, it would appear that interactive intervention is particularly effective at helping children initiate and maintain play activities with an unfamiliar peer and at enhancing social competence. Younger children ($2\frac{1}{2}$ to 3 years) appear to benefit more from interactive intervention than do older children ($3\frac{1}{2}$ to 6 years).

Directive Intervention. Both experimental and field studies have been used to assess directive intervention. In a controlled context, Finnie and Russell (1988) attempted to assess the relationship between directive intervention and preschool children's play with peers (age 4-5 years). During 12-minute play sessions, children who differed in peer status (popular, unpopular, average) were paired with average-status partners, and mothers were instructed to facilitate child-peer interactions by providing directive intervention for two successive, specified activities (i.e., blocks and puzzles). The content and skill of maternal interventions were coded on seven behavioral dimensions, including observing, avoidance, active/skillful and active/less skillful strategies, verbal instruction, and discipline strategy (power assertive versus inductive).

Results indicated that mothers of both high- and low-status children used active/skillful strategies most frequently, although mothers of low-status children used more active/unskilled strategies and were more likely to avoid intervention than were mothers of high-status children. Not surprisingly, appropriate and relevant interventions, generally representative of those used by mothers of the high-status group, were most effective at changing/improving children's social behavior.

Levitt and colleagues (Levitt, Weber, Clark, & McDonnell, 1985) also have contributed to our knowledge of the effects of directive maternal intervention on the social behavior of toddlers (aged 29-36 months). In this experimental study, toddlers were paired with unfamiliar peers in a play area divided by a lattice barrier. For half of a 10-minute play session, a set of toys was placed on one side of the barrier, outside of the reach of the other child. Halfway through the session, the toys were transferred to the other child's location. Mothers were told not to intervene until after their child had the toys for 4 minutes, and then only if the child had not spontaneously shared toys with the peer. While playing alone, none of the children shared toys, but after maternal directive intervention, 65% shared toys with the peer. During the second 5-minute interval, reciprocated sharing occurred only between those child-peer dyads that had shared the toys during the first 5-minute session.

The effects of directive intervention also have been evaluated in the context of object conflicts. Ross and colleagues (Ross, Tesla, Kenyon, & Lollis, 1991) conducted a study in which pairs of unfamiliar toddlers (aged 20-30 months) and their mothers met for a series of 18 40-minute play sessions. Mothers were instructed to behave naturally during child-peer interaction, but to refrain from interactive intervention during the play session. Observers then dictated a running record of each play session, recording both child activity and maternal interventions.

These findings showed that mothers' interventions are precipitated by the desire to deflect conflicts and often are intended to modify their own children's behavior, but not that of peers. For example, Ross et al.'s (1991) data show that mothers tended to resolve conflicts over their own child's possessions by telling the child to share but often responded to conflicts over peers' possessions by supporting the peer's position.

This last finding prompted Lollis and colleagues (Lollis et al., 1992) to evaluate further the goals and strategies that mothers implemented in their interventions. They found that, overall, mothers communicate a larger number of goals and strategies to older children and that, in conflict and contingent interactions, mothers tended to use more goals and strategies with males than females. These findings may indicate that maternal intervention becomes more verbal and explicit with older children, possibly because older children are better able to process and evaluate strategies.

Ladd and Golter (1988) used telephone-log interviews to assess the methods that parents use to supervise preschoolers' (aged 4-5 years) informal play activities in naturalistic settings. Their analyses revealed that parental supervisory style during preschool was predictive of children's classroom peer status in kindergarten. Children whose parents employed interactive forms of supervision (e.g., participating in children's play) tended to have lower levels of peer acceptance and were rated (by teachers) as aggressive and hostile. Mize and Ladd (1990) suggest that, with older preschoolers, interactive forms of supervision interfere with children's ability to develop independent and self-regulated play and relationship skills.

Monitoring. Investigations of monitoring have been conducted primarily among older children, yet the results of these studies may have implications for research on parents' roles as supervisors of young children's peer relations. Research on delinquent children frequently shows that parents are less likely to monitor and supervise their children's peer activities (Belson, 1975; Pulkinnen, 1982; Wilson, 1980). Patterson and Stouthamer-Loeber (1984), for example, report significant relationships between the lack of parental monitoring and negative outcomes such as court-reported delinquency, petty crime, rule breaking, and antisocial behavior. These investigators suggest, however, that the importance of parental monitoring may vary with the age of the child. Across the age span of their sample, they found that no significant relationship existed between behavior and monitoring among 4th-graders, yet a significant relationship did emerge for both 7th- and 10th-graders.

Dishion (1990) also has investigated the relationship between parental monitoring and adolescent peer relations. Included in this study were assessments of how well the child's activities were supervised by the parent, the child's perceptions of parental rules about volunteering information pertaining to daily social plans, and the amount of time spent together by parent and child on a daily basis. Analyses performed on composites formed from these measures revealed that monitoring was positively correlated with children's peer acceptance in each of two sample cohorts.

The relationship between parental monitoring and grade school children's (fourth and fifth grade) school performance (academic competence and behavior) was evaluated by Crouter and colleagues (Crouter, MacDermid, McHale, & Perry-Jenkins, 1990). They conducted individual telephone interviews with both mothers and grade-school-age children to assess children's daily experiences and the extent to which parents monitored these experiences. The key finding that emerged from Crouter et al.'s analyses was that boys who were less well monitored performed less well in school, exhibited poor conduct, and were identified by parents as having learning problems.

Although most of the studies on monitoring have been conducted with older children, it may be the case that parents use this type of supervision with preschoolers, particularly when children's peer activities take place outside of the home (e.g., at a peer's home, in the neighborhood). Parents' reliance on this type of supervision may be limited, however, to preschoolers who are old enough to play independently or to situations where supervision is provided by persons other than the parents.

Summary and Conclusions. More research has been conducted on parents' supervisory behaviors than on any other form of direct parental influence. The largest portion of this work has been designed to understand the relation between parents' supervision and children's interactive competence with peers. These styles, as they have been defined here and elsewhere (see Lollis et al., 1992), are termed *interactive intervention, directive intervention,* and *monitoring.*

The studies we have included are unique in that most have been conducted in laboratory or quasi-experimental (e.g., analogue) settings. The controls permitted by the settings have allowed investigators to operationalize specific supervisory strategies and tactics and to disentangle their potential effects from other potential influences on child behavior. However, some of the constraints inherent in these paradigms (e.g., use of laboratorylike playrooms and unfamiliar playmates) also limit the generalizability of this work. In particular, it is not entirely clear whether the findings reported in these studies are representative of the types of supervisory styles and outcomes that children experience in their everyday interactions with parents.

Although it has been hypothesized that parents' styles of supervising children's social activities vary with the age of the child, very little evidence that might support such a conclusion has emerged in recent literature. One exception is Bhavnagri's (1987) cross-sectional comparison of the effects of parents' interactive interventions on younger and older preschoolers' behavioral competence with peers. This investigator found that parents' interactive participation produced greater gains in competence in younger as compared with older preschoolers. Beyond these data, it would appear that investigators have studied different styles of parental supervision with different age groups of children. To shed greater light on this question, longitudinal designs are needed. In this way, researchers can determine when, in the course of child development, parents introduce and abandon specific styles of supervision.

At this point, data gathered on the effects of specific supervisory styles are far from conclusive, but recent studies have produced some promising leads. Bhavnagri and Parke (1991; Bhavnagri, 1987) have shown that younger preschoolers tend to exhibit higher levels of social competence (e.g., positive behaviors, longer play bouts with peers) while parents are engaged in interactive styles of supervision. Moreover, their data suggest that both mothers and fathers can be effective in this role with young children. Research by Lollis (1990) adds to our understanding of these potential effects by showing that the benefits that young preschoolers derive from interactive interventions may persist even after brief separations from the parent.

Directive intervention has been studied largely with older preschool-age children, and recent findings suggest that this form of supervision may be linked to parents' desires to maintain children's peer interactions and avert conflicts (see Lollis et al., 1992; Ross et al., 1991). In addition, Finnie and Russell (1988) have shown that the content of mothers' directive interventions (e.g., the type of advice given) is a significant correlate of children's competence in peer groups. Evidence also points to a linkage between older preschoolers' peer relationship problems (e.g., peer rejection) and parents' tendencies to rely on less developmentally mature forms of supervision. For example, Ladd and Golter (1988) found that parents who used interactive interventions with older preschoolers tended to have children who developed social difficulties after they entered grade school.

Because most investigators have focused on directive and interactive interventions, little or no data are available on the incidence and likely impact of parental monitoring with preschool children. Instead, research on monitoring—specifically parents' knowledge with children's whereabouts, activities, and peer companions—has been conducted primarily with samples of older children (e.g., children in middle childhood and adolescence). Overall, the research on this form of supervision suggests that the absence of parental monitoring is associated with maladjustment among children and especially among boys. These findings, along with data showing that higher levels of monitoring correlate positively with peer competence, suggest that monitoring is an important form of supervision and one that merits further research attention.

Parent as Consultant

Not all forms of direct parental management occur in the context of children's interactions with peers. Parents may advise or "consult" with children outside of their peer interactions and relationships. Lollis et al. (1992) have termed this type of direct parental management "decontextualized discussion." As consultants, parents may engage children in conversations about many aspects of their peer interactions and relationships, including how to initiate friendships, manage conflicts, maintain relationships, react to peer pressure and provocation, deflect teasing, repel bullies, and so on.

Parents may use these conversations to prepare children for social encounters or to resolve previously experienced interpersonal problems and difficulties. For example, to enhance children's success in new or unfamiliar peer situations, parents may initiate discussions about hypothetical or anticipated social activities, interactions, and events. Other forms of consulting may be reactive in nature, as when children request help with interpersonal problems or when parents recognize children's distress and become concerned about their performance in social situations. In such cases, parents may offer "expert" advice or assistance with problem solving—for example, helping the child analyze the problem, identify solutions, and weigh likely outcomes or consequences of particular strategies or actions. Or parents may adopt less directive roles, perhaps by acting as a sounding board for children's self-generated assessments and solutions (Kuczynski, 1984).

Research conducted by Cohen (1989) provides perhaps the best available information on the effects of consulting on peer relations. In her study, which was conducted with third-grade students and their families, mothers were asked to complete questionnaires on parent involvement, concerns about child sociability, and importance of child sociability. Cohen found that consulting was associated with positive child outcomes when mothers were supportive but noninterfering and that extremes in parental consulting behavior were predictive of socially withdrawn behavior in children.

Overinvolved mothers tended to be those who were highly concerned about their children's sociability and who valued sociability; it may be that these mothers recognized socially withdrawn behavior in their children and increased their involvement as an attempt to modify their children's behavior. Cohen (1989) suggests that maternal behavior that is too controlling, however, may interfere with the children's abilities to develop their own strategies for peer relations. Those mothers who did not value sociability, in contrast, provided less advice and support and also tended to have socially withdrawn children.

Russell and Finnie (1990) investigated the advice parents give children prior to their entry into peer-play situations. They asked mothers of popular and rejected preschool children (aged 4-5 years) to provide instructions/advice prior to the child's entry into an ongoing activity with two unfamiliar peers. Mothers were asked also whether they would consider giving the child feedback after the interaction was finished. The researchers found that mothers of neglected and rejected children were less likely to give group-oriented entry strategies to their children; mothers of neglected children also gave fewer active instructional strategies overall, providing instead passive strategies such as asking the peers' names. Mothers of popular and neglected children did not differ in the extent to which they said that they would provide feedback; none of the mothers of rejected children, however, indicated that they would offer any feedback to their children.

Summary and Conclusions. Of the four types of direct parental influences we have examined, the role of parent as consultant has received the least amount of research attention. We may infer from recent findings that parents employ different styles of consultation, ranging from styles that are intrusive and controlling to those that are supportive and noninterfering. Also consultation appears to be more common among parents who value their children's sociability and success with peers (Cohen, 1989).

As with supervision, evidence suggests that the quality of advice that parents offer during consultations has an important bearing on children's success in peer relations (Russell & Finnie, 1990).

Further research is needed to determine when parents begin to rely on consultation as a means of supporting and guiding children's social development. At present, we do not know when or how often parents employ consultation strategies with preschool-age children, nor do we understand the functions it may serve in young children's social lives. A better understanding is also needed of consultation process and outcomes, including studies of the dynamics of parent-child consultation at different ages (e.g., how often it occurs, who initiates it, and what topics tend to be discussed) and the types of effects it may have on children's peer relations and competence.

Expanding Research on
Direct Parental Influences:
New Directions and Findings

Much remains to be learned about parents' roles as facilitators of young children's peer relations and competence. One important objective within our own research program has been to gather further evidence on the role that parents play as mediators of children's peer relationships and play opportunities. A second objective has been to shed light on the potential antecedents of parents' involvement or participation in these roles—that is, the factors that may motivate or discourage parents from acting as designers, mediators, supervisors, and consultants.

Initiating Informal Peer Contacts:
Contributions of Parents and Children

As Bhavnagri and Parke (1991) have shown, the opportunities that children have to relate with peers in informal play settings and the contributions that these experiences may make to their overall social competence may depend not only on the frequency of their parents' initiations but also on those performed by the children themselves (and others). Ladd and Hart (1992) conducted an investigation to determine the frequency with which preschoolers' informal peer-play opportunities were initiated by parents, children, and peers. A second aim of this investigation was to determine the relative importance of parent and child initiations as predictors of preschoolers' social competence. Specifically we sought to determine whether the frequency of initiations performed by parents, by children, or by the combined initiations of both parties predicted preschoolers' social competence in informal and classroom settings.

The sample for this study consisted of 83 preschool children who were enrolled in one of four center-based preschools and were between 42 and 67 months of age at the outset of the study. A series of telephone-log interviews were conducted with each family to assess parents' initiations practices and children's peer relations and behavior on 16 days sampled during both the winter and spring months of the school year. During each of these calls, the interviewers recorded the amount of time that children spent in preschool or child care and made a log of all of the peer contacts that occurred outside the school context for that day. For each reported peer contact, interviewers also ascertained who had initiated the play opportunity and what role (if any) the parent and child played in the initiation process.

Data from these interviews were used to create several measures of children's informal peer relations, including: *contact frequency* (number of reported peer contacts), *range of partners* (number of different playmates), and *number of frequent play companions* (number of playmates present in 25% or more of the child's contacts). Classroom observations and sociometric ratings were used to assess children's social competence in child-care settings.

Frequency of Parents', Children's, and Peers' Initiations of Informal Play Opportunities With Peers. On average, children arranged 2.26 peer contacts during the sampled period—slightly fewer than were arranged by their parents ($M = 2.47$), and slightly more than were initiated by their peers ($M = 1.84$). These small differences proved to be statistically nonsignificant, as did differences between boys versus girls. The total number of informal peer contacts that children participated in over the 16 interview occasions averaged 9.62, with a range of 0 to 21.

Relation Between Children's Informal Peer Networks and the Frequency With Which Parents and Children Arrange Play Opportunities. When we examined qualities of children's non-school peer relations, we found that older children's peer contacts encompassed a larger range of partners than did their younger counterparts and that boys had significantly higher scores on this same measure than did girls. To determine the relative importance of parent and child initiations, we performed a hierarchical regression analysis in which each of the informal network variables was regressed on these two variables (and their interaction) after controlling for the amount of time children spent in child care and their age and gender. Scores for the frequency of parent and child initiations each accounted for significant and nonoverlapping proportions of variance in the range of partner scores. Thus the number of different play partners that children develop in informal settings appears to depend on the extent to which both parents and children initiate play opportunities in this context.

Relation Between the Frequencies of Parents' and Children's Initiations and Children's Social Competence in School. In contrast to the prior findings, differential relationships emerged between these two family variables and the various measures of children's classroom competence. Regression analyses revealed that children who initiated a larger number of peer contacts outside of school tended to be better liked by their classroom peers and engaged in fewer anxious behaviors at school. Parent initiations, in contrast, predicted the level of prosocial behavior (higher) and nonsocial behavior (lower) that children exhibited in classrooms and, among boys, greater acceptance by classmates.

These data show that, among preschool children (aged 3½-5½ years), parents are not the only persons who initiate informal play activities with peers. Rather, it would appear that many young children express a desire to spend time with peers and become the impetus for parents' efforts to arrange informal play opportunities.

Our findings also suggest a link between the frequency of parents' and children's social initiations and the type of peer companionship that children experience in both nonschool and school settings. Children in families where initiations were performed more frequently, either by the children or their parents, tended to develop a larger network of nonschool play companions. We also found that parents who frequently initiated peer contacts tended to have children who interacted in prosocial ways with peers and spent less time in unconstructive, solitary behaviors in classrooms. In particular, these children were observed to spend less time engaging in "tuned-out" behaviors and were less likely to act as passive bystanders, watching classmates from the periphery of their activities. Moreover, the frequency of parents' initiations predicted higher levels of prosocial behavior in the classroom and, among boys, greater peer acceptance. The latter finding is consistent with prior evidence linking the frequency of parents' initiations with early peer acceptance among boys (Ladd & Golter, 1988).

Finally children who take an active role in arranging informal peer activities were found to be less anxious in classroom settings and better liked by their preschool classmates. These findings may be attributable to variation in children's social maturity or independence or, alternatively, to differences stemming from their temperaments or learning experiences within the family.

Potential Antecedents
of Parents' Involvement

The second aim of our research was to assess the relationship between parents' perceptions of their children's progress in peer relations and their management behaviors. These aims were addressed in two related studies (Le Sieur, Profilet, & Ladd, 1992; Profilet & Ladd, 1992) conducted with a sample of 62 preschool children (34 girls, 28 boys; aged 43-72 months) and their mothers and teachers. Interviewers visited families in their homes and used questionnaires to gather data about mothers' perceptions of their children's *progress* in peer relations, *concerns,* and *policies* pertaining to children's informal peer relations. School data were obtained by asking teachers to rate each child's social behavior and peer relations in the classroom.

Progress perceptions, as conceived in this study, refer to mothers' views of their children's progress in social skills and peer relations, as compared with other children of the same age. Progress perceptions were assessed by having mothers rate their children's progress on 20 skill-related items using a 7-point scale ranging from *behind* to *ahead* of agemates. Psychometric analyses revealed that scores on this scale were internally consistent (alpha = .95) and stable (r over 2 months = .89).

Parental concerns refer to the degree of concern or worry that mothers have about their children's peer relations and social behaviors. Concern was measured by asking mothers to rate the same items employed on the progress scale using 7-point scales ranging from *not concerned* to *very concerned.* Psychometric analyses revealed that scores on this scale were internally consistent (alpha = .97) and stable (r over 2 months = .76).

Measures of parents' policies for informal peer relations were obtained by asking mothers to rate a series of items including (a) how often they encourage their child to get together with a friend or playmate (7-point scale ranging from *less than once a month* to *every day*), (b) the degree to which play contacts are typically sponsored by mother versus child (7-point scale ranging from *usually mother's idea* to *usually child's idea*), and (c) the degree to which mother versus child determines what the children will do together (7-point scale ranging from *parent decides* to *child and/or playmate decides*).

Relation Between Mothers' Perceptions of Children's Progress and Their Concerns. Correlational analyses revealed that mothers' progress perceptions and concerns were negatively related (r = −.26, p < .05). Thus mothers who tended to view their children as delayed in peer relations also reported higher levels of concern.

Relation Between Progress Perceptions and Their Management Behaviors. A median split on the progress measure was used to divide the sample into two groups, and one-way ANOVAs (groups: high vs. low progress) were used to explore differences in mothers' ratings of the frequency with which they encouraged children to arrange play activities with peers and the degree to which they allowed children to choose their own activities during play sessions with peers. Results indicated that mothers who viewed their children as ahead in peer relations encouraged their children to play with peers more often than did mothers who were inclined to see their children as behind; $F(1,60) = 4.92, p < .01$. In addition, mothers with higher progress perceptions tended to rate their children as having more control over their own play activities; $F(1,60) = 4.47, p < .05$.

Although preliminary, these findings suggest that parents' assessments of their children's early social abilities are related to the way they manage their children's peer relations. Mothers who tended to see their children as socially mature were less worried about their children's peer relations and more encouraging of their children's participation in informal peer relations (play activities in the home and neighborhood). These mothers also tended to see themselves as providing children with greater control over their own peer-play activities.

Conclusion

A primary aim of this chapter has been to expand our understanding of direct parental influences and their potential impact on the development of children's peer relations and competence. To do this, we proposed four parental roles, termed *designer, mediator, supervisor,* and *consultant.* These roles were defined in terms of specific parental behaviors or socialization practices that are hypothesized to affect various aspects of children's social development, including their access to social environments, contact with peers, and competence within peer interactions and relationships.

What we know about these pathways, however, is limited. Much of the evidence we have reviewed is of a descriptive or correlational nature and does not lend itself to strong causal inferences. Although it is clear that parents differ in the extent to which they manage children's peer relations, we know very little about why parents engage in these roles or what may motivate them to pursue different forms of management. Beyond simple descriptions of what parents do (e.g., arrange play activities), we lack a clear understanding of how parents accomplish these ends (e.g., specific processes) or how these processes influence children's social development and competence. We hope that investigators will view each of these limitations as an impetus for further investigation.

Relationships of Children Involved in Bully/Victim Problems at School

Peter K. Smith

Louise Bowers

Valerie Binney

Helen Cowie

For a child at school, perhaps the most important and salient aspects for happiness will be the quality of relationships with peers. This is not to deny the importance of early relationships with parents, generally thought to be crucial in the early years (e.g. Bowlby, 1988), and indeed to have continuing influence on the extent and quality of peer relationships. But, and especially if relationships with parents are rea-

AUTHORS' NOTE: Some of the work reported here was supported by Grant No. 8930636N from the Medical Research Council, London; some was supported by Grant No. R000232318 from the Economic and Social Research Council, Swindon, UK.

sonably satisfactory, by middle childhood peer relationships will occupy much of a child's time. This appears to be increasingly so through to adolescence; and the quality of friendships during these years is likely to affect later indicators of social adjustment, such as criminality, and mental health problems (Kupersmidt, Coie, & Dodge, 1990; Parker & Asher, 1987). Correlational evidence certainly supports such links, and various causal models have been proposed (Parker & Asher, 1987).

Most of the evidence on peer relationships in middle childhood comes from studies in schools. In modern urban societies, schools provide a prominent forum for same-age peer interaction, and for about 25% of the typical school day, children are engaged in playtime or dinner break activities, which allow for fairly unstructured peer interactions. The majority of such peer *interactions* are, in general terms, amicable and supportive, or playful; the majority of peer *relationships* are friendly or neutral. Observations in playgrounds indicate that actual fights between pupils are rare, taking up usually less than 1% of playground time (Humphreys & Smith, 1987; Pellegrini, 1989a).

Nevertheless some interactions are hostile, and some relationships are far from friendly. Psychologists have long been interested in aggressive interactions (for a review, see Parke & Slaby, 1983). However, many aggressive interactions are transient—ways of dealing with immediate conflicts that may arise between two individuals. Probably more insidious for children's developing relationships are situations in which a child (or children) *persistently* harasses or causes hurt to another child. In this more relationship oriented mode, we may think of "bullies" (who harass others) and "victims" (who are the recipients of this harassment). Research on bully/victim relationships does often tend to become a study of bullies or victims as individuals (and the evidence for stability of these categories across time [Olweus, 1991] goes some way to justify this), but the relationship concept is implicit in the definition.

The study of bully/victim relationships and associated problems in schools has shown a recent upsurge in interest in Scandinavia, the United Kingdom, North America, continental Europe, and Japan. These relationships appear to be prevalent and serious (Olweus, 1991; Smith, 1991b). In the United Kingdom, a survey of 6,758 pupils in Sheffield, based on anonymous pupil questionnaires, reported 27% of junior/middle school children and 10% of secondary school children were being bullied "sometimes" or more often; more frequent bullying of "once a week" or more was reported by 10% of junior/middle school children and 4% of secondary school children (Whitney & Smith, 1993). Comparable figures are available from Ireland, Spain, the Netherlands, and Japan; lesser but still significant figures are available from Scotland and Norway.

Bullying can have a devastating effect on the lives of victims. They suffer continuing loss of confidence and self-esteem in social relationships. They may resort to absenteeism to escape torment at school (Reid, 1983), and in the most severe cases victims have been known to commit suicide. For the child who bullies, too, an increased incidence of later problems of alcohol abuse, domestic violence, and violent crime in the community has been reported (Lane, 1989; Olweus, 1991).

School-based interventions to combat the problem have been implemented and have had some degree of success (Olweus, 1991; Smith, 1991b). But it is also important to understand why some children become bullies or victims and others do not. What part do child and family characteristics have in this matter? Also the nature of peer relationships that bullies and victims have is an area of interest and debate. Do bullies lack social skills, in some sense? Are bullying behaviors, by contrast, adaptive in some ways? Are bullies developing status and reputation in the peer group?

In this chapter we review these issues. First, however, we consider further what is meant by *bullying* and its relationship to such behaviors as teasing and playful fighting.

Definitions of Bullying, Teasing, and Playful Fighting

Bullying, and related terms such as *harassment,* can be taken to be a subset of aggressive behavior (e.g., Manning, Heron, & Marshall, 1978; Price & Dodge, 1989). As with aggressive behavior generally, bullying intentionally causes hurt to the recipient. This hurt can be both physical and psychological; although some bullying takes the form of hitting, pushing, and taking money, it also may involve telling nasty stories or social exclusion. It may be carried out by one child or a group.

Three further criteria particularly distinguish bullying. First, the hurt done is unprovoked, at least by any action that would normally be considered a provocation. (Being clumsy, for instance, might invoke some bullying but would not normally be considered a legitimate provocation.) Second, bullying is thought of as a repeated action; something that happens only once or twice would not be called bullying. Third, the child doing the bullying is generally thought of as being stronger or is perceived as stronger; at least, the victim is not (or does not feel him- or herself to be) in a position to retaliate very effectively (Smith, 1991b).

Teasing provides a category of behavior that overlaps with bullying, being persistently irritating but in a minor way or such that, dependent on context, it may or may not be taken as playful. Pawluk (1989) provides a useful analysis of how teasing may be construed. She draws attention to three factors: (a) the *commentary,* particularly how the teaser signals intent and the relation of the tease to prior events or context; (b) the *recipient response,* whether the person teased takes it in a serious or lighthearted way; and (c) the *audience response,* whether anyone else witnessing the teasing evaluates it as playful or hurtful.

In our own work on self-reports of bullying or being bullied, we have included *nasty teasing* as bullying. This inclusion emphasizes the importance of commentary or of recipient response and the finding from interviewing children that they, too, distinguished playful and more hurtful kinds of teasing (Ahmad & Smith, 1990).

Playful Fighting Is Usually Different From Bullying

Playful teasing might be signaled by laughing or smiling to mark what might otherwise be an ambiguous remark or action. This action has clear parallels with what happens in play fighting. Play fighting and chasing, or "rough-and-tumble play," is a typical form of behavior in children, taking up some 10% of playground time in middle childhood (Humphreys & Smith, 1987; Pellegrini, 1989a). It looks in many respects like real fighting but is clearly distinguishable in a number of respects by children and by trained adult observers (Boulton, 1991a; Costabile et al., 1991). It is often indexed by laughter or smiling. Play fighting and chasing normally show self-handicapping and restraint; participants do not fight or chase at full strength. This forbearance allows friendly play to continue, even between unequally matched partners. It often is characterized by reversal of roles, as first one child is on top, then the other.

Unlike bullying and nasty teasing, *play fighting* and *play chasing* seem generally to be activities often enjoyed and participated in by friends. A study of 5-, 8-, and 11-year-olds in England and in Italy found that about half of the children said they enjoyed play fighting, and over 80% said they enjoyed play chasing (Smith, Hunter, Carvalho, & Costabile, 1992). Smith and Lewis (1985) found that observed play partners for play fighting in 3- and 4-year-olds tended to be ranked as highly liked and that "best friends" participated in a greater number of play fighting episodes than expected by chance. Similarly Humphreys and Smith (1987) found that at 7, 9, and 11 years, play fighting partners ranked each other above chance for "liking," both when the points of view of the initiator and of the recipient of the play fighting bout were considered. Boulton (1991b) found that 8- and 11-year-olds liked play fighting partners at above chance levels.

There is evidence that play fighting can provide some benefits to the play participants. The two most frequently hypothesized benefits are that it may provide practice in fighting skills (Humphreys & Smith, 1987) and that it practices social skills (Pellegrini, 1988).

The hypothesis that play fighting improves fighting skills (which it resembles in form) would be consistent with children choosing friends as play partners but also would predict that children would chose partners matched for fighting ability. Humphreys and Smith (1987) found that although this was not the case at 7 and 9 years of age, there was evidence for this at 11 years. Boulton (1991b) reports that play fighting partners were closely matched for strength at both 8 and 11 years.

The hypothesis that play fighting advances social skills is supported by work with parent-infant physical play (MacDonald & Parke, 1984; Power & Parke, 1981), as well as peer-peer play (Pellegrini, 1988). It is argued that such forms of play develop communication skills of encoding and decoding (as in displaying or understanding play signals), the ability to regulate emotional display and strength of physical action (as in restraint), and the ability to take turns and to understand another's point of view (as in role reversals and self-handicapping).

Parke et al. (1987) reported correlational evidence to suggest that father-infant physical play correlates with emotional decoding ability; MacDonald (1987) found that children who were sociometrically *neglected* at nursery school had less parent-infant physical play at home; *rejected* children had more physical play at home, but it was characterized by overstimulation or avoidance of stimulation. These findings are patchy, but the general hypothesis that physical play and play fighting develop social skills is supported by corresponding findings from Pellegrini (1988) on peer play fighting. He found that, for *popular* children, frequency of play fighting correlated with a social skills measure. Also, *popular* children are best able to distinguish play fighting from real fighting on videotape episodes presented to them (Pellegrini, 1989b).

Play Fighting Can Turn
Into Fighting and Bullying

Just as teasing can be ambiguous, so too can play fighting. The conventions of handicap and self-restraint normally are recognized in play fights, but cheating may occur. This possibility was pointed out by Fagen (1981); a participant might take advantage of the "play convention" to actually harm another when that other has "consented" to be in an inferior position in a play bout. Some reports on play fighting in young children have found very low frequencies of such cheating (Fry, 1987; Humphreys &

Smith, 1987; Smith & Lewis, 1985), but instances were reported by Neill (1976) in a sample of 12- to 13-year-old boys. He reported that play fighting might be used as

> a means of asserting or maintaining dominance; once the weaker boy has registered distress the bond can be maintained by the fight taking a more playful form, but if he does not do so at the start of the fight, the stronger boy may increase the intensity of the fight until he does. (Neill, 1976, p. 219)

The sociometric status of children (Coie, Dodge, & Coppotelli, 1982) is another relevant factor here. Pellegrini (1988) found that play fighting seldom led to real fighting in most 5- to 9-year-old children but that it often did so in children who were sociometrically *rejected*. The actual nature of the rough-and-tumble bouts was not described in Pellegrini's study, however, so it is not certain what aspects of the rejected children's play fighting bouts led so often (in 25% of cases) to fighting or whether "cheating" was involved. However, rejected children are overrepresented among children nominated by peers as bullies and victims.

Bullies, Victims, and Social Relations With Peers

Overall, both bullies and victims tend to be disliked by peers, but the picture is by no means a simple one. On sociometric tests, our own studies suggest that bullies tend to be either *controversial* or *rejected* (Boulton & Smith, in press; Smith & Boulton, 1991). Thus they are collecting mainly "liked least" nominations from peers, but also, in the case of controversial children, some "liked most" nominations; they have a high social impact. On behavioral nominations (as used by Coie et al., 1982), bullies tend to be nominated often as "starting fights," and "disrupting" others, but sometimes as high in "leadership" (Boulton & Smith, in press; Whitney, Nabuzoka, & Smith, 1992). Some bullies can be quite liked and be leaders within their own network or gang (Cairns, Cairns, Neckerman, Gest, & Gariepy,

1988; Sluckin, 1981). Olweus (1991) also found that bullies were not necessarily less popular than other children. Using the Harter Self-Perception Profile (Harter, 1985), our own studies suggest that bullies do not have low self-esteem, except perhaps (accurately!) so far as the *behavioral conduct* scale is concerned. The case study of Sean (see Appendix) illustrates how a child can be confident and liked by some children and also be a bully.

Victims tend to be *rejected* on sociometric tests and to be nominated as "shy" and "seeking help" (Boulton & Smith, in press; Whitney et al., 1992). The perceived shyness of victims may be reflected in such measures as how often the children are alone and how lonely they report feeling. More victims than nonvictims report feeling lonely at school (Olweus, 1991). For some victims, at least, a natural tendency to withdraw may be a contributory factor. The case study of Graham (see Appendix) is an example; he was not a rewarding companion to be with. Other victims may wish to associate with others but, through factors such as prejudice, may be unable to do so as much as they wish. The case study of Farana (see Appendix) illustrates a child who, although quiet, was interested in forming friendships with others. (In her case, small group work in class did help her form the basis for new friendships.)

Typically victims of bullying appear to have a low opinion of themselves and to be anxious and insecure (Olweus, 1991), as do many socially withdrawn children (Rubin et al., 1990) and rejected children (Patterson et al., 1990). We found that victims generally perceived themselves as being less *physically competent* than did bullies and noninvolved children and that female victims perceived themselves as being less *well accepted* by their peers than did the other two groups (Boulton & Smith, in press).

There is good evidence for a distinction between *passive* or *withdrawn victims,* who do not often start fights or disrupt others, and *provocative victims* or "bully/victims," who do often start fights and tend to be the least liked children of all (Smith & Boulton, 1991). This distinction corresponds to that of Pikas (1989) between innocent victims and provocative victims and to corresponding categories in Stephenson and Smith (1989).

Our findings suggest that these bully/victims (who often are nominated as both bullies and victims by classmates) are seen as the least cooperative children. Bully/victims, like bullies, do not seem to show low self-esteem (Smith & Boulton, 1991) despite their objective unpopularity; however, given the disturbed nature of many of these children, it is possible that self-esteem tests such as the Harter are eliciting defensive or idealized responses. A case study of a bully/victim, Alan (see Appendix) illustrates how a victim can contribute to his or her own difficulties and be particularly disliked by classmates.

Bullying and Peer Relationships

One influential group of theorists (Dodge et al., 1986) see the cause of many problems in peer relationships as lying in a lack of appropriate social skills. Following an information-processing model of social interaction, they hypothesize that some children may interpret social signals incorrectly or have only a very limited range of response options available. Thus *aggressive children* may overreact to ambiguous signals and more readily select aggressive response options in a provocative situation. On the other hand, *withdrawn children* may lack the social skills of group entry. The evidence for the social skills deficit approach is mixed, however, and this approach leaves open the question of why some children lack these social skills (leaving aside cases of clear cognitive disability).

Applied to bullies and victims, the social skills approach would suggest that bullies have deficits similar to those of aggressive children, while victims may lack social skills of assertiveness and group entry. For bullies, however, the "deficit" label may be inappropriate. Rather than misinterpreting signals or having a limited range of response options, some bullies may simply be choosing goals of dominance and status reputation by aggressive and domineering means. Although this choosing might be interpreted into a social skills model as a difference in Step 4 ("evaluate the probable efficacy and consequences of the responses that he or she has generated and select an optimal choice," Dodge et al., 1986, p. 5), the perspective overall is a distinctly different one. Two sources of evidence–attributions of others' behavior, and "cheating" in play fighting–are relevant here.

Attributions Made by Bullies and Victims

Developing the ideas of Dodge and Frame (1982) that rejected and aggressive children may perceive ambiguous stimuli differently from other children, we have examined the way bullies, victims, and control children (who were neither bullies nor victims) perceived a videotape of fighting and bullying and described the feelings of the participants. Participating were 45 children, aged 9-11 years, 15 each of bully, victim, or control status, determined from peer nomination. They were shown a videotape depicting two incidents of physical fighting in the playground; in the second, another child intervened to stop it. They then were interviewed about how they interpreted these scenes, how the participants might have felt, whether they had experienced similar events, and why the children might be behaving that way (Smith, McWhinney, Boulton, & Cowie, in press).

When viewing the videotape, both bullies and victims tended to describe the two episodes as "bullying," whereas controls tended to describe it as "fighting." Other results suggested that bullies differed from both the victims and the controls in a number of respects. Most of the bullies (80%), but few of the controls or victims (30%), described the bullies in the videotape episodes as feeling "happy"; few of the bullies (27%), but most of the controls or victims (53%), described the victim as feeling "unhappy." Many bullies (47%), but few controls or victims (13%), thought that the bullying was happening because of some relatively unchangeable characteristic of the victim (such as physical appearance or color). Most bullies (67%) also thought that the bullying in the videotape was due to provocation and that if they themselves bullied others it was due to provocation.

In general, this and more detailed qualitative analysis of the interviews suggest that many bullies see little wrong in their bullying behavior; they are happy doing it; the playground is a tough place; and, though they show little awareness of the victim's feelings, they assert that the victim in one way or another often deserved the bullying. The case studies of Mark and Sean (see Appendix) both illustrate this.

"Cheating" in Play Fighting

Pellegrini (1988) found that, for rejected children, play fighting often "went wrong," turning into real fighting. Rejected children are often aggressive (Coie et al., 1982), and a lack of social skills could contribute to this aggression if playful signals or ambiguous contexts are mistakenly interpreted as aggressive. Evidence supports this scenario, both from ethnographic reports of playground behavior (Sluckin, 1981) and from the finding that rejected, aggressive children do interpret ambiguous cues as aggressive in test situations (Dodge & Frame, 1982). Such examples of play fighting going wrong might be thought of as "honest mistakes" (Fagen, 1981) if a signal is genuinely misunderstood.

But the alternative "cheating" hypothesis implies a different and more deliberate causation that Neill's (1976) observations, cited earlier, are more consistent with. Here, play fighting appears to be a context in which "cheating," and hence a public humiliation of the play partner, may be used to display dominance and, perhaps, to increase the status or reputation of the cheat or bully with the immediate peer group. Such ideas would link with the suggestion from many ethnographic and sociological writings that children who are aggressive or antisocial may have their own cliques or networks of allies (Cairns et al., 1988; Hargreaves, 1967) and may be establishing or managing a reputation as a tough and dominant person in this network (Emler & Reicher, 1993; Sluckin, 1981).

There may be an adaptive value for some children to achieve a "tough" reputation, in terms of their likely later career paths (Emler & Reicher, 1993). Draper and Harpending (1982) and Belsky, Steinberg, and Draper (1991) argue in a broader evolutionary context that high aggression may have been selected as an adaptive strategy for some children—specifically, those with low father involvement or experiencing uncertain predictability or availability of resources who might expect to engage in high male-male sexual competition as an adult. Whether or not this particular adaptive hypothesis is correct, it may be useful to think of aggressive, cheating kinds of play fighting, and bullying more generally, to be for some children a particular developmental pathway that may have advantages and that does not necessarily reflect lack of social skills in any narrow sense (Smith, 1991a).

Peer Relationships and Family Circumstances

Belsky, Steinberg, and Draper (1991) hypothesize a link between aggressive peer relationships and family-rearing experience at the level of adaptive significance rather than immediate causal pathways. Other theories are more relevant to causal links. Most of the relevant research has looked at correlates with high aggressiveness in children, rather than at bullying per se (and the background factors predisposing to being a victim are even less well explored). Two broad approaches are evident here.

One approach stems from attachment theory and especially from recent developments of the concept of *internal working models.* Following Bowlby (1969, 1988), theorists such as Bretherton (1985) and Main (1991) argue that a child develops internal working models of relationships that may be secure or insecure (avoidant, ambivalent, or disorganized). Unless there are changes in life circumstances (or an internal cognitive reevaluation that is thought unlikely to happen before adolescence), these patterns of attachment are hypothesized to show continuity into secure and insecure (dismissing, dependent/preoccupied, and controlling/disorganized) relationships in middle childhood and adulthood.

Insofar as the internal model of relationships developed with primary caregivers is generalized to others, these patterns may be expected to affect relations with peers as well as parents. Some evidence for this influence has appeared in the last few years—for example, linking child-mother attachment to qualities of friendship (Park & Waters, 1989) and to sociometric status at school (Cohn, 1990).

One study has made a specific link to bully/victim relationships. Troy and Sroufe (1987) characterized 38 children as having

either a secure, anxious-avoidant, or anxious-resistant attachment with their mothers; when the children were 4-5 years old,
they were assigned to same-gender play groups. All cases of
bullying occurred when a child with an avoidant attachment
history (the bully) was paired with a child with an anxious
attachment history (the victim). Children who had been securely attached were able to distance themselves and to avoid
bullying or being bullied.

No other studies have focused specifically on bullying, but
three have considered antisocial behavior. Fagot and Kavanagh
(1990) obtained attachment data at 18 months on 109 children,
with data on antisocial behavior up to 4 years of age. Most effects
of attachment type were nonsignificant, but anxious-avoidant
girls (not boys) were rated by teachers and observers of their
play groups as more difficult to deal with and as having more
difficulty with peers.

Turner (1991) concurrently assessed attachment quality and
play group behavior in 40 children. In contrast to Fagot and
Kavanagh (1990), Turner found that insecurely attached boys
showed more aggressive, assertive, and controlling behaviors to
peers; insecurely attached girls showed more positive, expressive behavior and compliance. The two studies differ somewhat
in age of assessment, actual measuring instruments, and culture
(U.S. and U.K., respectively), but the discrepancy certainly deserves further attention.

Booth et al. (1991) assessed attachment quality of 38 children
at 20 months. They measured social competence with an unfamiliar play partner in a laboratory playroom at 4 years. Insecurely
attached children (mostly Type D, disorganized) showed more
aggressive behavior and negative affect in their interactions. Unfortunately gender effects were not examined in this study.

The theoretical background to this approach is most thor-
oughly worked out by Renken et al. (1989). They suggest that
children with avoidant-insecure attachment relationships lack
trust and expect hostility and thus may develop aggressive patterns of interaction with peers. By contrast, children with ambiv-
alent-insecure attachment relationships with parents are likely to
be getting haphazard care and to doubt their own effectiveness

in influencing the caregiver. While staying somewhat dependent, they lack self-esteem and confidence in their own worth and are thus susceptible to being victimized by peers. Renken et al. (1989) report some (limited) confirmation of these associations.

This approach does not put so much emphasis on social skills as on the child's internal model of relationships. Social withdrawal, however, will in itself lead to less practice in important peer social skills, so many withdrawn children and many victims might indeed lack some social skills even if this may not be a primary cause for their condition.

The second approach is represented by a body of work on parenting styles not closely related to attachment theory. For example, Manning et al. (1978) reported that children with overcontrolling or dominating parents were found to harass other children more often at school. Using path analysis, Olweus (1980) reported that four factors contributed significantly to peer-rated aggression of boys: the boy's temperament (active, hot-headed), the mother's negativism (lack of warmth), the mother's permissiveness of aggression, and the parents' use of power-assertive methods. Loeber and Dishion (1984) found that parents who practiced inconsistent or highly aversive discipline techniques, coupled with physical punishment, were more likely to have a child who was aggressive toward others. Dishion (1990) used path analysis to show that ineffective parental discipline (rather more than lack of parental monitoring) led to antisocial behavior. These studies suggest that children growing up in such families are having aggressive behaviors modeled for them, and, in the absence of effective discipline and perhaps monitoring by parents, these behaviors develop and are used subsequently in peer interactions. (The case study of Sean [see Appendix] illustrates this, as Sean was reported to have a dominating father and a submissive mother who was unable to control him.) There is evidence that characteristics such as high aggressiveness can be transmitted across several generations (Caspi & Elder, 1988).

Patterson et al. (1989) have elaborated a developmental pathway embodying these ideas. Poor parental discipline and monitoring practices are presumed to lead to childhood conduct problems (such as aggression), in turn leading to academic failure and rejection by normal (nondeviant) peers. These outcomes, in turn, result in children who more frequently have commitment to a deviant peer group and who subsequently get involved in delinquent behavior.

Both these two approaches both focus on familial determinants of peer aggressiveness but have different emphases—one on internal models of relationships, and one on parental management and discipline practices. Are they reconcilable? Two further perspectives help in examining this question.

From a structural family systems viewpoint (P. Minuchin, 1988, S. Minuchin, 1974), the investigation of intergenerational boundaries would be relevant (as it has been in studies of structural family patterns underlying sexual abuse; Furniss, 1983). Family therapists assume that distortions in family structure, particularly weaknesses in the parental subsystem, result in children having to adopt roles such as scapegoat (victim) or bully in order to maintain family functioning. Different family patterns may be involved in bullying and victimization. From a psychodynamic viewpoint, lack of warmth or a high level of ambivalence in parent-child relationships might be implicated in bullying, while overprotective parenting might predispose to victimization. Degree of identification with the same-gender parent may be particularly important for both of these pathways. This approach may provide links between both attachment and management perspectives, placing both within the overall systems viewpoint.

Rubin et al. (1990) also have gone some way to integrate conceptual aspects of the two research traditions, basically proposing an integrative pathway model. They suggest a set of developmental pathways linking familial circumstances, infant temperament, mother-infant attachment, child-rearing techniques, self-esteem, and peer relationships. From this general model they postulate two main "deviant" pathways—one leading to aggressive or provocative peer problems, the other leading to passive/withdrawal problems and difficulties in initiating and maintaining relationships. The first pathway is linked to dispositional and temperamental traits in the child, such as being fussy and difficult to soothe, and to insecure-avoidant attachment patterns, leading to hostility, peer rejection, and externalizing problems. The second pathway is linked to dispositional and temperamental traits in the child, such as shyness, and to insecure-ambivalent attachment patterns, leading to anxiety, lack of social success, and internalizing problems such as withdrawal.

The first pathway might lead to bullying behavior, though the concept is not synonymous with high aggression. The second pathway might lead to being a victim. Anxiety and withdrawal may increase vulnerability to bullying, further lowering the individual's self-esteem, making him or her a still easier victim in the peer group. A vicious cycle can be set up, reinforced by the child's reputation in the peer group.

A Study of Family Influences
From Different Perspectives

The integrative models proposed are promising, but it is by no means certain that different factors—such as attachment relationships or parental management practices—have equal impact. Also the research is mostly on children defined by sociometric status, aggression, and withdrawal. In our own research, we are investigating aspects of family relationships from several points of view (Bowers et al., 1992, in press). We have focused on the family as perceived by the child; the child's own subjective view of relationships may reveal best his or her working models of relationships and relate most strongly to peer relationships (Patterson et al., 1990; Schaefer, 1965). We have related family characteristics to children nominated as bullies, victims, bully/victims (children nominated both as bullies and victims), and controls.

Children aged 8-11 years were selected from nine classes in three Sheffield middle schools, a total sample pool of about 200 children. On the basis of peer nomination, 20 bullies, 20 victims, 20 bully/victims, and 20 control children were chosen from this pool. These four subgroups were reasonably balanced for age, gender, and ethnicity and did not differ in mean family size/number of siblings. Children were interviewed individually on the Family Relations Test (FRT) (Bene & Anthony, 1957); the Parental Style Questionnaire (PSQ) (a measure of parental warmth and discipline modified from Parker, Tupling, & Brown, 1979); a family sculpt task, the FAST, in which family figures are represented on a spatial plot (Gehring & Wyler, 1986); and the Separation Anxiety Test (SAT) (a projective test based on attachment theory and modified from Klagsbrun & Bowlby, 1976).

The findings from the FRT on the total sample indicated that, for these children, who were approaching adolescence, the predominating role of parents in the child's life was moderated not only by friends and peers outside the family but also by siblings and other family members who are seen as within the family (such as aunts, grandparents). Siblings and some other family members captured a great deal of the involvement expressed by the children. Involvement with siblings was reasonably balanced but with appreciable negative elements; involvement with other family members, as also with mother and father but often with less intensity, was generally positive.

The results from the FRT, when combined with those from the PSQ and the FAST, yielded clear and interesting differences between the four subgroups of bullies, bully/victims, victims, and controls. Children involved in bullying others, whether bullies or bully/victims, shared some characteristics: They were more likely not to have a father at home, but to have another family member at first involvement rank (this was not just an artifact of absent fathers; only two of the nine children who ranked another family member first, lacked a father), and in the FAST test they more often marginalized one or more family members by putting them into a corner of the plot.

Bullies and bully/victims, however, differed in other respects. Bullies particularly indicated a lack of cohesion on the FAST test, by spreading out the figures widely, and a concern with power. Their FRT results indicated high ambivalent involvement with siblings and others, and the FAST results indicated that they saw siblings and others as powerful. Although poor relationships with parents often have been suggested as a factor in children's aggressiveness, these data highlighted the apparently relatively negative relationships with those siblings or other family members who often elicit high involvement at this age—in general, a family system lacking cohesion and warmth and with marked power relationships.

Bully/victims, by contrast, indicated on the PSQ more troubled relations directly with parents; they perceived parents lowest for accurate monitoring and warmth, yet highest for overprotection and for neglect, thus indicating inconsistent discipline/monitoring practices untempered by warm affection. This description is actually more similar to the picture of parental antecedents of bullying from Olweus (1980); in addition, however, these bully/victims indicated some increased obsession with self, both in terms of involvement (FRT) and power (FAST). Although they tended to put more power blocks under themselves and saw their mothers as relatively lacking in power, they also gave more negative items to themselves on the FRT. This distribution suggests an ambivalence about themselves that bears out the suggestion from other evidence (Stephenson & Smith, 1989) that bully/victims may be the most at risk of the four subgroups.

The picture for victims is different again from that of bully/victims; it is one of high and positive involvement with other family members, but perhaps to the extent of an enmeshed family structure. Victims tended to clump all figures together without separation on the FAST test; to have a parent more often at first or second involvement rank on the FRT, apparently unusual at this age; and to show high positive involvement generally with siblings and other family members.

Finally the control children represented their families as cohesive on the FAST test, but not as clumped as did the victims, and they did not have such high involvement with parents as victims did. They also perceived their parents as highest on accurate monitoring and lowest on both neglect and punitiveness. Mothers were seen to have equal power to fathers. In general, these parents seemed to be providing a warm, secure environment without being overinvolved with their children.

These results support many aspects of the models of Patterson et al. (1989) and Rubin et al. (1990), as applied to bullies and victims. However, an unexpected and contradictory finding was the lack of differences between subgroups on the SAT. The SAT is an attachment-based measure that is more applicable to older age groups than the Strange Situation. Shouldice and Stevenson-Hinde (1992) related SAT scores and attachment status derived from reunion after separation, at 4½ years. They concluded that the SAT cannot be used alone to determine attachment status at this age although some aspects of it are reliably associated with reunion classification. The use of the SAT with 8- to 10-year-olds shows promise, in that clearly avoidant, ambivalent, and secure responses were evident, but the reliability with which such scoring relates to other attachment-related criteria still may be problematic.

The results from the FAST could be related to predictions from attachment theory if one bears in mind that the organization of attachment changes through development. According to Main et al. (1985), an avoidant relationship in infancy translates into a dismissing relationship as an adult, while an ambivalent relationship in infancy translates into a dependent relationship in middle childhood and a preoccupied relationship model as an adult. The diffuse FAST plots of bullies and bully/victims, with use of corners, do suggest an avoidant internal working model of relationships moving to a dismissive one. It could also be argued that the clumped plots of victims and their high involvement with parents at this age indicate dependent relationships; the high cohesion and high positive involvement with siblings on the FRT may also show denial of feelings of independence and autonomy.

Overview of Bullies' and Victims'
Relationships With Others

It is clear that bullies and victims differ from other children in their peer relationships and in their family relationships; from what little evidence we have, this is true of bully/victims (or provocative victims) too. These differences (and the differences of rejected and aggressive children, who often overlap with the victims and bullies) can be described from various perspectives: in the case of peer relationships, social information-processing and deficit models, or models based on manipulation of conventions and management of reputation; in the case of family relationships, models based on internal working models and attachment, or parental management styles; or on family systems approaches.

It is tempting to say that all of these models may represent facets of the truth, at least for certain subgroups of children. Such a view may have something to recommend it; for example, the different approaches to family relationships may look primarily at different aspects of a complete system, as our own study indicates. However, models and theories can sometimes usefully confront each other, and, notably, it is difficult to reconcile the social skills deficit approach to evidence that some bullies are deliberately pursuing goals that humiliate others publicly and downplay others' feelings, possibly for their own advantage.

The social skills deficit model may have most relevance to victims of bullying who are shy and withdrawn (for example, see Graham, in Appendix). They may be enmeshed in over-intense or overinvolved family systems, consistent with dependent or preoccupied types of attachment relationships. It is possible that they thereby get less practice in the rougher sorts of social interaction, the teasing and play fighting that (both in family and peer contexts) actually may enhance social skills, and the control and interpretation of emotional expression.

So far as bullies are concerned, both our attributional data and our family data suggest that, by middle childhood, they are developing a general model of relationships as lacking warmth and concerned with power, consistent with the dismissing relationships postulated by attachment theorists. This involvement with power relations and lack of cohesion in families of bullies is, by 8-11 years of age, perceived as much or more with siblings and other family members as with parents. Furthermore, some bullies are, if not popular, at least controversial in the peer group; that is, they have their own friends and may be dominant and influential in the peer group. Rather than lacking social skills, they may be able to manipulate situations to their own ends (see Sean, in Appendix); they do, however, seem to ignore the unhappiness of victims and do not readily accept responsibility or blame for their own actions (see Mark, in Appendix).

Bully/victims appear to form a clear subgroup with a distinct identity from children who just bully others or from children who are just victims, a subgroup that deserves more attention in future research. So far, we have found this subgroup to overlap considerably with the aggressive-rejected subset of children from sociometric studies, who appear to have a distinct profile also from this tradition of research (Patterson et al., 1990). In contrast to bullies, the location of such bully/victims' own perceived problems in middle childhood continues to lie with lack of accurate monitoring and discipline practices of parents; and bully/victims are more likely to be involved with themselves in an ambivalent way. This ambivalence possibly could be linked to disorganized attachment patterns, if further research confirms the usefulness of attachment theory in this area. Alan (see Appendix) illustrates this type of child.

Finally it is worth noting that these arguments are not just academic ones. Given the problems associated with peer group bullying noted earlier, implications for treatment are important. The social skills approach already has led to associated training programs for highly aggressive children, though with only moderate success (Akhtar & Bradley, 1991). Insofar as parental management is important, working with parents would be appropriate (Patterson et al., 1989). Links to attachment problems might suggest, by middle childhood at least, the usefulness of counseling approaches to work through issues of relationships (Pikas, 1989). Finally, insofar as some children may be following strategies that are adaptive in terms of dominance and status, approaches may include not only moral development programs but also creating an institutional and peer environment that sanctions against, rather than ignores or condones, the kinds of continuing hurtful actions that occur in bully/victim relationships (Olweus, 1991; Smith & Thompson, 1991).

APPENDIX:
CASE STUDY REPORTS

The following ethnographic accounts, gathered by Helen Cowie from children involved in bullying or being bullied, their peers, and teachers, come from a middle school in a disadvantaged area of Sheffield, England. All of the children's names are pseudonyms.

Farana and Graham: Victims of Bullying

Farana and Graham are both very quiet children and are easily overlooked in class. When the teacher asks children to take partners for an activity, they are seldom chosen; at break time they are likely to be alone.

Farana was nominated as a victim by 42% of the children in her class. She considers herself to be lucky that there is one girl who occasionally will play with her, but for much of the time her experience of peer relationships is a negative one:

Some people hurt me in my class. They swear, sort of. They call me names . . . Sometimes they don't like me because I'm Pakistani. They don't like me. They think I'm *just* a Pakistani.

At break time Farana can never be sure that she will have a playmate:

HC: Some children get ignored by other children in the school and often feel lonely. Do you ever feel lonely like this?

Farana: Yes, when I've no friends—when Joanne's not my friend, when my sisters are inside at school.

HC: Have you tried to be friendly with them?

Farana: (quietly) Sometimes. They won't be my friends.

In fact, if Farana tries to join in group games, it is a common experience for her to find that someone will actively force her out:

HC: Is there anyone you don't get on with very well?

Farana: Yes, Chris. He don't let me take part.

HC: What does he do to keep you out?

Farana: He does nearly everything. He calls me names.

When Farana walks around on her own in the playground, she can be the target of further bullying. Her teacher, Mr. W., points out:

> She is vulnerable in the playground. Children like Darren will kick Farana. He can pick his people well! He picks people who aren't likely to hit back.

Farana is a shy child, and this in itself could make it difficult for her to relate easily to her peers, but with her sisters and in some supportive small groups in class she is accepted by others and can make effective contributions to group tasks. Because of the prejudiced attitudes of some of her peers, a major reason for her victimization seems to be that she is of Pakistani origin.

Graham was nominated as a victim by 50% of his classmates. His experience of peer relationships is similar to that of Farana, but the reasons that underlie his role as victim have more to do with his introverted personality and his lack of opportunity to develop appropriate social skills. His perception of children in his class is that "they are always fighting." He can name two children who sometimes will play with him. He likes them because they let him play football, but adds:

> Probably they are the only two people (in the class) who want to play with me.

Graham is not a popular choice when it comes to taking a partner because he is so shy and unforthcoming. Other children do not find him fun to be with.

As Ms. H., his teacher, says:

> He's very withdrawn. He doesn't give much to other children unless he is in a good mood . . . He is just a very introverted, withdrawn person.

Graham is vulnerable to attack in the playground simply because he is often on his own. He also is excluded from many activities, especially the prestigious football games that play an important part in the lives of boys of his age group. Probably the most alarming aspect of Graham's experience of peer relationships is that, although he is perceived as a victim by classmates, he does not believe that he has been bullied. Difficult as he finds it to talk about his loneliness and lack of contact with friends, the overriding impression is that Graham blames himself for his isolation.

Alan: A Bully/Victim

Alan was nominated as a bully by 55% of his classmates, and as a victim by 65%. He is a small boy who has been unhappy in his school for some time. As he says, with a deep sigh, "I keep saying to my mum, 'I want to leave this school 'cos people bully me before I bully them' but she says, 'No.' " His wish would be that "all the bad people left and friendly people came back into school."

Alan finds it hard to think of anything positive to say about his classmates and cannot name a particular friend. He talks mainly about arguments and fights that he defines as "bullying." In his words, "Only two people in the class *don't* bully me." There is no one person whom he would choose as a partner for classwork or for play.

He readily admits that he, too, "bullies" other children—for example, Richard—but thinks that usually they start the fight:

HC: What sort of things do you do when you are bullying Richard?

Alan: Well, he starts it first, like, comes to my table, punches me on the back, then we have a fight and then we get done [caught] by the teacher.

HC: Do you usually win these fights?

Alan: Yes, 'cos he's only little. Sometimes he cries, sometimes he tells.

Other children confirm his quarrelsome attitude. A typical comment is:

He thumps me in the back when we're working. He thumps me so I thump him back.

His teacher has noticed how difficult he finds it to cooperate with other children for any length of time:

Alan and Donna, they're either very good together and help each other or they argue and want to almost kill each other. [HC: Why?] Because they're both very painfully honest with each other. They say, "You did it" or "I didn't" or "Why have you got . . . ?" You know. They're both jealous of each other if the one has something that the other doesn't . . . I don't think they really like each other. But then they've got problems of their own. That comes out when they're together.

On the occasions when Alan is rash enough to annoy a stronger boy such as Mark, he gets into real trouble:

Mark: Alan drew this love heart and he gave it to Michelle. He said I drew it so I went up to him and went right hard on his nose.

HC: You punched him on the nose!

Mark: It didn't break . . . It only started bleeding.

HC: How do you think he felt when you made his nose bleed?

Mark: Sad.

HC: Sad. Did that worry you at all?

Mark: No. I knew what would happen when I did it.

HC: You mean, you knew you were going to punch him hard?

Mark: No, I do that automatically. When anyone gets me mad, I just swing me fist out . . . It was Alan's fault 'cos he drew the love heart and gave it to Michelle.

Alan certainly has contributed to his alienation from the rest of the class and can provoke attacks from other children. But a major difficulty for him is that he assumes that other children do not like him and does very little to try to win friends. As his teacher points out, he typically anticipates that he is not likely to be chosen in situations where children take partners:

> He will stand up and say, "I don't want to be with anybody." Whether he knew that nobody would pick him, I don't know. He had a hot temper and nobody wanted to be near him, I suppose.

Because Alan is quarrelsome, it is easy for others to blame him for any fights that occur. He is not a pleasant working partner and so, even in small group work, he does not sustain closeness with other children.

Mark: A Bully

Mark was nominated as a bully by 65% of his classmates. He is tall for his age (9 years) and physically fit. One of his hobbies is practicing karate. He sees the world as a threatening place, and it is important for him to be ready to defend himself:

> Karate is defense, so if someone came up and hit you, I've got license even to kill. You know, if you killed someone doing karate, yeah, you can't get done because it [the license] tells you that you're doing it for self-defense.

Mark has been bullying other children since he was first in school. Here he recalls an incident from the past:

Mark: When it was my ball, I brought it to school, he goes, "I'll pop it!" and I said, "Will ya?" and "I'll pop *your* brain!" Then he popped it and I gave him one . . . [pauses] . . . he had a broken nose. I broke his nose!

HC: You broke his nose?

Mark: He was on the floor before it got broken. I just stamped on it like that.

HC: You stamped on his nose? Were you sorry afterwards?

Mark: No . . . He admitted that he started the fight.

HC: That's quite a reaction on your part now, wasn't it? To break his nose, you must have stamped on it pretty hard.

Mark: (coolly) Not pretty hard 'cos on the side it's soft there.

HC: How do you think that he felt?

Mark: Nowt. He just ran out and went home.

This pattern of responding to other children with a strong counterattack has persisted. He shows no remorse for his over-reaction because he feels fully justified and is always convinced that the victim deserved all he got.

Other children have tried confronting Mark with specific examples of his aggressive behavior, but he does not find it easy to listen to honest feedback and reacts angrily to any hint of criticism from others. He will shout almost hysterically, "Shut up!" or "You liar!"

His teacher sees that some children tease and annoy Mark, but she has also noticed how quickly he goes on the defensive when faced with something that he does not like:

> He can be so silly. Someone will pull a face, and he'll go up and say, "Don't you do that again!" I think it's as if they offend him. He can be so aggressive. Then he'll take it to the extreme.

So far, it seems, no one has successfully challenged Mark. He has worked out that, although there are penalties for aggressive behavior, on the whole they are a small price to pay:

I just got to do lines for a few weeks and miss playtime.

Sean: A Bully

Sean was nominated as a bully by 68% of his classmates; at the same time he is viewed "controversially" in the sense that some children like him very much although others dislike him strongly. He is tall, physically fit, and attractive. He is aware of his power to draw attention to himself and explains it as being due to:

> Good looks . . . personality . . . I'm clever at sport and just share things and that.

At the beginning of the first year of middle school, his teacher acknowledged his skill in relating to other people but showed some concern:

> He's a very strong personality that usually acts for the good but has a very strong sense of devilment. And he has a very good general knowledge and lots of ideas . . . so he's a fun person to have around. But I think people's relations with him are tinged with fear. You've got to be friendly with him, otherwise . . . be-cause he is quite tough.

Sean himself does not deny that there have been times when he abused his power in the class:

HC: Have you ever bullied anybody?

Sean: No, but I hit someone for doing something little to me . . . It was Robert . . . He got on my nerves. Every time you tap him he says, "Stop tickling me!" So I just hit him.

And he freely admits that envious feelings make it hard for him to get on with children like Robert who have "always got the right answers and brag off about it." This "gets on my nerves" and, at times, causes Sean to "lose my temper and beat him up, 'cos Robert's right good. He's always going on trips and all this and I'm not because I'm not that good because he's better than good."

Sean has forged long-standing friendships with two other dominant boys in the class. They play football together at break and after school and make sure that only good players are in their team. He justifies excluding "crap players" on the grounds that:

> There's millions of footballs int' yard and they know they just want to annoy me 'cos they don't like me saying no to them.

The impression is that, although low-status children feel left out, favored children become highly positive about Sean's personal qualities of loyalty, liveliness, and sheer fun:

> He always plays football with me, and he's always been friends for years. [Steve, another bully]

> Sean makes me laugh. [Lottie, a popular girl]

His confidence and sense of fun allow him to play tricks on other people and get away with it:

> I put drawing pins on their seats and wiggly worms in their desks. Yes, and it's funny. They know I'm going to do it because I tell them I'm going to, and then they start screaming and they get right mad at me.

The kind of practical joke that misfires so badly for Alan is hugely successful for Sean and indicates his skill at judging how people relate to one another:

> Me and Ian write letters to each other and say, "Will you go out with me?" from boys to girls and we have a laugh. I wrote one from Lottie to Ian and from Ian to Lottie, and they both got them at the same time. And they both read them and they were both thinking "Yes," and when they said, "Yes" I said I was only messing about. And then if they said "No" I would say I was messing about, but if she said "Yes" Alan would say, "Thanks for going out with me."

References

Adams-Webber, J. R. (1979). *Personal construct theory: Concepts and applications*. New York: John Wiley.

Ahmad, Y., & Smith, P. K. (1990). Behavioral measures: Bullying in schools. *Newsletter of the Association for Child Psychology and Psychiatry, 12,* 26-27.

Ainsworth, M. D. S. (1982). Attachment: Retrospect and prospect. In C. M. Parkes & J. Stevenson-Hinde (Eds.), *The place of attachment in human behavior* (pp. 3-30). New York: Basic Books.

Ainsworth, M. D. S. (1989). Attachments beyond infancy. *American Psychologist, 44,* 709-716.

Ainsworth, M. D. S., Blehar, M. C., Waters, E., & Wall, S. (1978). *Patterns of attachment: A psychological study of the Strange Situation.* Hillsdale, NJ: Lawrence Erlbaum.

Akhtar, N., & Bradley, E. J. (1991). Social information processing deficits of aggressive children: Present findings and implications for social skills training. *Clinical Psychology Review, 11,* 621-644.

Allen, J. P., & Hauser, S. T. (1991, April). *Prediction of young adult attachment representations, psychological distress, social competence, and hard drug use from family interactions in adolescence.* Paper presented at the Society for Research in Child Development, Seattle, WA.

Arend, R., Gove, F., & Sroufe, L. A. (1979). Continuity of individual adaptation from infancy to kindergarten: A predictive study of ego-resiliency and curiosity in preschoolers. *Child Development, 50,* 950-959.

Asarnow, J. R., & Callan, J. W. (1985). Boys with peer adjustment problems: Social cognitive processes. *Journal of Consulting and Clinical Psychology, 53,* 80-87.

Asher, S. R. (1983). Social competence and peer status: Recent advances and future directions. *Child Development, 54,* 1427-1434.

213

Asher, S. R., & Renshaw, P. D. (1981). Children without friends: Social knowledge and social skill. In S. R. Asher & J. M. Gottman (Eds.), *The development of children's friendships* (pp. 273-296). New York: Cambridge University Press.

Asher, S. R., Renshaw, P. D., & Hymel, S. (1982). Peer relations and the development of social skills. In S. G. Moore & C. R. Cooper (Eds.), *The young child: Reviews of research* (Vol. 3, pp. 137-158). Washington, DC: National Association for the Education of Young Children.

Attili, G. (1989). Social competence versus emotional security: The link between home relationships and behavior problems in preschool. In B. H. Schneider, G. Attili, J. Nadel, & R. P. Weissberg (Eds.), *Social competence in developmental perspective* (pp. 293-311). Dordrecht, Netherlands: Kluwer.

Bakeman, R., & Brown, J. V. (1980). Early interaction: Consequences for social and mental development at three years. *Child Development, 51,* 437-447.

Barnett, P. A., & Gotlib, I. H. (1988). Psychosocial functioning and depression: Distinguishing among antecedents, concomitants, and consequences. *Psychological Bulletin, 104,* 97-126.

Barocas, R., Seifer, R., Sameroff, A. J., Andews, T. A., Croft, R. T., & Ostrow, E. (1991). Social and interpersonal determinants of developmental risk. *Developmental Psychology, 27,* 479-488.

Bartholomew, K. (1988). [Assessment of stability of self-report attachment ratings]. Unpublished raw data.

Bartholomew, K. (1989). *Attachment styles in young adults: Implications for self-concept and interpersonal functioning.* Unpublished doctoral dissertation, Stanford University, Stanford, CA.

Bartholomew, K. (1990). Avoidance of intimacy: An attachment perspective. *Journal of Social and Personal Relationships, 7,* 147-178.

Bartholomew, K., & Griffin, D. W. (in press). The metaphysics of measurement: The case of adult attachment. In K. Bartholomew & D. Perlman (Eds.), *Advances in personal relationships: Vol. 5. Adult attachment relationships.* London: Jessica Kingsley.

Bartholomew, K., & Horowitz, L. M. (1991). Attachment styles among young adults: A test of a four-category model. *Journal of Personality and Social Psychology, 61,* 226-244.

Bartholomew, K., & Larsen, S. G. (1991). *Interpersonal dependency and attachment in adulthood.* Unpublished manuscript.

Bartholomew, K., & Scharfe, E. (1992). *Attachment processes in young couples.* Unpublished manuscript.

Baumrind, D. (1967). Child care practices anteceding three patterns of preschool behavior. *Genetic Psychology Monographs, 75,* 43-88.

Bell, R. Q. (1968). A reinterpretation of the direction of effects in studies of socialization. *Psychological Review, 75,* 81-95.

Belsky, J. (1980). Child maltreatment. *American Psychologist, 35,* 320-335.

Belsky, J. (1984). The determinants of parenting: A process model. *Child Development, 55,* 83-96.

Belsky, J., Fish, M., & Isabella, R. (1991). Continuity and discontinuity in infant negative and positive emotionality: Family antecedents and attachment consequences. *Developmental Psychology, 27,* 421-431.

Belsky, J., & Pensky, E. (1988). Developmental history, personality, and family relationships: Toward an emergent family system. In R. A. Hinde & J. Stevenson-

Hinde (Eds.), *Relationships within families: Mutual influences* (pp. 193-217). Oxford, UK: Clarendon.

Belsky, J., Steinberg, L., & Draper, P. (1991). Childhood experience, interpersonal development, and reproductive strategy: An evolutionary theory of socialization. *Child Development, 62,* 647-670.

Belsky, J., Youngblade, L., & Pensky, E. (1989). Childrearing history, marital quality, and maternal affect: Intergenerational transmission in a low-risk sample. *Development and Psychopathology, 1,* 291-304.

Belson, W. A. (1975). *Juvenile theft: The causal factors.* New York: Harper & Row.

Bene, J., & Anthony, J. (1957). *Manual for the Family Relations Test.* London: National Foundation for Education Research.

Benoit, D., Vidovic, D., & Roman, J. (1991, April). *Transmission of attachment across three generations.* Paper presented at the Biennial Meeting of the Society for Research in Child Development, Seattle, WA.

Berg, M., & Medrich, E. A. (1980). Children in four neighborhoods: Physical environment and its effects on play and play patterns. *Environment and Behavior, 12,* 320-348.

Berndt, T. J. (1986). Children's comments about their friendships. In M. Perlmutter (Ed.), *Minnesota Symposia on Child Psychology: Vol. 18. Cognitive perspectives on children's social and behavioral development* (pp. 189-212). Hillsdale, NJ: Lawrence Erlbaum.

Bhavnagri, N. (1987). *Parents as facilitators of preschool children's peer relationships.* Unpublished doctoral dissertation, University of Illinois, Urbana-Champaign.

Bhavnagri, N., & Parke, R. D. (1985, April). *Parents as facilitators of preschool peer interaction.* Paper presented at the Biennial Meeting of the Society for Research in Child Development, Toronto, Canada.

Bhavnagri, N., & Parke, R. D. (1991). Parents as direct facilitators of children's peer relationships: Effects of age of child and sex of parent. *Journal of Social and Personal Relationships, 8,* 423-440.

Biringen, Z. (1990). Direct observation of maternal sensitivity and dyadic interaction in the home: Relations to maternal thinking. *Developmental Psychology, 26,* 278-284.

Black, B., & Hazen, N. L. (1990). Social status and patterns of communication in acquainted and unacquainted preschool children. *Developmental Psychology, 26,* 379-386.

Booth, C. L., Rose-Krasnor, L., & Rubin, K. H. (1991). Relating preschoolers' social competence and their mothers' parenting behaviors to early attachment security and high-risk status. *Journal of Social and Personal Relationships, 8,* 363-382.

Boulton, M. J. (1991a). A comparison of structural and contextual features of middle school children's playful and aggressive fighting. *Ethology and Sociobiology, 12,* 1119-1145.

Boulton, M. J. (1991b). Partner preferences in middle school children's playful fighting and chasing. *Ethology and Sociobiology, 12,* 177-193.

Boulton, M. J., & Smith, P. K. (in press). Bully/victim problems in middle school children: Stability, self-perceived competence, peer perceptions, and peer acceptance. *British Journal of Developmental Psychology.*

Bowers, L., Smith, P. K., & Binney, V. A. (1992). Cohesion and power in the families of children involved in bully/victim problems at school. *Journal of Family Therapy, 14,* 371-387.

Bowers, L., Smith, P. K., & Binney, V. A. (in press). Family relationships as perceived by children involved in bully/victim problems at school. *Journal of Personal and Social Relationships.*

Bowlby, J. (1969). *Attachment and loss.* New York: Basic Books.

Bowlby, J. (1973). *Attachment and loss: Vol 2. Separation.* New York: Basic Books.

Bowlby, J. (1977). The making and breaking of affectional bonds: I. Aetiology and psychopathology in the light of attachment theory. *British Journal of Psychiatry, 130,* 201-210.

Bowlby, J. (1980). *Attachment and loss: Vol. 3. Loss, sadness, and depression.* New York: Basic Books.

Bowlby, J. (1982). *Attachment and loss: Vol 1. Attachment* (2nd ed.). New York: Basic Books. (Original work published 1969)

Bowlby, J. (1988). *A secure base: Parent-child attachment and healthy human development.* New York: Basic Books.

Bradbard, M. R., Endsley, R. C., & Mize, J. (1991). *The ecology of parent-child communications about daily experiences in preschool and day care.* Manuscript submitted for publication.

Brennan, K. A., Shaver, P. R., & Tobey, A. E. (1991). Attachment styles, gender, and parental problem drinking. *Journal of Social and Personal Relationships, 8,* 451-466.

Bretherton, I. (1985). Attachment theory: Retrospect and prospect. In I. Bretherton & E. Waters (Eds.), *Growing points of attachment theory and research* (Monographs of the Society for Research in Child Development, Vol. 50, Serial No. 209, pp. 3-35). Chicago: University of Chicago Press.

Bretherton, I. (1990). Open communication and internal working models: Their role in the development of attachment relationships. In R. A. Thompson (Vol. Ed.), *Socioemotional development* (Vol. 36, pp. 57-113). R. A. Dienstbier (Series Ed.), *Nebraska Symposium on Motivation 1988.* Lincoln: University of Nebraska Press.

Bretherton, I., Biringen, Z., Ridgeway, D., Maslin, C., & Sherman, M. (1989). Attachment: The parental perspective. *Infant Mental Health Journal, 10,* 203-221.

Bretherton, I., Ridgeway, D., & Cassidy, J. (1990). Assessing internal working models of the attachment relationship: An attachment completion task for 3-year-olds. In M. Greenberg, D. Cicchetti, & E. M. Cummings (Eds.), *Attachment in the preschool years: Theory, research, and intervention* (pp. 273-308). Chicago: University of Chicago Press.

Bronfenbrenner, U. (1979). *The ecology of human development: Experiments by nature and design.* Cambridge, MA: Harvard University Press.

Bronfenbrenner, U. (1986). Ecology of the family as a context for human development: Research perspectives. *Developmental Psychology, 22*(6), 723-742.

Brown, G. W., & Harris, T. (1978). *Social origins of depression.* London: Tavistock.

Brownell, C. A. (1990). Peer social skills in toddlers: Competencies and constraints illustrated by same-age and mixed-age interaction. *Child Development, 61,* 838-848.

Bryant, B. (1985). The neighborhood walk: Sources of support in middle childhood. *Monographs of the Society for Research in Child Development, 50*(3, Serial No. 210).

Budd, K. S. (1985). Parents as mediators in the social skills training of children. In L. L'Abate & M. A. Milan (Eds.), *Handbook of social skills training and research* (pp. 245-262). New York: John Wiley.

Budd, K. S., & Itzkowitz, J. S. (1990). Parents as social skills trainers and evaluators of children. *Child and Family Behavior Therapy, 12,* 13-30.

Bugental, D. B., & Shennum, W. A. (1984). "Difficult" children as elicitors and targets of adult communication patterns: An attributional-behavioral transactional analysis. *Monographs of the Society for Research in Child Development, 49*(1, Serial No. 205).

Buhrmester, D. (1990). Intimacy of friendship, interpersonal competence, and adjustment during preadolescence and adolescence. *Child Development, 61,* 1101-1111.

Buss, D. M. (1984). Marital assortment for personality dispositions: Assessment with three data sources. *Behavior Genetics, 14,* 111-123.

Cairns, R. B., Cairns, B. D., Neckerman, H. J., Gest, S. D., & Gariepy, J. (1988). Social networks and aggressive behavior: Peer support of peer rejection. *Developmental Psychology, 24,* 815-823.

Carnelley [Fiala], K. B., & Janoff-Bulman, R. (1992). Optimism about love relationships: General vs. specific lessons from one's personal experiences. *Journal of Personal and Social Relationships, 9,* 5-20.

Case, R. (1991, April). *The role of primitive defenses in the regulation and representation of early attachment relations.* Paper presented at the Meeting of the Society for Research in Child Development, Seattle, WA.

Caspi, A., & Elder, G. H. (1988). Emergent family patterns: The intergenerational construction of problem behavior and relationships. In R. A. Hinde & J. Stevenson-Hinde (Eds.), *Relationships within families: Mutual influences* (pp. 218-240). Oxford, UK: Clarendon.

Cassidy, J. (1988). Child-mother attachment and the self in six-year-olds. *Child Development, 59,* 121-134.

Cassidy, J., & Kobak, R. (1988). Avoidance and its relation to other defensive processes. In J. Belsky & T. Nezworski (Eds.), *Clinical implications of attachment* (pp. 300-323). Hillsdale, NJ: Lawrence Erlbaum.

Chodorow, N. (1978). *The reproduction of mothering: Psychoanalysis and the sociology of gender.* Berkeley: University of California Press.

Cicchetti, D., & Carlson, V. (1989). *Child maltreatment: Theory and research on the causes and consequences of child abuse and neglect.* New York: Cambridge University Press.

Cicchetti, D., Lynch, M., Shonk, S., & Manly, J. T. (1992). An organizational perspective on peer relations in maltreated children. In R. D. Parke & G. W. Ladd (Eds.), *Family-peer relations: Modes of linkage.* Hillsdale, NJ: Lawrence Erlbaum.

Cicchetti, D., & Rizley, R. (1981). Developmental perspectives on the etiology, intergenerational transmission, and sequelae of child maltreatment. In R. Rizley & D. Cicchetti (Eds.), *Developmental perspectives on child maltreatment* (pp. 31-56). San Francisco: Jossey-Bass.

Cicchetti, D., & Toth, S. L. (1991). A developmental perspective on internalizing and externalizing disorders. In D. Cicchetti & S. L. Toth (Eds.), *Rochester Symposium on Developmental Psychopathology: Vol. 2. Internalizing and externalizing expressions of dysfunction* (pp. 1-19). Hillsdale, NJ: Lawrence Erlbaum.

Cillessen, T., & Ferguson, T. J. (1989). Self-perpetuation processes in children's peer relationships. In B. H. Schneider, G. Attili, J. Nadel, & R. P. Weissberg (Eds.), *Social competence in developmental perspective* (pp. 203-221). Dordrecht, Netherlands: Kluwer.

Clarke-Stewart, K. A., VanderStoep, L. P., & Killian, G. A. (1979). Analysis and replication of mother-child relations at two years of age. *Child Development, 50,* 777-793.

Cochran, M., & Riley, D. (1988). Mothers' reports of children's personal networks: Antecedents, concomitants, and consequences. In S. Salzinger, J. Antrobus, & M. Hammer (Eds.), *Social networks of children, adolescents, and college students* (pp. 113-148). Hillsdale, NJ: Lawrence Erlbaum.

Cohen, J. S. (1989). *Maternal involvement in children's peer relationships during middle childhood.* Unpublished doctoral dissertation, University of Waterloo, Waterloo, Ontario, Canada.

Cohen, J. S., & Woody, E. (1991, April). *Maternal involvement in children's peer relationships: The contributions of mothers' experiences, values, and beliefs.* Paper presented at the Biennial Meeting of the Society for Research in Child Development, Seattle, WA.

Cohn, D. A. (1990). Child-mother attachment at six years and social competence at school. *Child Development, 61,* 152-162.

Cohn, D. A., Patterson, C., & Christopoulos, C. (1991). The family and children's peer relations. *Journal of Social and Personal Relationships, 8,* 315-346.

Cohn, D. A., Silver, D., Cowan, P. A., Cowan, C. P., & Pearson, J. J. (1991, April). *Working models of childhood attachment and marital relationships.* Paper presented at the Biennial Meeting of the Society for Research in Child Development, Seattle, WA.

Coie, J. D., Dodge, K. A., & Coppotelli, H. A. (1982). Dimensions and types of social status: A cross-age perspective. *Developmental Psychology, 18,* 557-569.

Collins, N. L. (1991). *Adult attachment styles and explanations for relationship events: A knowledge structure approach to explanation in close relationships.* Unpublished doctoral dissertation, University of Southern California, Los Angeles.

Collins, N. L., & Read, S. J. (1990). Adult attachment, working models, and relationship quality in dating couples. *Journal of Personality and Social Psychology, 58,* 644-663.

Cooper, C. R., & Cooper, R. G. (1992). Links between adolescents' relationships with their parents and peers: Models, evidence, and mechanisms. In R. D. Parke & G. W. Ladd (Eds.), *Family-peer relations: Modes of linkage.* Hillsdale, NJ: Lawrence Erlbaum.

Costabile, A., Smith, P. K., Matheson, L., Aston, J., Hunter, T., & Boulton, M. (1991). Cross-national comparison of how children distinguish serious and playful fighting. *Developmental Psychology, 27,* 881-887.

Costanzo, P. R. (1991). Morals, mothers, and memories: The social context of developing social cognition. In R. Cohen & A. Siegel (Eds.), *Context and development* (pp. 91-132). Hillsdale, NJ: Lawrence Erlbaum.

Crittenden, P. M. (1988). Relationships at risk. In J. Belsky & T. Nezworski (Eds.), *Clinical implications of attachment* (pp. 136-174). Hillsdale, NJ: Lawrence Erlbaum.

Crittenden, P. M., & Ainsworth, M. D. S. (1989). Child maltreatment and attachment theory. In D. Cicchetti & V. Carlson (Eds.), *Child maltreatment: Theory and research on the causes and consequences of child abuse and neglect* (pp. 432-463). New York: Cambridge University Press.

Crouter, A. C., MacDermid, S. M., McHale, S. M., & Perry-Jenkins, M. (1990). Parental monitoring and perceptions of children's school performance and conduct in dual- and single-earner families. *Developmental Psychology, 26*(4), 649-657.

Crowell, J. A., & Feldman, S. S. (1988). Mothers' internal models of relationships and children's behavioral and developmental status: A study of mother-child interaction. *Child Development, 59,* 1273-1285.

Davis, K. E., & Kirkpatrick, L. A. (1991). *Attachment style, gender, and relationship stability: A longitudinal analysis.* Unpublished manuscript.

Denham, S. A., McKinley, M., Couchoud, E. A., & Holt, R. (1990). Emotional and behavioral predictors of preschool peer ratings. *Child Development, 61,* 1145-1152.

Denham, S. A., Renwick, S. M., & Holt, R. W. (1991). Working and playing together: Prediction of preschool social-emotional competence from mother-child interaction. *Child Development, 62,* 242-249.

DeVault, M. V. (1957). Classroom sociometric mutual pairs and residential proximity. *Journal of Educational Research, 50,* 605-610.

Dishion, T. (1990). The family ecology of boys' peer relations in middle childhood. *Child Development, 61,* 874-892.

Dix, T. H., & Grusec, J. E. (1985). Parent attribution processes in the socialization of children. In I. E. Sigel (Ed.), *Parental belief systems: The psychological consequences for children* (pp. 201-233). Hillsdale, NJ: Lawrence Erlbaum.

Dix, T. H., & Lochman, J. E. (1990). Social cognition and negative reactions to children: A comparison of mothers of aggressive and nonaggressive boys. *Journal of Social and Clinical Psychology, 9,* 418-438.

Dix, T. H., Ruble, D. N., & Zambarano, R. J. (1989). Mothers' implicit theories of discipline: Child effects, parent effects, and the attribution process. *Child Development, 60,* 1373-1391.

Dodge, K. A. (1986). A social information processing model of social competence in children. In M. Perlmutter (Ed.), *Minnesota Symposia on Child Psychology: Vol. 18. Cognitive perspectives on children's social and behavioral development* (pp. 77-125). Hillsdale, NJ: Lawrence Erlbaum.

Dodge, K. A., Bates, J. E., & Pettit, G. S. (1990). Mechanisms in the cycle of violence. *Science, 250,* 1678-1683.

Dodge, K. A., Coie, J. D., Pettit, G. S., & Price, J. M. (1990). Peer status and aggression in boys' groups: Developmental and contextual analyses. *Child Development, 61,* 1289-1309.

Dodge, K. A., & Frame, C. L. (1982). Social cognitive biases and deficits in aggressive boys. *Child Development, 53,* 620-635.

Dodge, K. A., Pettit, G. S., McClaskey, C. L., & Brown, M. M. (1986). Social competence in children. *Monographs of the Society for Research in Child Development, 51*(1, Serial No. 213).

Dodge, K. A., & Somberg, D. (1987). Hostile attributional biases among aggressive boys are exacerbated under conditions of threats to the self. *Child Development, 58,* 213-224.

Doumas, D. (1990). *Conceptualization and implications of adult attachment styles.* Unpublished honors thesis, Stanford University, Stanford, CA.

Draper, P., & Harpending, H. (1982). Father absence and reproductive strategy: An evolutionary perspective. *Journal of Anthropological Research, 38,* 255-273.

Duck, S. W. (1973). *Personal relationships and personal constructs: A study of friendship formation.* New York: John Wiley.

Duck, S. W. (1990). Relationships as unfinished business: Out of the frying pan and into the 1990s. *Journal of Social and Personal Relationships, 7,* 5-24.

Dunn, J., Brown, J., & Beardsall, L. (1991). Family talk about feeling states and children's later understanding of others' emotions. *Developmental Psychology, 27,* 448-455.

Dunn, J., & Munn, P. (1985). Becoming a family member: Family conflict and the development of social understanding in the second year. *Child Development, 56,* 480-492.

East, P. (1991). The parent-child relationships of withdrawn, aggressive, and sociable children: Child and parent perspectives. *Merrill-Palmer Quarterly, 37,* 425-444.

Easterbrooks, M. A., Davidson, C. E., & Chazan, R. (1991, April). *Representations of self, attachment, and the social context.* Paper presented at the Biennial Meeting of the Society for Research in Child Development, Seattle, WA.

Easterbrooks, M. A., & Lamb, M. (1979). The relationship between quality of infant-mother attachment and infant competence in initial encounters with peers. *Child Development, 50,* 380-387.

Egeland, B. R. (1991, August). *Developmental consequences of maltreatment: Research findings and implications for intervention.* Paper presented at the Annual Meeting of the American Psychological Association, San Francisco, CA.

Egeland, B. R., & Farber, E. A. (1984). Infant-mother attachment: Factors related to its development and changes over time. *Child Development, 55,* 753-771.

Egeland, B. R., Jacobvitz, D., & Papatola, K. (1987). Intergenerational continuity of abuse. In R. J. Gelles & J. B. Lancaster (Eds.), *Child abuse and neglect: Biosocial dimensions* (pp. 255-276). Hawthorne, NY: Aldine.

Egeland, B. R., Jacobvitz, D., & Sroufe, L. A. (1988). Breaking the cycle of abuse. *Child Development, 58,* 1080-1088.

Egeland, B. R., & Sroufe, L. A. (1981). Developmental sequelae of maltreatment in infancy. In R. Rizley & D. Cicchetti (Eds.), *Developmental perspectives on child maltreatment* (pp. 77-92). San Francisco: Jossey-Bass.

Emler, N., & Reicher, S. (1993). *A social psychology of adolescence and delinquency.* Oxford, UK: Blackwell.

Epstein, S. (1980). The self-concept: A review and the proposal of an integrated theory of personality. In E. Staub (Ed.), *Personality: Basic aspects and current research* (pp. 82-131). Englewood Cliffs, NJ: Prentice-Hall.

Epstein, S. (1983). *The Mother-Father-Peer Scale.* Unpublished manuscript, University of Massachusetts, Amherst.

Epstein, S. (1987). Implications of cognitive self-theory for psychopathology and psychotherapy. In N. Cheshire & H. Thomas (Eds.), *Self, symptoms, and psychotherapy* (pp. 43-58). New York: John Wiley.

Erickson, M. F., Sroufe, L. A., & Egeland, B. (1985). The relationship between quality of attachment and behavior problems in preschool in a high-risk sample. In I. Bretherton & E. Waters (Eds.), *Growing points of attachment theory and research* (Monographs of the Society for Research in Child Development, Vol. 50, Serial No. 209, pp. 147-166). Chicago: University of Chicago Press.

Fagen, R. (1981). *Animal play behavior.* New York: Oxford University Press.

Fagot, B., & Kavanagh, K. (1990). The prediction of antisocial behavior from avoidant attachment classifications. *Child Development, 61,* 864-873.

Feeney, J. A., & Noller, P. (1990). Attachment style as a predictor of adult romantic relationships. *Journal of Personality and Social Psychology, 58,* 281-291.

Feeney, J. A., Noller, P., & Callan, V. J. (in press). Attachment style, communication, and satisfaction in the early years of marriage. In K. Bartholomew & D. Perlman (Eds.), *Advances in personal relationships: Vol. 5. Adult attachment relationships.* London: Jessica Kingsley.

Fenigstein, A., Scheier, M. F., & Buss, A. H. (1975). Public and private self-consciousness: Assessment and theory. *Journal of Consulting and Clinical Psychology, 43,* 522-527.

Fiala [Carnelley], K. B. (1991). *Attachment and psychosocial functioning of depressed, remitted depressed, and nondepressed women and their partners.* Unpublished doctoral dissertation, University of Massachusetts, Amherst.

Fine, G. A. (1981). Friends, impression management, and preadolescent behavior. In S. R. Asher & J. M. Gottman (Eds.), *The development of children's friendships* (pp. 29-52). New York: Cambridge University Press.

Finkelstein, N. W., Dent, C., Gallacher, K., & Ramey, C. T. (1978). Social behavior of infants and toddlers in a day-care environment. *Developmental Psychology, 14,* 257-262.

Finnie, V., & Russell, A. (1988). Preschool children's social status and their mothers' behavior and knowledge in the supervisory role. *Developmental Psychology, 24,* 789-801.

Fonagy, P., Steele, H., & Steele, M. (1991). Maternal representations of attachment during pregnancy predict the organization of infant-mother attachment at one year of age. *Child Development, 62,* 891-905.

Fontana, V. (1968). Further reflections on maltreatment of children. *New York State Journal of Medicine, 68,* 2214-2215.

Fox, N. A., Kimmerly, N. L., & Schafer, W. D. (1991). Attachment to mother/attachment to father: A meta-analysis. *Child Development, 62,* 210-225.

Fraiberg, S., Adelson, E., & Shapiro, V. (1975). Ghosts in the nursery: A psychoanalytic approach to the problems of impaired infant-mother relationships. *Journal of the American Academy of Child Psychiatry, 14,* 387-421.

Franz, C. E., McClelland, D. C., & Weinberger, J. (1991). Childhood antecedents of conventional social accomplishment in mid-life adults: A 36-year prospective study. *Journal of Personality and Social Psychology, 60,* 586-595.

Fry, D. P. (1987). Differences between playfighting and serious fights among Zapotec children. *Ethology and Sociobiology, 8,* 285-306.

Furniss, T. (1983). Family process in the treatment of interfamilial child sexual abuse. *Journal of Family Therapy, 5,* 263-278.

Galdston, R. (1965). Observations on children who have been physically abused and their parents. *American Journal of Psychiatry, 122,* 440-443.

Gallagher, J. J. (1958). Social status of children related to intelligence, propinquity, and social perception. *Elementary School Journal, 59,* 225-231.

Garbarino, J., & Gilliam, G. (1980). *Understanding abusive families.* Lexington, MA: Lexington.

Gehring, T. M., & Wyler, I. L. (1986). Family Systems Test (FAST): A three-dimensional approach to investigate family relationships. *Child Psychiatry and Human Development, 16,* 235-248.

George, C., Kaplan, N., & Main, M. (1987). *The adult attachment interview.* Unpublished manuscript, University of California, Berkeley.

George, C., & Main, M. (1979). Social interactions of young abused children: Approach, avoidance, and aggression. *Child Development, 50,* 306-318.

George, C., & Solomon, J. (1989). Internal working models of caregiving and security of attachment at age six. *Infant Mental Health Journal, 10,* 222-237.

Gilligan, C. (1982). *In a different voice: Psychological theory and women's development.* Cambridge, MA: Harvard University Press.

Goodnow, J. J. (1988). Parents' ideas, actions, and feelings: Models and methods from developmental and social psychology. *Child Development, 59,* 286-320.

Goodnow, J. J., & Collins, W. A. (1990). *Development according to parents: The nature, sources, and consequences of parents' ideas.* Hillsdale, NJ: Lawrence Erlbaum.

Goodnow, J. J., Knight, R., & Cashmore, J. (1985). Adult social cognition: Implications of parents' ideas for approaches to development. In M. Perlmutter (Ed.), *Minnesota Symposia on Child Psychology: Vol. 18. Cognitive perspectives on children's social and behavioral development* (pp. 287-329). Hillsdale, NJ: Lawrence Erlbaum.

Gottman, J. M. (1983). *How children become friends* (Monographs of the Society for Research in Child Development, Vol. 48, Serial No. 201). Chicago: University of Chicago Press.

Green-Eichberg, C. (1987). *Quality of infant-parent attachment: Related to mother's representation of her own relationship history.* Paper presented at the Biennial Meeting of the Society for Research in Child Development, Baltimore, MD.

Grossmann, K., Fremmer-Bombik, E., Rudolph, J., & Grossmann, K. E. (1988). Maternal attachment representations as related to patterns of infant-mother attachment and maternal care during the first year. In R. A. Hinde & J. Stevenson-Hinde (Eds.), *Relationships within families: Mutual influences* (pp. 241-260). Oxford, UK: Clarendon.

Grossmann, K. E., & Grossmann, K. (1991). Attachment quality as an organizer of emotional and behavioral responses in a longitudinal perspective. In C. M. Parkes, J. Stevenson-Hinde, & P. Marris (Eds.), *Attachment across the life cycle* (pp. 93-114). London: Routledge.

Grossmann, K. E., Grossmann, K., & Schwan, A. (1986). Capturing the wider view of attachment: A reanalysis of Ainsworth's Strange Situation. In C. E. Izard & P. B. Read (Eds.), *Measuring emotions in infants and children* (Vol. 2, pp. 124-171). Cambridge, UK: Cambridge University Press.

Grossmann, K., Grossmann, K. E., Spangler, G., Suess, G., & Unzner, L. (1985). Maternal sensitivity and newborns' orientation responses as related to quality of attachment in Northern Germany. In I. Bretherton & E. Waters (Eds.), *Growing points of attachment theory and research* (Monographs of the Society for Research in Child Development, Vol. 50, Serial No. 209, pp. 233-256). Chicago: University of Chicago Press.

Gurucharri, C., Phelps, E., & Selman, R. (1984). Development of interpersonal understanding: A longitudinal and comparative study of normal and disturbed youths. *Journal of Consulting and Clinical Psychology, 52,* 26-36.

Hargreaves, D. (1967). *Social relations in a secondary school.* London: Routledge & Kegan Paul.

Harrison-Greer, L. L. (1991). *Styles of attachment in marital relationships.* Unpublished master's thesis, York University, Toronto.

Harrist, A. W. (1991). *Synchronous and nonsynchronous parent-child interaction: Relations with children's later competence with peers.* Unpublished doctoral dissertation, University of Tennessee, Knoxville.

Hart, C. H., DeWolf, M., Wozniak, P., & Burts, D. (1992). Maternal and paternal disciplinary styles: Relations with preschoolers' playground behavioral orientations and peer status. *Child Development, 63,* 879-892.

Hart, C. H., Ladd, G., & Burleson, B. (1990). Children's expectations of the outcomes of social strategies: Relations with sociometric status and maternal disciplinary styles. *Child Development, 61,* 127-137.

Harter, S. (1985). *Manual for the Self-Perception Profile for Children.* Denver, CO: University of Denver.

Hartup, W. W. (1983). Peer relations. In E. M. Hetherington (Ed.), *Handbook of child psychology: Vol. 4. Socialization, personality, and social development* (pp. 103-198). New York: John Wiley.

Hartup, W. W. (1985). Relationships and their significance in cognitive development. In R. A. Hinde, A. Perret-Clermont, & J. Stevenson-Hinde (Eds.), *Social relationships and cognitive development* (pp. 66-82). Oxford, UK: Clarendon.

Hartup, W. W. (1989). Social relationships and their developmental significance. *American Psychologist, 44,* 120-126.

Hartup, W. W., Laursen, B., Stewart, M. I., & Eastenson, A. (1988). Conflict and the friendship relations of young children. *Child Development, 59,* 1590-1600.

Haskett, M. E., & Kistner, J. A. (1991). Social interactions and peer perceptions of young physically abused children. *Child Development, 62,* 979-990.

Hazan, C., & Hutt, M. J. (1991). *From parents to peers: Transitions in attachment.* Unpublished manuscript, Cornell University, Department of Human Development, Ithaca, NY.

Hazan, C., Hutt, M. J., & Markus, H. (1991). *Continuity and change in inner working models of attachment.* Unpublished manuscript, Cornell University, Department of Human Development, Ithaca, NY.

Hazan, C., & Shaver, P. R. (1987). Conceptualizing romantic love as an attachment process. *Journal of Personality and Social Psychology, 52,* 511-524.

Hazan, C., & Shaver, P. R. (1990). Love and work: An attachment-theoretical perspective. *Journal of Personality and Social Psychology, 59,* 270-280.

Herrenkohl, R. C., & Herrenkohl, E. C. (1981). Some antecedents and consequences of child maltreatment. In R. Rizley & D. Cicchetti (Eds.), *Developmental perspectives on child maltreatment* (pp. 57-76). San Francisco: Jossey-Bass.

Hertzberger, S. (1983). Social cognition and the transmission of abuse. In D. Finkelhor, R. Gelles, G. Hotaling, & M. Straus (Eds.), *The darkside of families: Current family violence research* (pp. 317-329). Beverly Hills, CA: Sage.

Hetherington, E. M., & Martin, B. (1986). Family factors and psychopathology in children. In H. C. Quay & J. S. Werry (Eds.), *Psychopathological disorders of childhood* (3rd ed., pp. 332-390). New York: John Wiley.

Hoffman, M. L., & Saltzstein, H. D. (1967). Parent discipline and the child's moral development. *Journal of Personality and Social Psychology, 5,* 45-47.

Horowitz, L. M., Rosenberg, S. E., Baer, B. A., Ureno, G., & Villasenor, V. S. (1988). Inventory of interpersonal problems: Psychometric properties and clinical applications. *Journal of Consulting and Clinical Psychology, 56,* 885-892.

Howes, C. (1983). Patterns of friendship. *Child Development, 54,* 1041-1053.

Howes, C. (1988). Peer interaction of young children. *Monographs of the Society for Research in Child Development, 53*(1, Serial No. 217).

Howes, P. W., Markman, H. J., & Lindahl. K. M. (1991). *Contributions of attachment theory to the study of marriage: Theoretical and empirical relations.* Unpublished manuscript.

Humphreys, A. P., & Smith, P. K. (1987). Rough and tumble, friendship, and dominance in schoolchildren: Evidence for continuity and change with age. *Child Development, 58,* 201-212.

Hunter, P. S., & Kilstrom, N. (1979). Breaking the intergenerational cycle in abusive families. *American Journal of Psychiatry, 136,* 1320-1322.

Hymel, S., Rubin, K. H., Rowden, L., & LeMare, L. (1990). Children's peer relationships: Longitudinal prediction of internalizing and externalizing problems from middle to late childhood. *Child Development, 61,* 2004-2021.

Isabella, R. A., & Belsky, J. (1991). Interactional synchrony and the origins of infant-mother attachment: A replication study. *Child Development, 63,* 373-384.

Jacobson, J. L., & Wille, D. E. (1986). The influence of attachment pattern on developmental changes in peer interaction from the toddler to the preschool period. *Child Development, 57,* 338-347.

Jacobson, R. S., & Straker, G. (1982). Peer group interaction of physically abused children. *Child Abuse and Neglect, 6,* 321-327.

Jacobvitz, D., Fullinwider, N., & Loera, L. (1991, August). *Representation of childhood family patterns, the self, and intimacy in romantic relationships.* Paper presented at the Biennial Meeting of the Society for Research in Child Development, Seattle, WA.

Jones, G. P., & Dembo, M. H. (1989). Age and sex role differences in intimate friendships during childhood and adolescence. *Merrill-Palmer Quarterly, 35,* 445-462.

Kaplan, N., & Main, M. (1985, April). Internal representations of attachment at six years as indicated by family drawings and verbal responses to imagined separations. In M. Main (chair). *Attachment: A move to the level of representation.* Symposium conducted at the meeting of the the Society for Research in Child Development, Toronto, Canada.

Kashani, J. H., Deuser, W., & Reid, J. C. (1991). Aggression and anxiety: A new look at an old notion. *Journal of the American Academy of Child and Adolescent Psychiatry, 30,* 218-223.

Kaufman, J., & Zigler, E. (1987). Do abused children become abusive parents? *American Journal of Orthopsychiatry, 57,* 186-192.

Kelly, G. A. (1970). A brief introduction to personal construct theory. In D. Bannister (Ed.), *Perspectives in personal construct theory* (pp. 1-29). New York: Academic Press.

Kempe, C. H., Silverman, F., Steele, B., Droegemueller, W., & Silver, H. (1962). The battered child syndrome. *Journal of the American Medical Association, 181,* 17-24.

Kirkpatrick, L. A., & Shaver, P. R. (1990). Attachment theory and religion: Childhood attachments, religious beliefs, and conversion. *Journal for the Scientific Study of Religion, 29,* 315-334.

Kirkpatrick, L. A., & Shaver, P. R. (1992). An attachment-theoretical approach to romantic love and religious belief. *Personality and Social Psychology Bulletin, 18,* 266-275.

Klagsbrun, M., & Bowlby, J. (1976). Response to separation from parents: A clinical test for young children. *Projective Psychology, 21,* 7-27.

Klimes-Dougan, B., & Kistner, J. (1990). Physically abused preschoolers' responses to peers' distress. *Developmental Psychology, 26,* 599-602.

Kobak, R. R. (1991, August). *Attachment strategies in marital relationships.* Paper presented at the Biennial Meeting of the Society for Research in Child Development, Seattle, WA.

Kobak, R. R., & Hazan, C. (1991). Attachment in marriage: The effects of security and accuracy of working models. *Journal of Personality and Social Psychology, 60,* 861-869.

Kobak, R. R., & Sceery, A. (1988). Attachment in late adolescence: Working models, affect regulation, and representations of self and others. *Child Development, 59,* 135-146.

Koestner, R., Franz, C., & Weinberger, J. (1990). The family origins of empathic concern: A 26-year longitudinal study. *Journal of Personality and Social Psychology, 58,* 709-717.

Krappman, L. (1986, December). *Family relationships and peer relationships in middle childhood.* Paper presented at the Family Systems and Life-Span Development Conference at the Max Planck Institute, Berlin, Germany.

Kuczynski, L. (1984). Socialization goals and mother-child interaction: Strategies for long-term and short-term compliance. *Developmental Psychology, 20,* 1061-1073.

Kupersmidt, J. B., Coie, J. D., & Dodge, K. A. (1990). The role of poor peer relationships in the development of disorder. In S. R. Asher & J. D. Coie (Eds.), *Peer rejection in childhood* (pp. 274-305). Cambridge, UK: Cambridge University Press.

Ladd, G. W. (1990). Having friends, keeping friends, making friends, and being liked by peers in the classroom: Predictors of children's early school adjustment? *Child Development, 61,* 312-331.

Ladd, G. W. (1991). Introduction: Family-peer relations during childhood: Pathways to competence and pathology? *Journal of Social and Personal Relationships, 8,* 307-314.

Ladd, G. W., & Coleman, C. (in press). Young children's peer relationships: Forms, features, and functions. In B. Spodek (Ed.), *Handbook of research on the education of young children* (2nd ed.). New York: Macmillan.

Ladd, G. W., & Golter, B. (1988). Parents' management of preschoolers' peer relations: Is it related to children's social competence? *Developmental Psychology, 24,* 109-117.

Ladd, G. W., & Hart, C. H., (1991, July). *Parents' management of children's poor relationships: Patterns associated with social competence.* Paper presented at the biennial meeting of the International Society for the Study of Behavioral Development, Minneapolis, MN.

Ladd, G. W., & Hart, C. H. (1992). Creating informal play opportunities: Are parents' and preschoolers' initiations related to children's competence with peers? *Developmental Psychology, 28,* 1179-1187.

Ladd, G. W., Hart, C. H., Wadsworth, E. M., & Golter, B. S. (1988). Preschooler's peer networks in nonschool settings: Relationship to family characteristics and school adjustment. In S. Salzinger, J. Antrobus, & M. Hammer (Eds.), *Social networks of children, adolescents, and college students* (pp. 61-92). Hillsdale, NJ: Lawrence Erlbaum.

Ladd, G. W., & Mize, J. (1983). A cognitive-social learning model of social skill training. *Psychological Review, 90,* 127-157.

Ladd, G. W., & Price, J. M. (1987). Predicting children's social and school adjustment following the transition from preschool to kindergarten. *Child Development, 57,* 446-460.

Ladd, G. W., Price, J. M., & Hart, C. H. (1988). Predicting preschoolers' peer status from their playground behaviors. *Child Development, 59,* 986-992.

Ladd, G. W., Profilet, S. M., & Hart, C. H. (1992). Parents' management of children's peer relations: Facilitating and supervising children's activities in the peer culture. In R. D. Parke & G. W. Ladd (Eds.), *Family-peer relations: Modes of linkage.* Hillsdale, NJ: Lawrence Erlbaum.

LaFreniere, P., & Sroufe, L. A. (1985). Profiles of peer competence in the preschool: Interrelations between measures, influence of social ecology, and relation to attachment history. *Developmental Psychology, 21,* 56-68.

Lamb, M. E., & Nash, A. (1989). Infant-mother attachment, sociability, and peer competence. In T. J. Berndt & G. W. Ladd (Eds.), *Peer relationships in child development* (pp. 219-245). New York: John Wiley.

Lane, D. A. (1989). Violent histories: Bullying and criminality. In D. P. Tattum & D. A. Lane (Eds.), *Bullying in schools* (pp. 95-104). Stoke-on-Trent: Trentham.

Latty-Mann, H., & Davis, K. E. (1988, November). *Adult children of alcoholics (ACOAs): Family dynamics and patterns of romantic relating.* Paper presented at the Annual Meeting of the National Council on Family Relations, Philadelphia, PA.

Le Sieur, K. D., Profilet, S. M., & Ladd, G. W. (1992, April). *Arranging preschool children's peer contacts: A look at parent/child contributions and gender effects.* Paper presented at the Annual Meeting of the American Educational Research Association, San Francisco, CA.

Levitt, M. J., Weber, R. A., Clark, M. C., & McDonnell, P. (1985). Reciprocity of exchange in toddler sharing behavior. *Developmental Psychology, 21,* 122-123.

Levy, M. B., & Davis, K. E. (1988). Love styles and attachment styles compared: Their relations to each other and to various relationship characteristics. *Journal of Social and Personal Relationships, 5,* 439-471.

Lieberman, A. F. (1977). Preschoolers' competence with a peer: Relations with attachment and peer experience. *Child Development, 48,* 1277-1287.

Loeber, R., & Dishion, T. J. (1984). Boys who fight at home and school: Family conditions influencing cross-setting consistency. *Journal of Consulting and Clinical Psychology, 52,* 759-768.

Lollis, S. P. (1990). Maternal influence on children's separation behavior. *Child Development, 61,* 99-103.

Lollis, S. P., Ross, H. S., & Tate, E. (1992). Parents' regulation of children's peer interactions: Direct influences. In R. D. Parke & G. W. Ladd (Eds.), *Family-peer relations: Modes of linkage.* Hillsdale, NJ: Lawrence Erlbaum.

Lytton, H. (1990). Child and parent effects in boys' conduct disorder: A reinterpretation. *Developmental Psychology, 26,* 683-697.

Maccoby, E. E. (1990). Gender and relationships: A developmental account. *American Psychologist, 50,* 513-520.

Maccoby, E. E., & Martin, J. A. (1983). Socialization in the context of the family: Parent-child interaction. In E. M. Hetherington (Ed.), *Handbook of child psychology: Vol. 4. Socialization, personality, and social development* (pp. 1-102). New York: John Wiley.

MacDonald, K. B. (1987). Parent-child physical play with rejected, neglected, and popular boys. *Developmental Psychology, 23,* 705-711.

MacDonald, K. B., & Parke, R. (1984). Bridging the gap: Parent-child play interaction and peer interactive competence. *Child Development, 55,* 1265-1277.

Main, M. (1991). Metacognitive models, metacognitive monitoring, and singular (coherent) model of attachment: Findings and directions for future research. In C. M. Parkes, J. Stevenson-Hinde, & P. Marris (Eds.), *Attachment across the life cycle* (pp. 127-159). London: Routledge.

Main, M., & George, C. (1985). Responses of abused and disadvantaged toddlers to distress in agemates: A study in the day-care setting. *Developmental Psychology, 21,* 407-412.

Main, M., & Goldwyn, R. (1984). Predicting rejection of her own infant from mother's representation of her own experience: Implications for the abused-abusing intergenerational cycle. *Child Abuse and Neglect, 8,* 203-217.

Main, M., & Goldwyn, R. (in press). Intention-based attachment classification: Related to infant-mother and infant-father attachment. *Developmental Psychology.*

Main, M., Kaplan, N., & Cassidy, J. (1985). Security in infancy, childhood, and adulthood: A move to the level of representation. In I. Bretherton & E. Waters (Eds.), *Growing points of attachment theory and research* (Monographs of the Society for Research in Child Development, Vol. 50, Serial No. 209, pp. 66-104). Chicago: University of Chicago Press.

Main, M., & Solomon, J. (1986). Discovery of a new, insecure-disorganized/disoriented attachment pattern. In M. Yogman & T. B. Brazelton (Eds.), *Affective development in infancy* (pp. 95-124). Norwood, NJ: Ablex.

Main, M., & Solomon, J. (1990). Procedures for identifying insecure-disorganized/disoriented infants: Procedures, findings, and implications for the classification of behavior. In M. Greenberg, D. Cicchetti, & E. M. Cummings (Eds.), *Attachment in the preschool years: Theory, research, and intervention* (pp. 121-160). Chicago: University of Chicago Press.

Main, M., & Weston, D. R. (1981). The quality of the toddler's relationship to mother and father: Related to conflict behavior and the readiness to establish new relationships. *Child Development, 52,* 932-940.

Manning, M., Heron, J., & Marshall, T. (1978). Styles of hostility and social interactions at nursery, at school, and at home: An extended study of children. In L. A. Hersov, M. Berger, & D. Shaffer (Eds.), *Aggression and antisocial behavior in childhood and adolescence* (pp. 29-58). Elmsford, NY: Pergamon.

Masten, A. S., Morison, P., & Pellegrini, D. S. (1985). A Revised Class Play method of peer assessment. *Developmental Psychology, 21,* 523-533.

Masters, J. C., & Furman, W. (1981). Popularity, individual friendship selection, and specific peer interaction among children. *Developmental Psychology, 17,* 344-350.

McCabe, V. (1984). Abstract perceptual information for age level: A risk factor for maltreatment? *Child Development, 55,* 267-276.

McCrae, R. R., & Costa, P. T. (1988). Recalled parent-child relations and adult personality. *Journal of Personality, 56,* 417-434.

McFadyen-Ketchum, S. (1991, April). *A situational assessment of age and gender differences in peer competence.* Paper presented at the Biennial Meeting of the Society for Research in Child Development, Seattle, WA.

McNally, S., Eisenberg, N., & Harris, J. D. (1991). Consistency and change in maternal child-rearing practices and values: A longitudinal study. *Child Development, 62,* 190-198.

Medrich, E. A., Roizen, J. A., Rubin, V., & Buckley, S. (1982). *The serious business of growing up: A study of children's lives outside school.* Berkeley: University of California Press.

Melnick, B., & Hurley, J. R. (1969). Distinctive personality attributes of child-abusing mothers. *Journal of Consulting and Clinical Psychology, 33,* 746-749.

Melson, G. F., & Kim, J. (1990). Separations and reunions of preschoolers and their parents at nursery school. *Early Childhood Research Quarterly, 5,* 117-134.

Mikulincer, M., Florian, V., & Tolmacz, R. (1990). Attachment styles and fear of personal death: A case study of affect regulation. *Journal of Personality and Social Psychology, 58,* 273-280.

Mikulincer, M., & Nachshon, O. (1991). Attachment styles and patterns of self-disclosure. *Journal of Personality and Social Psychology, 61,* 321-331.

Miller, J. B. (1989). Memories of peer relations and styles of conflict management. *Journal of Social and Personal Relationships, 6,* 487-504.

Mills, R. S. L., & Rubin, K. H. (1990). Parental beliefs about problematic social behaviors in early childhood. *Child Development, 61,* 138-151.

Mills, R. S. L., & Rubin, K. H. (1992). A longitudinal study of maternal beliefs about children's social behavior. *Merrill-Palmer Quarterly, 38,* 494-512.

Milner, J. S., & Wimberly, R. C. (1980). Prediction and explanation of child abuse. *Journal of Consulting and Clinical Psychology, 36,* 875-884.

Minuchin, P. (1988). A systems perspective on development. In R. A. Hinde & J. Stevenson-Hinde (Eds.), *Relationships within families: Mutual influences* (pp. 7-26). Oxford, UK: Clarendon.

Minuchin, S. (1974). *Families and family therapy.* Cambridge, MA: Harvard University Press.

Mize, J., & Ladd, G. W. (1988). Predicting preschoolers' peer behavior and status from their interpersonal strategies: A comparison of verbal and enactive responses to hypothetical social dilemmas. *Developmental Psychology, 24,* 782-788.

Mize, J., & Ladd, G. W. (1990). A cognitive-social learning approach to social skill training with low-status preschool children. *Developmental Psychology, 26,* 388-397.

Moore, E. G. (1986). Family socialization and the IQ test performance of traditionally and transracially adopted black children. *Developmental Psychology, 22,* 317-326.

Moore, R., & Young, D. (1978). Children outdoors: Toward a social ecology of the landscape. In I. Altman & J. F. Wohlwill (Eds.), *Children and the environment* (pp. 83-130). New York: Plenum.

Mueller, E., & Brenner, J. (1977). The origins of social skills and interaction among playgroup toddlers. *Child Development, 48,* 854-861.

Nash, A. (1989, April). *The role of adults in infant-peer interactions.* Poster presented at the Biennial Meeting of the Society for Research in Child Development, Kansas City, MO.

Neill, S. R. St.-J. (1976). Aggressive and nonaggressive fighting in 12- to 13-year-old preadolescent boys. *Journal of Child Psychology and Psychiatry, 17,* 213-220.

O'Hearn, R. E., & Davis, K. E. (1992). *Classification of adult romantic attachment: A test of Bartholomew's dimensional model.* Unpublished manuscript, University of South Carolina, Columbia.

Olweus, D. (1980). Familial and temperamental determinants of aggressive behavior in adolescents—A causal analysis. *Developmental Psychology, 16,* 644-660.

Olweus, D. (1991). Bully/victim problems among schoolchildren: Basic facts and effects of a school-based intervention program. In K. Rubin & D. Pepler (Eds.), *The development and treatment of childhood aggression* (pp. 441-448). Hillsdale, NJ: Lawrence Erlbaum.

Park, K. A., & Waters, E. (1989). Security of attachment and preschool friendships. *Child Development, 60,* 1076-1081.

Parke, R. D., & Bhavnagri, N. (1989). Parents as managers of children's peer relationships. In D. Belle (Ed.), *Children's social networks and social supports* (pp. 241-259). New York: John Wiley.

Parke, R. D., & Collmer, C. W. (1975). Child abuse: An interdisciplinary analysis. In E. M. Hetherington (Ed.), *Review of child development research* (Vol. 5, pp. 509-590). Chicago: University of Chicago Press.

Parke, R. D., MacDonald, K. B., Beitel, A., & Bhavnagri, N. (1988). The role of the family in the development of peer relationships. In R. DeV. Peters & R. J. McMahon (Eds.), *Social learning and systems approaches to marriage and the family* (pp. 17-44). New York: Bruner/Mazel.

Parke, R. D., & Slaby, R. G. (1983). The development of aggression. In P. Mussen (Ed.), *Handbook of child psychology* (4th ed., Vol. 4, pp. 547-642). New York: John Wiley.

Parke, R. D., & Tinsley, B. R. (1984). Historical and contemporary perspectives on fathering. In K. A. McCluskey & H. W. Reese (Eds.), *Life span developmental psychology: Historical and generational effects* (pp. 203-248). New York: Academic Press.

Parker, G., Tupling, H., & Brown, L. B. (1979). A parental bonding instrument. *British Journal of Medical Psychology, 52,* 1-10.

Parker, J. G., & Asher, S. R. (1987). Peer acceptance and later personal adjustment: Are low-accepted children "at risk"? *Psychological Bulletin, 102,* 357-389.

Pastor, D. L. (1981). The quality of mother-infant attachment and its relationship to toddlers' initial sociability with peers. *Developmental Psychology, 17,* 326-335.

Patterson, C. J., Kupersmidt, J. B., & Griesler, P. C. (1990). Children's perceptions of self and of relationships with others as a function of sociometric status. *Child Development, 61,* 1335-1349.

Patterson, C. J., Vaden, N. A., & Kupersmidt, J. B. (1991). Family background, recent life events, and peer rejection during childhood. *Journal of Social and Personal Relationships, 8,* 347-361.

Patterson, G. R. (1982). *A social learning approach: Vol. 3. Coercive family process.* Eugene, OR: Castalia.

Patterson, G. R., DeBaryshe, B. D., & Ramsey, E. (1989). A developmental perspective on antisocial behavior. *American Psychologist, 44,* 329-335.

Patterson, G. R., & Stouthamer-Loeber, M. (1984). The correlation of family management practices and delinquency. *Child Development, 55,* 1299-1307.

Patterson, G. R., & Yoerger, K. (1991, April). *A model for general parenting is too simple: Mediational models work better.* Paper presented at the Biennial Meeting of the Society for Research in Child Development, Seattle, WA.

Pawluk, C. J. (1989). Social construction of teasing. *Journal for the Theory of Social Behavior, 19,* 145-167.

Pellegrini, A. D. (1988). Elementary school children's rough-and-tumble play and social competence. *Developmental Psychology, 24,* 802-806.

Pellegrini, A. D. (1989a). Elementary school children's rough-and-tumble play. *Early Childhood Research Quarterly, 4,* 245-260.

Pellegrini, A. D. (1989b). What is a category? The case of rough-and-tumble play. *Ethology and Sociobiology, 10,* 331-341.

Pellegrini, D. S. (1985). Social cognition and competence in middle childhood. *Child Development, 56,* 253-264.

Pepler, D. J., & Rubin, K. H. (1991). *The development and treatment of childhood aggression.* Hillsdale, NJ: Lawrence Erlbaum.

Pettit, G. S. (1992). Developmental theories. In V. Van Hasselt & M. Hersen (Eds.), *Handbook of social development: A life span perspective* (pp. 3-28). New York: Plenum.

Pettit, G. S., Cullen, S., Brown, E. G., & Sinclair, J. J. (n.d.). *Parents' perceptions of social problem situations for preschool children.* Unpublished manuscript, Auburn University, Auburn, AL.

Pettit, G. S., Dodge, K. A., & Brown, M. (1988). Early family experience, social problem-solving patterns, and children's social competence. *Child Development, 59,* 107-120.

Pettit, G. S., & Harrist, A. W. (1993). Children's aggressive and socially unskilled behavior with peers: Origins in early family relations. In C. H. Hart (Ed.), *Children on playgrounds: Research perspectives and applications* (pp. 240-270). Albany: State University of New York Press.

Pettit, G. S., Harrist, A. W., Bates, J. E., & Dodge, K. A. (1991). Family interaction, social cognition, and children's subsequent relations with peers at kindergarten. *Journal of Social and Personal Relationships, 8,* 383-402.

Pettit, G. S., & Sinclair, J. J. (1991, July). *Synchronous and asynchronous family interaction patterns in early childhood: Contexts for the social transmission of interpersonal style.* Paper presented at the Biennial Meeting of the International Society for the Study of Behavioral Development, Minneapolis, MN.

Phillips, K., Fulker, D. W., Carey, G., & Nagoshi, C. T. (1988). Direct marital assortment for cognitive and personality variables. *Behavior Genetics, 18,* 347-356.

Piaget, J. (1970). *Structuralism.* New York: Basic Books.

Pianta, R., Egeland, B., & Erickson, M. F. (1989). The antecedents of maltreatment: Results of the mother-child interaction research project. In D. Cicchetti & V. Carlson (Eds.), *Child maltreatment: Theory and research on the causes and consequences of child abuse and neglect* (pp. 203-253). New York: Cambridge University Press.

Pikas, A. (1989). The common concern method for the treatment of mobbing. In E. Roland & E. Munthe (Eds.), *Bullying: An international perspective* (pp. 91-104). London: David Fulton.

Potashin, R. (1946). A sociometric study of children's friendships. *Sociometry, 9,* 48-70.

Powell, T. H., Salzberg, C. L., Rule, S., Levy, S., & Itzkowitz, J. S. (1983). Teaching mentally retarded children to play with their siblings using parents as trainers. *Education and Treatment of Children, 6,* 343-362.

Power, T. G., & Parke, R. D. (1981). Play as a context for early learning. In L. M. Laosa & I. E. Sigel (Eds.), *Families as learning environments for children* (pp. 147-178). New York: Plenum.

Price, J. M., & Dodge, K. A. (1989). Reactive and proactive aggression in childhood: Relations to peer status and social context dimensions. *Journal of Abnormal Child Psychology, 17,* 455-471.

Profilet, S. M., & Ladd, G. W. (1992, April). *Mothers' perceptions and concerns about their preschool children's progress in peer relations.* Paper presented at the Annual Meeting of the American Educational Research Association, San Francisco, CA.

Pulkinnen, L. (1982). Self-control and continuity from childhood to late adolescence. In P. B. Baltes (Ed.), *Life span development and behavior* (Vol. 4, pp. 63-105). New York: Academic Press.

Putallaz, M. (1983). Predicting children's sociometric status from their behavior. *Child Development, 54,* 1417-1426.

Putallaz, M. (1987). Maternal behavior and children's sociometric status. *Child Development, 58,* 324-340.

Putallaz, M., Costanzo, P. R., & Smith, R. B. (1991). Maternal recollections of childhood peer relationships: Implications for their children's social competence. *Journal of Social and Personal Relationships, 8,* 403-422.

Putallaz, M., & Heflin, A. H. (1986). Toward a model of peer acceptance. In J. M. Gottman & J. G. Parker (Eds.), *Conversations of friends: Speculations on affective development* (pp. 292-314). Cambridge, UK: Cambridge University Press.

Putallaz, M., & Heflin, A. H. (1990). Parent-child interaction. In S. R. Asher & J. D. Coie (Eds.), *Peer rejection in childhood* (pp. 189-216). Cambridge, UK: Cambridge University Press.

Quinton, D., Rutter, M., & Liddle, C. (1984). Institutional rearing, parenting difficulties, and marital support. *Psychological Medicine, 14,* 107-124.

Raush, H. L., Barry, W. A., Hertel, R. K., & Swain, M. A. (1974). Communication, conflict, and marriage. San Francisco: Jossey-Bass.

Reid, K. (1983). Retrospection and persistent school absenteeism. *Educational Research, 25,* 110-115.

Renken, B., Egeland, B., Marvinney, D., Mangelsdorf, S., & Sroufe, L. A. (1989). Early childhood antecedents of aggression and passive-withdrawal in early elementary school. *Journal of Personality, 57,* 257-281.

Renscorla, L. (1989, April). *Academic experiences for preschool children: An investigation of parental attitudes.* Paper presented at the Biennial Meeting of the Society for Research in Child Development, Kansas City, MO.

Ricks, M. H. (1985). The social transmission of parental behavior: Attachment across generations. In I. Bretherton & E. Waters (Eds.), *Growing points of attachment theory and research* (Monographs of the Society for Research in Child Development, Vol. 50, Serial No. 209, pp. 211-227). Chicago: University of Chicago Press.

Rogosa, D. (1978). A critique of cross-lagged correlation. *Psychological Bulletin, 88,* 245-258.

Rohner, R. (1960). *Handbook for the study of parental acceptance and rejection.* Storrs: University of Connecticut, Center for the Study of Parental Acceptance and Rejection.

Roopnarine, J. L., & Adams, G. R. (1987). The interactional teaching patterns of mothers and fathers with their popular, moderately popular, or unpopular children. *Journal of Abnormal Child Psychology, 15,* 125-136.

Ross, H. S., & Lollis, S. P. (1989). A social relations analysis of toddler peer relationships. *Child Development, 60,* 1082-1091.

Ross, H. S., Tesla, C., Kenyon, B., & Lollis, S. (1991). Maternal intervention in toddler peer conflict: The socialization of principles of justice. *Developmental Psychology, 6,* 994-1003.

Ross, M. (1989). The relation of implicit theories to the construction of personal histories. *Psychological Review, 96,* 341-357.

Rothenberg, B. B. (1970). Children's social sensitivity and the relationship to interpersonal competence, intrapersonal comfort, and intellectual level. *Developmental Psychology, 2,* 335-350.

Rowe, D. C. (1989). Families and peers: Another look at the nature-nurture question. In T. J. Berndt & G. W. Ladd (Eds.), *Peer relationships in child development* (pp. 274-299). New York: John Wiley.

Rubin, K. H., & Asendorpf, J. B. (Eds.). (1993). *Social withdrawal, inhibition, and shyness in childhood.* Hillsdale, NJ: Lawrence Erlbaum.

Rubin, K. H., Hymel, S., Mills, R. S. L., & Rose-Krasnor, L. (1991). Conceptualizing different developmental pathways to and from social isolation in childhood. In D. Cicchetti & S. L. Toth (Eds.), *Rochester Symposium on Developmental Psychopathology: Vol. 2. Internalizing and externalizing expressions of dysfunction* (pp. 91-122). Hillsdale, NJ: Lawrence Erlbaum.

Rubin, K. H., & Krasnor, L. R. (1986). Social-cognitive and social behavioral perspectives on problem solving. In M. Perlmutter (Ed.), *Minnesota Symposia on Child Psychology: Vol. 18. Cognitive perspectives on children's social and behavioral development* (pp. 1-76). Hillsdale, NJ: Lawrence Erlbaum.

Rubin, K. H., LeMare, L. J., & Lollis, S. (1990). Social withdrawal in childhood: Developmental pathways to peer rejection. In S. R. Asher & J. D. Coie (Eds.), *Peer rejection in childhood* (pp. 217-249). Cambridge, UK: Cambridge University Press.

Rubin, K. H., & Mills, R. S. L. (1990). Maternal beliefs about adaptive and maladaptive social behaviors in normal, aggressive, and withdrawn preschoolers. *Journal of Abnormal Child Psychology, 18,* 419-435.

Rubin, K. H., & Mills, R. S. L. (1992). Parents' thoughts about children's socially adaptive and maladaptive behaviors: Stability, change, and individual differences. In I. E. Sigel, J. J. Goodnow, & A. V. McGillicuddy-deLisi (Eds.), *Parental belief systems: The psychological consequences for children.* Hillsdale, NJ: Lawrence Erlbaum.

Rubin, K. H., Mills, R. S. L., & Rose-Krasnor, L. (1989). Maternal beliefs and children's competence. In B. H. Schneider, G. Attili, J. Nadel, & R. P. Weissberg (Eds.), *Social competence in developmental perspective* (pp. 313-331). Dordrecht, Netherlands: Kluwer.

Rubin, K. H., & Rose-Krasnor, L. (1986). Social cognitive and social behavioral perspectives on problem solving. In M. Perlmutter (Ed.), *Minnesota Symposia on Child Psychology: Vol. 18. Cognitive perspectives on children's social and behavioral development* (pp. 1-68). Hillsdale, NJ: Lawrence Erlbaum.

Rubin, K. H., & Rose-Krasnor, L. (in press). Interpersonal problem solving and social competence in children. In V. B. van Hasselt & M. Hersen (Eds.), *Handbook of social development: A life span perspective.* New York: Plenum.

Rubin, Z., & Sloman, J. (1984). How parents influence their children's friendships. In M. Lewis (Ed.), *Beyond the dyad* (pp. 223-250). New York: Plenum.

Russell, A., & Finnie, V. (1990). Preschool children's social status and maternal instructions to assist group entry. *Developmental Psychology, 26,* 603-611.

Rutter, M. (1979). Protective factors in children's responses to stress and disadvantage. In M. Kent & J. Rolf (Eds.), *Primary prevention of psychiatry: Vol 3. Social competence in children* (pp. 65-88). Hanover, NH: University Press of New England.

Rutter, M. (1988). Functions and consequences of relationships: Some psychopathological considerations. In R. A. Hinde & J. Stevenson-Hinde (Eds.), *Relationships within families: Mutual influences* (pp. 332-353). Oxford, UK: Clarendon.

Sameroff, A. J., & Chandler, M. J. (1975). Reproductive risk and the continuum of caretaking causality. In F. D. Horowitz (Ed.), *Review of child development research* (Vol. 4, pp. 187-244). Chicago: University of Chicago Press.

Schaefer, E. S. (1965). A configurational analysis of children's reports of parent behavior. *Journal of Consulting Psychology, 29,* 552-557.

Segoe, M. (1939). Factors influencing the selection of associates. *Journal of Educational Research, 27,* 32-40.

Selman, R. L. (1980). *The growth of interpersonal understanding: Developmental and clinical analyses.* New York: Academic Press.

Senchak, M., & Leonard, K. E. (1992). Attachment styles and marital adjustment among newlywed couples. *Journal of Social and Personal Relationships, 9,* 51-64.

Shantz, C. U. (1987). Conflicts between children. *Child Development, 58,* 283-305.

Shaver, P. R., & Hazan, C. (1992). Adult romantic attachment: Theory and evidence. In D. Perlman & W. Jones (Eds.), *Advances in personal relationships: Vol. 4* (pp. 29-70). London: Jessica Kingsley.

Shaver, P. R., Hazan, C., & Bradshaw, D. (1988). Love as attachment: The integration of three behavioral systems. In R. J. Sternberg & M. L. Barnes (Eds.), *The psychology of love* (pp. 68-99). New Haven, CT: Yale University Press.

Shouldice, A., & Stevenson-Hinde, J. (1992). Coping with security distress: The Separation Anxiety Test and attachment classification at 4.5 years. *Journal of Child Psychology and Psychiatry, 33,* 331-348.

Shure, M. B. (1981). Social competence as a problem-solving skill. In J. D. Wine & M. D. Smye (Eds.), *Social competence* (pp. 158-185). New York: Guilford.

Sigel, I. E. (1982). The relationship between parental distancing strategies and the child's cognitive behavior. In L. M. Laosa & I. E. Sigel (Eds.), *Families as learning environments for children* (pp. 47-86). New York: Plenum.

Simpson, J. A. (1990). The influence of attachment styles on romantic relationships. *Journal of Personality and Social Psychology, 59,* 971-980.

Simpson, J. A., Rholes, W. S., & Nelligan, J. S. (1992). Support-seeking and support-giving within couples in an anxiety-provoking situation: The role of attachment styles. *Journal of Personality and Social Psychology, 62,* 434-446.

Skinner, E. A. (1985). Determinants of mother-sensitive and contingent-responsive behavior: The role of childrearing beliefs and socioeconomic status. In I. E. Sigel (Ed.), *Parental belief systems: The psychological consequences for children* (pp. 51-82). Hillsdale, NJ: Lawrence Erlbaum.

Sluckin, A. M. (1981). *Growing up in the playground: The social development of children.* London: Routledge & Kegan Paul.

Smith, P. B., & Pederson, D. R. (1988). Maternal sensitivity and patterns of infant-mother attachment. *Child Development, 59,* 1097-1101.

Smith, P. K. (1991a). Hostile aggression as social skills deficit or evolutionary strategy? *Behavioral and Brain Sciences, 14,* 315-316.

Smith, P. K. (1991b). The silent nightmare: Bullying and victimization in school peer groups. *The Psychologist, 4,* 243-248.

Smith, P. K., & Boulton, M. J. (1991, July). *Self-esteem, sociometric status, and peer-perceived behavioral characteristics in middle school children in the United Kingdom.* Paper presented at the Eleventh Meeting of ISSBD, Minneapolis, MN.

Smith, P. K., Hunter, T., Carvalho, A. M. A., & Costabile, A. (1992). Children's perceptions of playfighting, playchasing, and real fighting: A cross-cultural interview study. *Social Development, 1,* 211-229.

Smith, P. K., & Lewis, K. (1985). Rough-and-tumble play, fighting, and chasing in nursery school children. *Ethology and Sociobiology, 6,* 175-181.

Smith, P. K., McWhinney, K., Boulton, M. J., & Cowie, H. (in press). *Self- and other-attributions in bullies and victims in middle childhood.* Unpublished manuscript.

Smith, P. K., & Thompson, D. A. (Eds.). (1991). *Practical approaches to bullying.* London: David Fulton.

Sperling, M. B., Berman, W. H., & Fagen, G. (1991, March). *Assessment of adult attachment: An integrative taxonomy from attachment and psychoana-*

lytic theories. Paper presented at the Midwinter Meetings of the Society for Personality Assessment, New Orleans, LA.

Sperling, M. B., & Borgaro, S. (1991). *Attachment insecurity and reciprocity as mediators of interpersonal attraction*. Unpublished manuscript.

Spinetta, J. J. (1978). Parental personality factors in child abuse. *Journal of Consulting and Clinical Psychology, 46,* 1409-1414.

Spinetta, J. J., & Rigler, D. (1972). The child-abusing parent: A psychological review. *Psychological Bulletin, 77,* 296-304.

Sroufe, L. A. (1983). Infant-caregiver attachment and patterns of adaptation in preschool: The roots of maladaptation and competence. In M. Perlmutter (Ed.), *Minnesota Symposia on Child Psychology: Vol. 16. Development and policy concerning children with special needs* (pp. 41-83). Hillsdale, NJ: Lawrence Erlbaum.

Sroufe, L. A., Egeland, B., & Kreutzer, T. (1990). The fate of early experience following developmental change: Longitudinal approaches to individual adaptation in childhood. *Child Development, 61,* 1363-1373.

Sroufe, L. A., & Fleeson, J. (1986). Attachment and the construction of relationships. In W. Hartup & Z. Rubin (Eds.), *Relationships and development* (pp. 51-71). Hillsdale, NJ: Lawrence Erlbaum.

Sroufe, L. A., & Waters, E. (1977). Attachment as an organizational construct. *Child Development, 48,* 1184-1199.

Steele, B. F., & Pollock, D. (1968). A psychiatric study of parents who abuse infants and small children. In R. E. Helfer & C. H. Kempe (Eds.), *The battered child* (pp. 103-148). Chicago: University of Chicago Press.

Stephenson, P., & Smith, D. (1989). Bullying in the junior school. In D. P. Tattum & D. A. Lane (Eds.), *Bullying in schools* (pp. 45-57). Stoke-on-Trent: Trentham.

Stevenson-Hinde, J., Hinde, R., & Simpson, A. (1986). Behavior at home and friendly or hostile behavior in preschool. In D. Olweus, J. Block, & M. Radke-Yarrow (Eds.), *Development of antisocial and prosocial behavior* (pp. 127-145). New York: Academic Press.

Sullivan, H. S. (1953). *The interpersonal theory of psychiatry. New York:* Norton.

Swann, W. B. (1983). Self-verification: Bringing social reality into harmony with the self. In J. Suls & A. G. Greenwald (Eds.), *Psychological perspectives on the self* (Vol. 2, pp. 33-66). Hillsdale, NJ: Lawrence Erlbaum.

Swann, W. B. (1987). Identity negotiation: Where two roads meet. *Journal of Personality and Social Psychology, 53,* 1038-1051.

Swann, W. B., Pelham, B. W., Hixon, J. G., & de la Ronde, C. (1991). *The self-concept and preference for relationship partners*. Unpublished manuscript, University of Texas, Austin.

Thompson, R. A., & Lamb, M. E. (1983). Security of attachment and stranger sociability in infancy. *Developmental Psychology, 19,* 184-191.

Thompson, R. A., Lamb, M. E., & Estes, D. (1982). Stability of infant-mother attachment and its relationship to changing life circumstances in an unselected middle-class sample. *Child Development, 53,* 144-148.

Tinsley, B. R., & Parke, R. D. (1984). Grandparents as support and socialization agents. In M. Lewis (Ed.), *Beyond the dyad* (pp. 161-194). New York: Plenum.

Trickett, P. K., & Susman, E. J. (1989). Perceived similarities and disagreements about childrearing practices in abusive and nonabusive families: Intergenerational and concurrent family processes. In D. Cicchetti & V. Carlson (Eds.), *Child maltreatment: Theory and research on the causes and consequences of child abuse and neglect* (pp. 280-301). New York: Cambridge University Press.

Troy, M., & Sroufe, L. A. (1987). Victimization among preschoolers: Role of attachment relationship history. *Journal of the American Academy of Child and Adolescent Psychiatry, 26,* 166-172.

Turner, P. (1991). Relations between attachment, gender, and behavior with peers in preschool. *Child Development, 62,* 1475-1488.

Vandell, D. L., Henderson, V. K., & Wilson, K. S. (1988). A longitudinal study of children with day-care experiences for varying quality. *Child Development, 59,* 1286-1292.

van Vliet, W. C. (1981). The environmental context of children's friendships: An empirical and conceptual examination of the role of child density. In A. E. Osterberg, C. P. Tiernan, & R. A. Findlay (Eds.), *Proceedings from the 12th Annual Conference of the Environmental Design Research Association* (pp. 216-224). Washington, DC: Environmental Design Research Association.

Vaughn, B., Egeland, B., Sroufe, L. A., & Waters, E. (1979). Individual differences in infant-mother attachment at twelve and eighteen months: Stability and change. *Child Development, 50,* 971-975.

Vygotsky, L. S. (1978). *Mind in society: The development of higher mental processes.* Cambridge, MA: Harvard University Press.

Wahler, R. G., & Dumas, J. E. (1986). Maintenance factors in coercive mother-child interactions: The compliance and predictability hypotheses. *Journal of Applied Behavior Analysis, 19,* 13-22.

Ward, M. J., & Carlson, E. A. (1991). The predictive validity of the Adult Attachment Interview for adolescent mothers. Unpublished manuscript.

Waters, E. (1978). The reliability and stability of individual differences in infant-mother attachment. *Child Development, 49,* 483-494.

Waters, E., Wippman, J., & Sroufe, L. A. (1979). Attachment, positive affect, and competence in the peer group: Two studies in construct validation. *Child Development, 50,* 821-829.

Weiss, B., Dodge, K. A., Bates, J. E., & Pettit, G. S. (1992). Some consequences of early harsh discipline: Child aggression and a maladaptive social information processing style. *Child Development, 63,* 1321-1335.

Weiss, R. S. (1982). Attachment in adult life. In C. M. Parkes & J. Stevenson-Hinde (Eds.), *The place of attachment in human behavior* (pp. 171-184). New York: Basic Books.

Westen, D. (1991). Social cognition and object relations. *Psychological Bulletin, 109,* 429-455.

Whitney, I., Nabuzoka, N., & Smith, P. K. (1992). Bullying in schools: Mainstream and special needs. *Support for Learning, 7,* 3-7.

Whitney, I., & Smith, P. K. (1993). A survey of the nature and extent of bullying in junior/middle and secondary schools. *Educational Research, 35.*

Wilson, H. (1980). Parental supervision: A neglected aspect of delinquency. *British Journal of Criminology, 20,* 203-235.

Wolfe, D. A. (1985). Child abusive parents: An empirical review and analysis. *Psychological Bulletin, 97,* 462-482.

Yeates, K. O., Schultz, L. H., & Selman, R. L. (1991). The development of interpersonal negotiation strategies in thought and action: A social-cognitive link to behavioral adjustment and social status. *Merrill-Palmer Quarterly, 37,* 369-406.

Zahn-Waxler, C., Denham, S., & Ianotti, R. J. (1992). Peer relations in childhood with a depressed caregiver. In R. D. Parke & G. W. Ladd (Eds.), *Family-peer relations: Modes of linkage.* Hillsdale, NJ: Lawrence Erlbaum.

Zahn-Waxler, C., & Radke-Yarrow, M. (1990). The origins of empathic concern. *Motivation and Emotion, 14,* 107-130.

Zahn-Waxler, C., Radke-Yarrow, M., & King, R. A. (1979). Child-rearing and children's prosocial initiations toward victims of distress. *Child Development, 50,* 319-330.

Zigler, E., & Hall, N. W. (1989). Physical and child abuse in America: Past, present, and future. In D. Cicchetti & V. Carlson (Eds.), *Child maltreatment: Theory and research on the causes and consequences of child abuse and neglect* (pp. 38-75). New York: Cambridge University Press.

Author Index

Subject Index

About the Contributors

Kim Bartholomew received her Ph.D. from Stanford University, Stanford, CA, in 1989 and is currently an Assistant Professor in the Department of Psychology at Simon Fraser University, Burnaby, British Columbia, Canada. Her primary research interests include adult attachment relationships and intergenerational transmission of interpersonal patterns.

Valerie Binney is Consultant Clinical Psychologist in the Child and Family Service, Doncaster NHS Healthcare Trust; and Honorary Lecturer in the Department of Psychology, University of Sheffield, Sheffield, England. Her interests lie in the clinical applications of attachment theory and children's internal representations of social relationships.

Louise Bowers currently is training to be a forensic psychologist with the prison service. She was employed previously by the University of Sheffield, Sheffield, England, as a Research Associate, first investigating family factors characteristics of bullies and victims in middle childhood, and second evaluating a cooperative group work intervention project with the same group of children.

Philip R. Costanzo is a Professor of Psychology and Chair of the Department of Psychology, Social and Health Sciences at Duke University, Durham, North Carolina. His work has been at the interface of social, clinical, and developmental psychology; his research has been particularly concerned with the relationships between parental and peer socialization and the development of social cognition and social relationships. He has co-edited *The Social Psychology of Mental Health* with Diane Ruble and Molly Oliveri; and has co-authored the standard reference book *Theories of Social Psychology* with Marvin Shaw. He also has authored or co-authored chapters and articles on research and theoretical problems at the interface of social and developmental psychology.

Helen Cowie is Director of Counseling Courses at Bretton Hall College of the University of Leeds, England. She has published extensively in professional journals on children's writing processes, cooperative group work, and issues around bullying in school. She has co-authored *Understanding Children's Development* with Peter K. Smith; and the series *Working Together, Learning Together* with Jean Rudduck.

Steve Duck is the founding editor of the *Journal of Social and Personal Relationships*, the editor of *Handbook of Personal Relationships*, and the editor or author of 25 other books on personal relationships. He also founded the International Network on Personal Relationships (the professional organization for the field) and two series of international conferences on relationships. He is presently the Daniel and Amy Starch Research Professor at the University of Iowa, Iowa City.

Tovah P. Klein is a doctoral candidate in the Clinical Psychology Program at Duke University, Durham, North Carolina. Her area of interest includes processes of intergenerational transmission between parents and their children, especially as these influences affect children's abilities to relate to others. Her current research is examining one potential mechanism of transmission—social framing. This work is looking at social frames or filters used by parents to interpret social interactions and to convey meaning to their children.

Gary W. Ladd received his Ph.D. from the University of Rochester, Rochester, NY, and worked for more than a decade as Professor of Child Development and of Psychology at Purdue University, West Lafayette, Indiana. Currently he is Professor of Educational Psychology at the University of Illinois, Urbana-Champaign. He has been employed as a school psychologist in both Indiana and New York State and serves as a consultant to several early childhood and elementary schools. He has published numerous empirical studies, theoretical articles, and reviews of research in the area of children's social development. Included in his recent work are the books *Peer Relationships in Child Development,* co-authored with Thomas R. Berndt, and *Family-Peer Relationships: Modes of Linkage,* co-authored with Ross D. Parke. He is currently Associate Editor for the journal *Child Development* and has served on the editorial boards of other journals, including *Developmental Psychology* and the *Journal of Consulting and Clinical Psychology.* He is conducting research on the contributions of families, peers, and teachers to children's early school adjustment and on the linkages between children's family and peer relations.

Karen D. Le Sieur received her B.A. from Duke University, Durham, North Carolina, and currently is pursuing a doctorate in Educational Psychology at the University of Illinois, Urbana-Champaign. Her interests focus on the effects of family stress on children's early social development and school adjustment, and family-peer relations. She has served as Research Assistant for Gary Ladd on two longitudinal research projects that evaluate the process of early school adjustment, and has presented a paper on parent/child contributions to early peer interactions at the 1992 AERA conference.

Judi Beinstein Miller is Professor of Psychology at Oberlin College, Oberlin, Ohio, where she has taught for 20 years. She received her Ph.D. in Communication from the University of

Pennsylvania, Philadelphia, in 1972 and taught Communication prior to Psychology. She has published research on interpersonal conflict, adolescent-parent relationships, relationship expectations, and gender differences in interaction. She currently is investigating factors that promote insight into close relationships.

Rosemary S. L. Mills received her Ph.D. in Psychology from University of Toronto, Ontario, Canada. She completed a postdoctoral fellowship at the University of Waterloo, Ontario, Canada, before joining the Department of Family Studies at the University of Manitoba, Winnipeg, Canada. Her primary research interests are in parent-child relations and their role in children's socioemotional development.

Jacquelyn Mize received her Ph.D. in Child Development from Purdue University, West Lafayette, Indiana, and is an Associate Professor of Family and Child Development at Auburn University, Auburn, Alabama. Her research interests focus on children's peer relationships and social skills in the preschool years. Her published works have appeared in the journals *Developmental Psychology, Psychological Review,* and *Child Care Quarterly.* Currently she is engaged in research on the processes by which parents contribute to young children's social competence.

Gregory S. Pettit received his Ph.D. in Child Development from Indiana University and is an Associate Professor of Family and Child Development at Auburn University, Auburn, Alabama. His published works have appeared in the journals *Child Development, Developmental Psychology, Journal of Applied Developmental Psychology, Behavioral Assessment,* and several edited volumes on children's social development and interpersonal relationships. He has served on the editorial boards of *Child Development, Developmental Psychology,* and the *Journal of Social and Personal Relationships.* His current research is concerned with familial influences on children's peer relationships.

Susan M. Profilet received her M.A. in Educational Psychology at the University of Illinois, Urbana-Champaign. She currently is a doctoral student in Educational Psychology at the University of Illinois, Urbana-Champaign. Her research interests include parental involvement in young children's peer relations, and she has completed an investigation of mothers' perceptions and concerns about their preschool children's peer relations. Included in her work is a chapter in *Family-Peer Relationships: Modes of Linkage* co-authored with Gary W. Ladd and Craig H. Hart. She has won several awards, including a William Chandler Bagley Scholarship and the Janet Tritsch Memorial Award for Excellence in Undergraduate Research. She currently is working on a longitudinal study of children's early school adjustment.

Martha Putallaz is Associate Professor in the Department of Psychology, Social and Health Science, at Duke University, Durham, North Carolina, and is a member of the faculty of the Carolina Consortium on Human Development. Her program of research concerns the mutual influence of parents and peers on the development and evolution of children's social competence and social relationships.

Kenneth H. Rubin is Professor of Psychology at the University of Waterloo, Ontario, Canada. His research interests focus on the origins and consequences of adaptive and maladaptive relationships and behaviors in childhood. He is Fellow of the Canadian and American Psychological Associations and a recipient of a Killam Research Fellowship. He was associate editor of *Child Development* (1980-1983) and currently sits on several journal editorial boards. He has served as president of the Developmental Division of the Canadian Psychological Association and is currently Membership Secretary-Treasurer of the International Society for the Study of Behavioral Development.

Peter K. Smith is Professor of Psychology at the University of Sheffield, Sheffield, England. He is co-author, with Helen Cowie, of *Understanding Children's Development;* and with David Thompson, of *Practical Approaches to Bullying.* He has contributed more than 100 articles to academic books and journals. A Fellow of the British Psychological Society, he is associate editor of the *International Journal of Behavioral Development,* and European editor of *Ethology and Sociobiology.*